THE IMPASSE OF THE
LATIN AMERICAN LEFT

THE IMPASSE OF THE
LATIN AMERICAN LEFT

RADICAL AMÉRICAS   A series edited by Bruno Bosteels and Geo Maher

FRANCK GAUDICHAUD,
MASSIMO MODONESI, AND
JEFFERY R. WEBBER

Duke University Press   Durham and London   2022

© 2022 Duke University Press. All rights reserved
Typeset in Whitman and Trade Gothic by
Westchester Publishing Services

Library of Congress Cataloging-in-Publication Data
Names: Gaudichaud, Franck, author. | Modonesi, Massimo, [date] author. | Webber, Jeffery R., author.
Title: The impasse of the Latin American Left / Franck Gaudichaud, Massimo Modonesi, and Jeffery R. Webber.
Other titles: Radical Américas.
Description: Durham: Duke University Press, 2022. | Series: Radical Américas | Includes bibliographical references and index. Identifiers:
LCCN 2021035741 (print)
LCCN 2021035742 (ebook)
ISBN 9781478015581 (hardcover)
ISBN 9781478018216 (paperback)
ISBN 9781478022824 (ebook)
Subjects: LCSH: New Left—Latin America. | Right and left (Political science)—Latin America—History—21st century. | Latin America—Politics and government—1980– | BISAC: HISTORY / Latin America / General | POLITICAL SCIENCE / World / Caribbean & Latin American
Classification: LCC F1414.3 .G39 2022 (print) | LCC F1414.3 (ebook) | DDC 320.53098— dc23/eng/20211018
LC record available at https://lccn.loc.gov/2021035741
LC ebook record available at https://lccn.loc.gov/2021035742

COVER ART: Map. Courtesy Vector Map/Shutterstock.

CONTENTS

INTRODUCTION · 1

1. CONFLICT, BLOOD, AND HOPE · 11
Popular Movements and Progressive Politics
in the Storm of the Latin American Class Struggle

**2. WORLD MARKET, PATTERNS OF
ACCUMULATION, AND IMPERIAL DOMINATION** · 75
The Political Economy of the Latin American Left

3. LATIN AMERICAN PROGRESSIVISM · 109
An Epochal Debate

CONCLUSION · 143

COVID-19 Postscript · 151   Acknowledgments · 167
Notes · 169   Index · 197

INTRODUCTION

In the first five years of the twenty-first century, Latin America produced a wave of electoral defeats of the previously invincible supporters of neoliberalism, along with a corresponding opening to one of the most significant processes of change in political leadership in the region's history. In a short sequence, which accelerated between 2002 and 2006, Venezuela, Brazil, Argentina, Bolivia, Uruguay, Ecuador, Nicaragua, and El Salvador all witnessed self-declared anti-neoliberal parties and presidents form governments. As a result, in the first decade of the twenty-first century more progressive Latin American governments were in office than had been witnessed since the 1930s and 1940s.

These governments managed to install a certain degree of hegemony that allowed them to sustain themselves for surprisingly long periods—varying from ten to almost twenty years in office—which included three constituent processes and various presidential reelections, including changes in the executive leadership of the governing parties (except in the cases of Bolivia and Nicaragua). However, in the last several years, for many reasons that will be analyzed in this book, this process entered a phase of exhaustion—the so-called end of the cycle—which manifested itself in an electoral defeat in Argentina in 2015, an institutional coup d'état in Brazil in 2016 and the subsequent election of a far-right government there in 2018, negative referendum results for the reelection of Evo Morales in Bolivia in 2016 and his overthrow in a coup in 2019, and the slim victory of Lenín Moreno (Rafael Correa's successor in the PAIS Alliance) in Ecuador in 2017, followed by Moreno's sharp turn to the right once in office. This phase of exhaustion has also been made evident in explosive form in the Venezuelan crisis since 2013, as well as that of the regime of Daniel Ortega in Nicaragua since 2018.

Attempting to provide an integral account of the ascent, consolidation, and crisis of these political experiences, this book aims to offer an interpretive framework capable of meeting the analytical challenges related to two fundamental elements—historicity and political characterization, both of which give our analysis a significance beyond the specific Latin American context.

The historicity of the progressive cycle is evident in the short term, as it constitutes a significant chapter in the history of the present—a chapter that we can provisionally describe as two decades of Latin American progressivism. These decades have been marked by a line of tension between neoliberalism, anti-neoliberalism, and post-neoliberalism, as well as by the discontinuity that progressive governments introduced, in terms of their discourse and their practices, relative to the preceding neoliberal cycle. Hence the expression "an epoch of change" is justified. At the same time, and this calls into question its political character, the period's scope in terms of "epoch making" is not as evident, at least in the sense that Antonio Gramsci suggested, in that epochal change involves a profound and durable break, a qualitative difference that can delineate the distance separating mere change from transformation, the latter of which surpasses the strictly political level so as to also reach structural and cultural levels.

In this sense, the governments that proclaimed themselves to be post-neoliberal or revolutionary were evaluated through these prisms from their right and from their left, and, in both cases, were judged as having gone too far or fallen short of their respective proclamations and aspirations. The historiography of the coming decades, weighing the impact of these phenomena that we cannot yet fully measure, will allow us to evaluate the depth of this most recent progressive period over the medium to long term.

That very depth could be compared, mutatis mutandis, with the impact of the progressive Latin American governments of the 1930s and 1940s, which were the consequence of another wave or cycle of popular mobilization, and which functioned as a compromise solution, as a way of tempering and deactivating conflict, thereby opening up an epoch of passive revolution that proved quite successful in the short term. That epoch lasted until another cycle of mobilization and conflict appeared, beginning between the close of the 1940s and the middle of the 1950s, and ending in the 1970s with the militarist wave that devastated the diverse expressions—national-popular and revolutionary socialist—of popular movements built and strengthened over the course of at least half a century of history.

Beyond its historical scope, the Latin American progressive experience, in terms of its political characterization, has raised its own contribution to the debates and processes of renovation and reconfiguration of the various lefts on a global scale, now three decades since the fall of the Berlin Wall. Apart from the details and specificities that will appear over the course of the book, we can argue that Latin America at the beginning of the twenty-first century was characterized by the eruption of a progressive project that looked to a post-neoliberal horizon, which was weakened by its populist characteristics and ended up being cornered by a combination of protests arising from below and by the restorative reaction of neoliberal and even oligarchic right-wing forces. Without delving into the often semantic academic disputes over the meaning of "post-neoliberalism" in twenty-first century Latin America, we deliberately treat the progressive projects as having introduced a contested and never fully realized post-neoliberal horizon to politics in various countries, rather than treating post-neoliberalism as an accomplished fact of these governments.

The notion of progressivism is conceptually vast and ambiguous, as is the actual field of left, center-left, and national-popular expressions that captured state power. This was understood by progressive leaders themselves as they sought a minimum common denominator, in the same way that critics, opponents, and analysts tried to find evidence of an overarching model or shared framework.

As a result, "progressive" became an elusive but omnipresent term, developing into the qualifying adjective with which these governments have been conventionally characterized. It has become a key word in the lexicon of live debates, as much in the political arena as in the academic one. Yet, in relation to the content that it attempts to designate, the notion of progressivism has the distinct virtue of pointing to constitutive aspects of the projects and practices of these governments.

In effect, this notion belongs to the language through which it was historically developed, from the Marxist left, to describe social democratic and populist programs and sociopolitical forces that sought to transform and reform capitalism by introducing a dose of intervention and state regulation, along with the redistribution of wealth and, in the case of Latin America, anti-imperialism and developmentalism. This last aspect, today presented as neo-developmentalism, connects with the notion of progress and helps to define the horizon and character of the project, as well as the criticisms, from environmentalist and postcolonial perspectives, which directly call into question the very ideas of progress and development in their expressions over past centuries, as well as in their prolongation in the twenty-first century.

It should be noted that, alongside progressivism, another polemical concept—on which we will not unduly detain ourselves because of the complexity involved—runs through contemporary Latin American debate: that of populism. Suffice it to note the ambivalence of a concept that, on the one hand, served the right in its conservative and reactionary criticisms of progressivism for its statism, welfarism, clientelism, and authoritarianism, and, on the other hand, left-opponents of progressivism, whose critique of populism stressed the inconsistent record of progressive governments toward anti-neoliberalism and anti-capitalism. Left critics of populism also criticized what they saw as its coerced multiclassism, which in reality disguised a substantial continuity of division between classes and, most important, the emergence of specific elite groups, class fractions, and bureaucracies under progressivism that occupied crucial positions in the prevailing relations of domination.

The siege on the progressive project and practice, under the banner of populism, intensified around 2013, as the effects of the global crisis of 2008 began to impact on Latin America in political terms. Governments no longer had the resources to ensure both the accumulation and the redistribution of wealth. From below and to the left of progressivism, sometimes even breaking off from the perimeters of alliances and coalitions with progressive governments, others from an independence that had never actually been forsaken, there sprouted diverse experiences of struggles, mobilizations, and protests that, without managing to articulate a left alternative and remaining dispersed or sporadic, illustrated cracks and ruptures in the left flank of progressive hegemony.

However, in the context of a crisis that became organic, it was right-wing Latin American forces, as we pointed out at the outset, that took advantage of the conjuncture to recover the political initiative that they had lost in the mid-2000s. Witness the assumption of the presidency by center-right Luis Lacalle Pou in Uruguay in 2019, far-right Jair Bolsonaro in Brazil in 2019, Jeanine Áñez in Bolivia also in 2019, conservative Mauricio Macri in Argentina in 2015, and the return to power of reactionary Sebastián Piñera in Chile in 2018. However, the return of the right represents only its relative recovery, which is showing its limits very quickly, not only because it has not been able to extend and generalize itself, but also because, in countries such as Brazil and Argentina, the restorative project of neoliberal elites and old oligarchies presented itself in a brutal manner, without hesitation or gestures toward constructing consensus, demonstrating rapacity and cynicism in the exercise of government, alongside incompetence in the economic domain. Moreover, important exceptions should be noted to these electoral trends, most prominently the election to the presidency of center-leftist Andrés Manuel López

Obrador in Mexico in 2018, as well as the return of center-left Peronism to the presidency of Argentina in 2019 in the figure of Alberto Fernández, with Cristina Fernández de Kirchner (no relation) as vice president.

In the current scenario, which remains open to multiple outcomes, it must be recognized that progressivism, in spite of its undebatable crisis and its evident miseries, has neither died nor been tossed into the dustbin of history; rather, it remains an option that is positioned as an alternative to the right-wing trajectory on the disputed terrain of state power, while social and anticapitalist lefts—the movements and organizations in struggle—remain on the respectable but bounded terrain of resistance, finding it difficult to serve as centers for the accumulation and expansion of sociopolitical forces. Therefore, despite its defeats, its crises, and the inexorable advance of the end of a historical and political cycle in which a certain progressive hegemony reigned, from various perspectives there continues to be an insistence on the formula of a new progressivism that would not renounce but would simply amend the limits or errors of the old.[1]

Argument

Three interrelated arguments lie at the core of this book. They move through three levels of analysis—the political, the economic, and the ideological—to weave together an overarching portrait of the phenomenon of progressivism in twenty-first century Latin America.

First, at the political level, we home in on the dynamic conflicts and shifting balance of forces between popular movements from below, on the one hand, and on the other hand the capacities of the dominant classes to maintain their power and exercise hegemony through consent, coercion, or co-optation/integration. Crucially, we argue that the era of progressivism in the twenty-first century was made possible by the preceding period of plebeian upsurge in the 1990s, fueled by a multitude of social movements whose demands and practices pivoted around a triad of territory, autonomy, and horizontalism. This plebeian upsurge of popular rebellions helped to usher in a crisis of neoliberal hegemony in the early 2000s, which eventually found formal political expression in a series of electoral victories for left as well as center-left parties. The governments that these progressive parties formed achieved hegemonic rule between 2006 and 2013, institutionalizing social movements through incorporation into the apparatuses of the state, rolling out targeted redistributive social programs and instituting forms of state capitalism that violated some of the precepts of neoliberalism without altering the underlying socioproductive matrices of these societies. This period of progressive hegemony was far from homogeneous in political terms. Colombia and Mexico continued to be governed by neoliberal-conservative regimes closely aligned with the United States. A second bloc of center-left, social-liberal (Brazil and Uruguay) or left-wing populist governments (Argentina and Nicaragua) exercised some autonomy from the United States and offered qualified state support for their local bourgeoisies. And a third bloc (Venezuela, Bolivia, and Ecuador) oscillated between popular nationalism, anti-imperialism, and neo-developmentalism, entering into conflict periodically with both Washington and local oligarchies. The specificities of each case were, of course, determined by complex relations between popular movements, parties, the state, and progressive governments themselves. A shifting blend of co-optation, symbolic reward, and the institutionalization of movements characterized, to different extents, all the progressive experiences of this era. Between 2013 and 2020, however, the political project of progressivism was largely exhausted and a shift to the right occurred in two dominant and interrelated ways. First, there were shifts to the right *within* progressive ruling parties and governments in response to the end of the commodities boom and declining state revenues. Second, progressive parties were defeated—either electorally or through extra-constitutional means—and various right-wing parties assumed national office in a number of countries. The new right in power, however, has lacked both the coherent project of political rule and the vision of economic development that defined the orthodox neoliberal right of the 1980s and 1990s. The international context has changed dramatically since, and the new right has insufficient ideological, political, and economic bearings to effectively navigate the new terrain.

A second argument of this book is that, at the economic level, few signs are evident of genuine democratic advances having been made at the high mark of progressivism in the political realm. Progressive governments of various stripes failed to translate their political momentum into a transformation of class structures or improvement of Latin America's subordinate position within the international division of labor. Indeed, the latter worsened in several respects as the move to primary exports and away from industrialization advanced apace. Center-left governments, such as those in Brazil and Argentina in the mid-2000s, modestly broke with orthodox neoliberalism in key respects, while leaving other facets of that mode of accumulation in place. In more radical experiments, such as those in Bolivia and Venezuela, more significant confrontations with neoliberal orthodoxy were partially inaugurated, but rarely developed to fruition. The high period of progressivism accompanied a commodities boom between 2003 and 2011, and the concomitant intensification of extractive capitalism in the region partially accounted for the almost uniformly high rates of economic growth and increases in state revenues. Rents from mining, agro-industry, and natural gas and oil extraction were directed by progressive governments toward targeted antipoverty programs, improving the lives of the most impoverished, while employment rates improved and domestic consumption increased. Poverty fell (in select cases, dramatically) and income inequality—in the most unequal region of the world, it should be stressed—was slightly reduced. Basic social services in health and education were improved, as was infrastructure in marginal urban neighborhoods and impoverished rural areas. These gains, however, were generally contingent on a favorable international economic environment, and they have receded dramatically as the global crisis of capitalism that began in 2007–2008 hit Latin America sharply a few years later. Across the period of the commodities boom and the subsequent era of declining growth and state austerity—problems amplified dramatically through the multipronged crisis of COVID-19 beginning at the outset of 2020—the economics and politics of the region have been deeply affected by imperial strategies of both the United States and, to an increasing extent, China. The high period of progressive hegemony witnessed attempts to forge regional integration projects that would counter the historic domination of the region by the United States, but these efforts have been largely undermined by the economic and political crises that have accelerated since 2013, and in addition the new bilateral ties China has with various Latin American countries are deeply asymmetrical.

The third argument of this book is that, at the ideological level, on the critical Latin American left we have witnessed a shift from an overarching anti-neoliberal consensus in the 1990s to a much more complex field of debate early in the twenty-first century, with a rough schematic line dividing those currents of thought more favorable to progressive governments from those more critical of them. The new divisions pivot on the political weight in different left traditions allotted to party and government hegemony versus subaltern autonomy, as well as along a series of divisive strategic questions: the socioeconomic question (post-neoliberalism, neo-developmentalism, and anti-capitalism); the economic-environmental question (extractivism and dependency); the question of the state and democracy (populism, clientelism, transformism, and passive revolution); and the question of cultural diversity (plurinationalism and postcoloniality). Against this backdrop, we propose the Gramscian concept of passive revolution as the most fruitful lens through which to understand the intricacies of Latin American progressivism early in this century. We argue that a series of passive revolutions have unfolded, and are in some cases still unfolding, in countries with progressive governments in office. Specifically, to say that across these cases, with all their specificities, the era of progressivism has been an era of passive revolutions, is to say that there has been a combination of transformation and conservation of sociopolitical relations of domination directed from the state in an effort to absorb and de-escalate class struggle from below. There has also been a recomposition of modes of capitalist accumulation through socioeconomic reforms that have benefited the subaltern classes but that have simultaneously been designed for their demobilization and even control from above. Far-reaching change has frequently occurred in the ideological composition of the personnel occupying the state machinery, with changes to the modalities of political domination. However, these events have not been accompanied by parallel transformation of the underlying property relations and class structures of the relevant societies.

Structure

The book is organized into three chapters. In the first chapter, we propose a periodization of the complex relations among class struggles, progressivisms, lefts, and popular movements from the 1990s to the present. We stress, in the first instance, plebeian eruption, those movements and resistances that fractured neoliberal hegemony and the Washington consensus. Next, we discuss the ascent of progressive governments—ranging from the center-left to the national-popular and anti-imperialist—beginning in 1998 with the election of Hugo Chávez in Venezuela. The second half of the first decade of the current century appears as a "golden age" of progressivisms, of the Bolivarian experience and of a partial redistribution of the revenue from exports through diverse frameworks of state capitalism. Finally, we emphasize the political ebb of the "pink tide," the authoritarian drifts, the formation of new castes in power, the tensions between progressive governments and popular movements, and the return of right-wing forces beginning in

2013—a period "in tension" that also can be characterized by new dynamics of struggle and collective action, coming from conservative sectors of society as well as from antagonistic or even emancipatory social movements.

In the second chapter, we analyze the political economy of the Latin American left, bringing together in complex ways the rhythms of capitalist accumulation and crisis in the region, with the international dynamic of the world market and the geopolitical maneuvers of both American and Chinese imperialism in the twenty-first century. The chapter surveys the ascent, the consolidation, and finally the crisis of neoliberalism in Latin America during the 1980s and 1990s, the boom in primary commodity prices and the consolidation of the electoral left between 2003 and 2011, and the economic and political repercussions of the latest crisis of global capitalism—the great slump of 2008—which began to affect Latin America seriously in 2012. The chapter explains the dialectical relationship between political and economic temporalities in Latin America over the last few decades, emphasizing ruptures and continuities in the region's political economy during the several phases of progressive rule. It also maps the multiple attempts made to forge regional integration projects relatively free from the historic domination of the United States.

In the third chapter, we analyze intellectual debates on the Latin American left over this historical period, and in particular since the establishment of progressive governments in office. We outline the general coordinates of the debate and review its principal arguments from the distinct perspectives of the national-popular, populism, anti-capitalism, autonomism-libertarianism, environmentalism, and postcolonialism. We highlight a theoretical-political tension in the background, on the antipodes of the debate, between a tendency oriented toward hegemony and another toward autonomy, between the defense of initiatives from above, from the state, on the basis of multiclass alliances, and through limited and measured reforms, and the criticism of this perspective from a vantage point emphasizing agency from below and the necessity of anti-systemic radicalism.

Finally, the book ends with some conclusions that seek to order and summarize the main ideas of the book and open windows into the future, particularly in the new context of the COVID-19 global pandemic.

We hope that our interpretation stimulates further analysis and critical assessment of the political experiences that disrupted the neoliberal order in Latin America and represented a watershed moment in history, the consequences of which live on, and about which we need to reflect. The intellectual and political stakes could not be higher. The right—including the extreme-right—is in ascendance in the region, and in order to understand and to resist this phenomenon, it is necessary to evaluate as soberly and thoroughly as possible how the internal contradictions of the preceding era of progressive hegemony helped to make the right-wing resurgence possible.

TRANSLATED BY DAVID BRODER

1. CONFLICT, BLOOD, AND HOPE POPULAR MOVEMENTS AND PROGRESSIVE POLITICS IN THE STORM OF THE LATIN AMERICAN CLASS STRUGGLE

*Popular Movements between Resistance,
Participation, and Repression*

Latin America often still stands, in the global collective imagination, as the region of revolutions (as well as dictatorships). Even beyond romantic images of the "heroic guerrilla fighter," Latin America has indeed been shaken by profound social upheavals across the twentieth and early twenty-first centuries. Added to that, the subaltern classes have frequently burst onto a political arena long controlled by imperialism and the ruling classes. The region has thus seen great moments of rupture in the established order and numerous projects of revolutionary, populist, and national anti-imperialist hues. These latter have often been crushed or defeated by various forms of counterrevolution, state authoritarianism, paramilitaries, and US interventions.[1] It is worth noting briefly that it was, in a sense, the Mexican Revolution beginning in 1910 that kicked off the "short" twentieth century, a few years before the 1917 Russian Revolution, with a peasant and indigenous uprising that was simultaneously a national and modernizing revolution. We could continue with a long list of radical collective experiences that forged Latin America's modern politics and its class relations. By way of example, we could mention the Salvadoran revolution or Augusto César Sandino's armed struggle in the 1930s; the revolutionary process led by peasants and miners in Bolivia in 1952, which gave rise to what was for many years one of the bastions of the South American working class (the COB—Bolivian Workers' Central); of course, one of the great—and rare—successful revolutions, the victory of Castroism in Cuba in 1959, which continues to be a point of reference for militants six decades later; the "Chilean road to socialism" during the Allende government in Chile (1970–1973); or the Sandinista experience in Nicaragua starting with the flight of the Anastasio Somoza clan in 1979 (lasting until the electoral defeat of 1990).[2] And if appeals to "twenty-first century socialism" repeatedly flourished during the Hugo Chávez years in Venezuela, this was because the idea of socialism had not been completely buried by the rubble of the Berlin Wall, and it continued to burrow its tunnels through the multicolored terrain of Latin–Indo–Afro-America's (or Abya Yala's) political and social left. And it is also worth remembering the importance that the idea of breaking with dependent capitalism had in the 1960s and 1970s, and the place then occupied by the multiple organizations of the revolutionary left—which had emerged from various ideological currents in countries such as Argentina, Brazil, and Uruguay—as well as by the armed struggle in Central America, up until the early 1990s. As for the notion of "popular power," it has been one of the collective grammars running through Latin America's great social mobilizations. While designating a concept that is simultaneously vague and flexible, it has embodied a dynamic visible during periods of revolutionary crisis (as in Cuba or Chile) but also in multiple local experiments limited to a particular neighborhood, factory, or territory. This *poder popular* has also consisted of a series of social and political experiences arising "from below," with the creation of new (and often limited) forms of collective appropriations that are opposed in whole or in part to the dominant social formation and the established powers.[3] In other terms, this means putting into question the ways in which work is organized, social hierarchies are established, and the mechanisms of symbolic, racial, gender, and material domination come into being. Across multiple parts of its territory, Latin America has been shaken by these "sparks of self-management" in its identities and in its social geography, each of which is itself inextricably linked to its anchoring in that region. This praxis of self-organization is always there, in filigree, in the open veins of the processes that we will go on to analyze. But as we will see, it is also very often mistreated, suffocated, or repressed, or simply the victim of its own limitations.

At the base of these dynamics are numerous mobilized popular actors, sometimes massive social movements as well, along with a sharp, contradictory, and often violent class struggle. This plays out under the pressure of the vagaries of globalized capitalism, and it evolves in a nonlinear fashion, which depends on multiple internal and external factors: the turns, and the weight, of the global market; the impact of imperialist strategies and imperialist interventions; economic and state structures; the forms, resources, and repertoires of social organizations; the local bourgeoisies' capacity to exercise their hegemony; the (re)composition of the electoral and party-political space; the transformation of political regimes; and other factors.[4]

Let's focus first on the "left turn," the progressive "wave," and the "end" of neoliberalism. The shift in the politics and the governments of many South American countries (and some Central American ones, too) in the mid-2000s surprised many observers. For a time, a very optimistic—and in certain cases, hagiographic—narrative speaking of the "pink tide" took hold, even in the writings of renowned intellectuals who were far from always being well in touch with the history of Latin America.[5] But as the theologian and sociologist François Houtart, who was also executive secretary of the World Forum for Alternatives, emphasized in 2016, the challenge—in particular for countries like Bolivia, Venezuela, and Ecuador, which have most sparked hopes among a global left lacking for examples to follow—was still to find a concrete route toward a new post-neoliberal and even in certain regards post-capitalist paradigm.[6] So for some social movement militants and political leaders, the first step was to go further than any mere capitalist modernization project, or still less a new model based on extractivism— the simple framework of rearranging the relation of forces among national development, regional bourgeoisies, and foreign capital. From this point of view, we think that today it is fundamental that we elaborate a critical review of the last two decades, encompassing the period that opened up at the beginning of the 2000s in the fight against neoliberal hegemony, up until the current period of retreat for progressivism and the deep crisis of Bolivarianism (2013–2020), passing via their institutionalization in various kinds of redistributive state capitalism between 2007 and 2013.

In general terms, thinking about popular movements—their relations with the political and institutional fields, their influence on the pattern of social and economic transformations, and their capacities to orient words and things—clearly demands a whole theoretical and epistemological debate on the very definition of popular and social movements in Latin America, or indeed that of the characteristics of the class struggle in the region. Such a debate evidently goes beyond the limits of this short book.[7] It is nonetheless essential that we underline some points that ought to be self-evident. First, that in the Latin American context, the very concept of social movements can refer to a huge variety of movements, collectives, and actors—without this term necessarily referring to emancipatory or anti-systemic mobilizations. Indeed, over the last fifteen years, but particularly since 2010, the countries of the "left turn" have also seen a large number of collective mobilizations of a conservative or reactionary character, and in some cases they have been able to put hundreds of thousands of people demonstrating in the streets. We need only think, for example, of how in Brazil the right and civil-society forces (for instance, collectives like Vem para a rua, Revoltados on line, and Movimento Brasil Livre) have been able to mobilize in hundreds of cities over several weeks, beginning in late 2014 and then again in 2015 and 2016—initially in calling for the removal of center-left president Dilma Rousseff, and subsequently in the context of the Lava Jato anti-corruption operation. Such supposedly "anti-political" demonstrations were in fact systematically opposed to the Workers' Party, and refrained from overly disturbing the interim neoliberal Michel Temer's presidency (2016–2018). Such movements have also formed the hard-core base of the far-right presidency of Jair Bolsonaro since 2019.[8] These "anti-corruption" mobilizations could count on the support of the big media conglomerates (including Globo) and on financing from large companies, and they have been led by both right-wing and far-right militants. We might equally point to the reactionary mobilizations in Bolivia's Santa Cruz region in 2008, opposed to Evo Morales's government and favoring the secession of Bolivia's eastern *media luna*, and which would play a key role in the 2019 coup d'état that overthrew Evo Morales and installed Jeanine Áñez in the presidency;[9] the mobilizations of the big agrarian producers' unions in Argentina, against Cristina Fernández de Kirchner and her program of export taxes (again, in 2008); the hostile reactions, backed by Catholic or evangelical churches in multiple countries, against any proposal legalizing abortion; or the mobilization of the Venezuelan opposition between 2002 and 2004. Following the historian Valério Arcary, we might start out from a few basic criteria that allow us to identify whether social movements are reactionary, progressive, or potentially emancipatory in character—namely, their "sociohistorical" lineage and their declared intentions; their composition in terms of their base in some class (or class fraction); the political subject that they mobilize and the ideological orientation of their leaders; and the consequences and main results of their collective actions.[10]

Another essential problem is that many sociological generalizations and "labels"—as, for example, the terms "indigenous movement" or "labor movement"—do not always allow us to identify the numerous internal tensions and differentiations that cut across these movements, their corporatist or "movementist" tendencies, their more or less vertical composition and modus operandi, and such like. These are, then, normative terms that are useful for interpretative purposes but also demand closer scrutiny. Here, we will privilege the concept of "popular movements," in the sense in which it is used by many Latin American authors from critical-Marxist backgrounds. It refers to social antagonism and collective actions coming from below, which take place in the context of the material power relations peculiar to dependent capitalism and aspire either fully or partly to transform these relations. These popular movements can be thought of as "new critical radicalisms"; they are antagonistic, potentially emancipatory, and a force for the self-organization of the subalterns.[11]

Lastly, when we think about the social and the political during the "progressive cycle," we also need to keep in mind that class conflicts consist not only of the resistance and the organizational possibilities of those "from below," but also (and sometimes above all) the capacity of the dominant to exercise their own hegemony through consent, coercion, or co-optation/integration. And in Latin America we find ample confirmation of this. This chapter thus tries to draw together the insights of numerous recent works on the changing relations between class struggles, popular movements, and states and governments over this period.[12] To this end, we will also propose a general periodization in light of recent progressive experiences, trying to identify some of the common themes running through this time frame, even while also remaining conscious of the great national and regional disparities that distinguish each process and the sometimes arbitrary character of the chronological milestones we have chosen.

The rest of this chapter is divided into three sections, organized around a periodization of the left into distinct phases since 1990. First, we explore the height of the neoliberal era between 1990 and 1999, focusing on the upsurge of Latin American popular movements toward the end of the decade, and examining the role of these struggles within the international "alterglobalization" movement. Second, we analyze another period, between 2006 and 2013, and show how popular movements then were institutionalized under progressive governments; we unpack the character of these governments' redistributive social policies; and we highlight the state-capitalist forms of accumulation they tended to pursue. Third, and finally, we examine the period stretching between 2013 and 2020, one marked by a crisis of the Venezuelan "Bolivarian Revolution"—an authoritarian drift in the repressive orientation of various progressive governments that marked a return of the neoliberal right to power in several countries in the region.

The emphasis in this chapter is on the politics of these distinct phases. In chapter 2, economic dimensions of these phases are explored, and in chapter 3, the core intellectual and theoretical currents and disputes within the left are explained in relation to these phases.

Neoliberalism, Alter-Globalization, and the "Plebeian Upsurge" (1990–1999)

During the period between 1950 and 1975, class conflicts throughout Latin America were concentrated in two main branches.[13] On the one hand were the movements around land, peasant struggles, and struggles over the *latifundio* and agrarian reform. On the other hand, class conflicts were powerfully shaped by the demands of the urban proletariat (and semi-proletariat) and by a trade union movement that became especially influential in semi-industrialized countries like Mexico, Brazil, and Argentina.[14] Without doubt, the 1970s and 1980s profoundly remodeled this landscape. This was the era of great strategic defeats for the forces of the left, for the workers' movement, and for populist projects in general; and so, too, the era that saw a series of coups d'état and dictatorships, as well as long and bloody civil wars in Central America.[15] At the core of the inter-American Cold War, the whole set of social relations was reconfigured, but so, too, was the capacity of the subaltern classes to intervene politically, as a whole generation of militants experienced repression, torture, and exile. These dark years, a period of state terrorism (and Operation Condor), still weigh down on public life in the region. These years allowed local elites (and Washington) to "tame" the simmering collective rebellions and to get rid of the specter of revolution that had been haunting the region since the Cuban Revolution. This latter revolution did, of course, survive. But it did so in a condition of political isolation, with a people suffocated by the longest blockade in contemporary history and prey to constant attacks (as well as numerous internal contradictions). It has been six decades since Fidel Castro's troops entered Havana; and in the new era following the collapse of his Soviet ally, with everyday life on the island characterized by drastic difficulties, the death of the *líder máximo* (maximum leader) and the "updating" of the Cuban model also mark the beginning of a new era for all Latin America, at least as much as does the more recent crisis of the "progressive cycle."

The "lost decade" of the 1980s and the "long night of neoliberalism" in the 1990s and 2000s are thus the fruit of a field of ruins in which the Latin American ruling classes, imperialism, and the various armed forces used brute force to impose a lasting change in class relations, in their own favor. Both the social actors and the foci of mobilization have been substantially altered, while the historic forces of the revolutionary left have often been overwhelmed or disoriented in this new context. Without doubt, aided by the change in the international situation, the breadth of opposition, and the economic crisis, the whole region has seen the gradual establishment of constitutional systems affording the difficult return of the rule of law and free elections. This is an evident advance with respect to the previous era—a hard-fought and even essential one. However, these successive waves of "democratic transitions" have mostly given rise to so-called "low-intensity" parliamentary democracies resulting from a pact between the ruling classes, the moderate opposition to the dictatorships, the armed forces, and the economic elites. These civilian regimes are based on the consolidation or deepening of the neoliberal capitalist model—which had often begun during the authoritarian period, and sometimes very early on, as in Chile—and frequently resulted in a sweeping amnesty for those responsible for human rights violations. The foreign debt crisis[16] opened the doors even wider to the International Monetary Fund (IMF), which imposed its famous "structural adjustments" on the states of Latin America: privatization after privatization, state disengagement from public policy, wage cuts, an end to customs barriers, and so on. This offensive sharpened in the 1990s and 2000s; if the region's economies did manage to put a halt to runaway inflation, this came at the cost of severe social regression, an increase in the asymmetry of North–South relations, and a gigantic contradiction between the democratic pretensions of the established regimes and the prevalent regime of capital accumulation.[17] One striking example of this were the years of Carlos Menem in Argentina (1989–1999).

In such conditions, it is unsurprising that citizens grew increasingly disenchanted with political and electoral systems that often served only a handful of families, who themselves saw this as a mode of government sufficiently functional to their interests. And, we ought to add, the new political systems were characterized by continuing very high levels of political violence, impunity, and the proliferation of criminal or narcotrafficking networks.

In parallel to this crisis of democracy, in this same period the region confirmed its place as the region par excellence for class, gender, territorial, and socioethnic inequalities and antagonisms. According to the Argentinian economist Claudio Katz,

> between 1980 and 2003 the official unemployment rate rose from 7.2% to 11%, the minimum wage fell by an average of 25%, and informal

employment grew from 36% to 46%. In parallel to this Latin American capitalists' loss of position on the international stage was confirmed, with just a few exceptions, like Chile. This retreat was compounded with stagnation in GDP per capita, a fall in foreign investment (particularly as compared to China and south-east Asia) and soaring debts. In these conditions, cyclic phases of prosperity become ever more dependent on the international financial or trade conjuncture.[18]

What, then, does it mean to speak of "democratic governability" at the beginning of the twenty-first century? What does this mean for an inhabitant of the favelas of Rio de Janeiro, for the Haitian whose official mean income is around $300 a year, for the landless peasant of north-eastern Brazil, for an indigenous Mapuche, for the Mexican woman working in a *maquiladora*, for a day-laborer on a Central American plantation or a kid on the streets of Bolivia? This may seem a pitifully banal remark, but it is at the heart of the sociopolitical convulsions we have seen in recent years.

To summarize, we can say that the force driving the progressive and national-popular experiences of the 2000s results from the mounting rejection both of the "Washington Agenda"—or rather, the effects of neoliberalism on the everyday lives of millions of Latin Americans—and of a political caste held responsible (and not wrongly) for this situation. This is no uniform phenomenon, nor is it limited to the countries of the "left turn" in the recent period; far from it. But in these countries, it has managed to crystalize or be canalized by the center-left or by new progressive or national-popular political forces, into a perspective of winning elections and conquering state power.

We ought to say that the 1990s were also a landscape of deep economic crises, demonstrating neoliberalism's inability to stabilize itself in the long term. This was particularly notable in the collapse of three major Latin American economies: Mexico in 1994, Brazil in 1999, and Argentina in 2002. This period was the theater for the anger and the dissatisfaction of those "from below" that would subsequently fuel the reorganization of multiple forms of resistance, with the return of an explosive charge of social antagonism. We could date the advent of the new riots against neoliberalism back as early as April 1984, with the popular revolt in the Dominican Republic, or to February 27, 1989, with the Caracazo, the day when "the Venezuelan people woke up": a few months before the fall of the Berlin Wall, the residents of Caracas, most of them living in the poor neighborhoods (80 percent of the population) revolted against the brutal implementation of IMF measures by

Venezuelan President Carlos Andrés Pérez (or CAP; at the time he was also the vice president of the Socialist International). The government's political response was brutal, as it deployed the army and authorized it to fire on the crowds. The repression resulted in over 1,000 deaths in four days.[19]

Popular movements now returned to center stage, albeit in an uneven and combined way, depending on the different countries and their national histories. But this time they emerged in a context of neoliberal fragmentation, and thus with the mobilization of new actors. As the sociologist Bernard Duterme of the Tricontinental Center emphasizes:

> Three decades of recession, institutional repression, and then the neoliberal ideological offensive have made profound changes to classic Latin American social movements. Before the dictatorships, these movements—of peasants, workers and students—aligned with the "national-popular" and "developmentalist" project, coupled to the creation of a welfare state within a form of capitalism that would be independent of the countries of the global North. Over the last fifteen years (1990–2005) as these countries came out of military regimes, new oppositional social forces have emerged—movements of residents in poor neighborhoods, women's movements, the movements of landless peasants and of the unemployed, indigenous movements, and so on. These movements have forced new themes onto the agenda of social struggle, articulated to a renewed critique of capitalism. Paradoxically driven by both new forms of exclusion and the relative opening-up of political space, generated by the liberalization of the sub-continent and the evolution of its socio-economic structures, these new actors have socially and culturally asserted themselves from the margins of the traditional forms of mediation and representation.[20]

The problematic of popular social movements and their relationship with the political has transformed substantially, confirming the (neoliberal) institutional mechanisms' inability to resolve sociopolitical crises within a legal and constitutional framework. Among the most pervasive characteristics of these new mobilizations is the importance of their relationship with territory, territoriality, the neighborhood, or community organization. This responds to transnational capital's own new means of expansion, and to a pattern of accumulation centered on the monopoly appropriation of natural resources (and no longer on an industrialization strategy). This return to the territorial level also reflects the declining weight of traditional (meaning trade union and political) organizations in the workplace, as well as of the spread of precarity or unemployment in a context of privatizations and lay-offs in the industrial sector. Here the boundaries of exploitation and exclusion are displaced, and the territorial level thus becomes an essential site of sociopolitical confrontation. One example of these disputes is the emergence of the *piqueteros* movement in Argentina: the unemployed transpose their resistance from the factory to the territorial level, blocking the roads with pickets in order to draw the attention of the public authorities and the media, demanding the granting of state aid, and then gradually introducing a rich process of self-organization and productive (subsistence) activities in their neighborhoods.[21] But we see this territorial aspect of mobilization developing also outside the cities, with the proliferation of socioenvironmental movements in defense of water, nature, and *buen vivir* (living well), in opposition to big extractive projects like hydroelectric dams, the oil and gas industries, or open-cast mines, and indeed in opposition to the rapid growth of genetically modified (GM) agribusiness or forest monoculture with its "green deserts."[22] Where indigenous movements were already important social forces, they also became prominent forces in the resistance against neoliberalism. These oppositional actors ally the defense of their ancestral territories with direct confrontation against multinational companies. They assert their quest for identity and demand the decolonization of their states, while also calling for social justice and authorities of a new "color," faced with the structural racism that constitutes the cement of the oligarchic republics born of the nineteenth century. Among others, the Confederation of Indigenous Nationalities in Ecuador (CONAIE—Confederación de Nacionalidades Indígenas del Ecuador) is paradigmatic of this axis of conflict. Created in 1986 with the goal of uniting local or regional indigenous communities and associations, this organization became the spearhead of social struggles in Ecuador. In 1990, the CONAIE organized one of the biggest uprisings that the country had ever seen, using various repertoires of action: blockading agricultural land, demonstrating, and occupying major properties and institutions. Although this uprising was repressed, it nonetheless marked the date when indigenous Ecuadorians burst onto the political scene, and the beginning of ten years of tensions that would bring down several governments.[23]

Other important traits of these popular movements include the clear demand for direct forms of action with a greater degree of horizontalism or self-managed democracy, in which the assembly serves as a privileged space of deliberation and decision-making. This also involves a widespread critique of forms of engagement based on delegation, as well as "traditional" ways of doing politics and indeed the party-political left's forms of intervention within social movements. Hence the Landless Rural Workers' Movement (MST—Movimento dos Trabalhadores Rurais Sem Terra) in Brazil has built up its strength on these bases since its creation in 1985, even while also standing in continuity with a tradition of Brazilian peasant resistance. Organizing mass occupations of large landholdings as it demanded agrarian reform, the MST simultaneously promotes participatory democracy, emancipatory pedagogy, and self-education. It moreover practices agro-ecology in its thousands of *assentamentos* (land it has taken over that has now been legally recognized) and *acampamentos* (occupations). The MST has become the main landless rural workers' movement in Latin America, and indeed to this date it is one of the most important mass popular movements on the planet. It is estimated that the movement currently organizes some 1.5 million people, and that it has built 1,800 schools and conquered "from below" approximately 7 million hectares of land (twice the area of Denmark).[24]

One last characteristic of this cycle of struggles, also worth mentioning, is the widespread assertion of a greater demand for "autonomy" and a much more complex, more flexible, and less instrumental relationship with the political terrain and political parties. This concern for autonomy does not imply an outright rejection of politics, but rather has to do with an emphasis on self-determination or even the construction of new utopian horizons, in the here and now. This tends to challenge the "classic" grammars of both the revolutionary and the social-democratic left with regard to the state and taking power.

> Thus the demand for autonomy highlights an important transformation in the process by which political subjectivities are constructed, as the result of changes that have taken place within contemporary society over recent decades. Moreover, we can say that the articulation of territorial identity, direct action, the spread of models based on assemblies and the demand for autonomy have molded a new militant ethos—that is to say, a combination of political and ideological orientations that configure collective action and express themselves through new models of militant: social and territorial militants, social-environmental militants, and cultural activists, among others.[25]

In the 1990s, the embodiment par excellence of this tendency was the rapid emergence of the Zapatista Army of National Liberation (Ejército Zapatista de

Liberación Nacional—EZLN), on January 1, 1994, in the Lacandon Jungle of Chiapas, Mexico. In the same year in which the conservative intellectual Jorge Castañeda published his *Utopia Unarmed*,[26] these new Zapatistas' cry "Ya Basta!" (Enough!) declared their opposition to neoliberal integration under the North American Free Trade Agreement (NAFTA). They wagered on a renewed resistance, which would conjugate social and political democracy, equality and diversity, in the aim of building "a world where many worlds fit." According to "Sub-Comandante Marcos," the aim was to reject the uniformity of globalized commodification and to respect indigenous identities—albeit without dumping internationalism—while also remaining at a distance from the central state.[27] While maintaining their capacity for armed self-defense, the Zapatistas now began to build an experience unique worldwide, with their various "Good Government Councils" based on the distribution of responsibilities and supported by a rich structure of organized indigenous communities. Their capacity to build in the long term did much to fuel the left's debates on the means of fighting neoliberalism and the strategic question of the state. Following in the wake of *zapatismo*, the region became the beacon for a "new internationalism," the forerunner of the alter-globalization movement[28] and the organization of the first World Social Forum in Porto Alegre (Brazil, 2001), a counter-summit set up in opposition to the economic forum held by the great powers in Davos, Switzerland. This new internationalism was also expressed in the continent-wide anti-debt campaign and the MST's participation, in 1992–1993, in the formation of the Vía Campesina, the global expression of dozens of rural organizations fighting for food sovereignty and peasant farming.[29] In April 1997 the Continental Social Alliance (ASC) was founded in Belo Horizonte (Brazil). This coordination would bring together social movements from thirty-five Latin American and Caribbean countries in order to fight against the proposed Free Trade Area of the Americas (FTAA): between 1998 and 2005, the ASC organized three "People's Summits of the Americas," counterposed to the Summits of the Americas bringing together heads of state and government. Each of these alternative summits, until the ultimate collapse of the FTAA project at the summit in Mar del Plata, Argentina, in 2005, mobilized social movements, NGOs, and trade unions from around the region, allowing them to set out a common agenda for struggle.

These collectives also include the women's and feminist movements, seeking to reorganize themselves after a period of strong growth and institutionalization:

During the 1980s feminism thus developed and diversified considerably. At the same time, it grew apart from its initial global perspective (change the world, put an end to oppression) to specialize in a series of more particular questions. The existence of major international financing also contributed greatly to the formation of networks focused on particular questions (decriminalization of abortion, the fight against violence, political participation, etc.), and the movement gradually restructured itself around these networks. The 1990s were marked by a sort of growth-crisis: clearer tensions developed between "pure, hardline" feminists (*de huesos colorados*) more critical of the parties and political practices of the left—and these feminists were often criticized for a certain elitism and/or radicalism—and those who upheld the feminism of the popular sectors, who were sometimes characterized as populist and maternalistic. Two major tendencies crystallized, against the backdrop of the professionalization-institutionalization-recuperation of the movement and a loss of ideological bearings.[30]

The hardening and indeed the reorganization of social relations concerning sex, race, and class forced feminists to propose new organizing strategies, which would bear fruit over the following decade.

The privatization of strongly unionized public sectors, the fall in unionization levels to below 15 percent, the profound transformations of the working class, and deindustrialization—all knocked the stuffing out of the unions as an actor, and fueled workers' loss of class identities. Pension systems were privatized to varying degrees in twelve Latin American countries. Informal sections of the economy became increasingly important, in some countries covering over 60 percent of the economically active population. The bastions of the industrial working class that had previously formed the hard core of the Southern Cone's strongly organized and politicized trade unionism were hit hard, and the corporatist link between the state and the trade union movement was deeply shaken (sometimes to the point of destruction), even though some arrangements with the established union bureaucracies were maintained.[31] The trade union movement was divided over what attitude to adopt in the face of these changes, with some favoring a militant, confrontational response and others an attempt to negotiate with neoliberal governments in order to alleviate the effects of reforms.[32] In Brazil, the trade union movement contributed to the restoration of democracy in 1985, while the majority wing of the movement, organized in the

Unified Workers' Central (CUT), maintained an oppositional stance against the neoliberal governments of the 1990s (Fernando Collor, Itamar Franco, Fernando Henrique Cardoso) while also establishing strong links with the Workers' Party (PT). Nonetheless, during this decade the number of strikes halved and strikers' demands became fundamentally defensive. Argentina's main union *central*, the General Confederation of Labor (CGT), opted for negotiation with the government, demobilizing its members in exchange for a few concessions and suffering splits by the more-critical Argentinian Workers' Central (CTA) and Argentinian Workers' Movement (MTA). Argentinian trade unionism nonetheless went through a "hibernation period" in the 1990s. Similarly, in this same decade the main union *central* in Venezuela, the Venezuelan Workers' Confederation (CTV), accelerated its slide into discredit by signing up to benefit changes unfavorable to workers. In parallel to this, a new generation of "class struggle" militants began to resist—including against the main unions' own leaderships—and to build joint action with other popular actors.[33]

Thus at the end of the 1990s a complex panorama was taking shape. Despite the multiple contradictions, the fragmentation, and the difficulties, these different movements began what we here propose to call a *long wave of the Latin American class struggle*. They did so in what was—it is worth emphasizing—an extremely hostile context, as repression multiplied and neoliberalism continued its advance almost everywhere (from Menem's government in Argentina to the Alberto Fujimori dictatorship in Peru). At first these were essentially defensive, protest mobilizations. The plurality of both their demands and the subjects in struggle means that we can speak of a "plebeian upsurge" that was neither strictly proletarian nor even popular (it also integrated sections of the middle classes). It was directly linked to what the Bolivian sociologist René Zavaleta Mercado has called the *"abigarrada"* (motley, multicolored) social identity of the actors mobilized during this neoliberal period.[34] It was precisely this "polymorph mobilized people"—an original hybridization of forms of community organization, urban collectives, and modern class and trade union reference points—that the progressivisms and the governmental left would purport to embody at the ballot box. It was also these peoples in resistance who would facilitate the onset of the progressive cycle, in some cases vaunting a *destituent* power "from below," capable of bringing down governments. This would transform the region's political characteristics, indeed in a lasting way.

Popular Rebellions, the Crisis of Neoliberal Hegemony,
and the "Turn to the Left" (2000–2006)

Above we saw that the movements of the 1990s were imbued with a strong demand for autonomy, and also influenced by the Zapatistas' proposed route of transforming the world without "taking"—or even concerning themselves with—state power (following in the line of John Holloway's theories).[35] This meant insisting more on the "power to do" (*potential*) of concrete local self-organization than on the "power over" (*potentas*) involved in the left's political-party and state projects. This situation was further reinforced by the collapse of a whole swathe of social-democratic and historical populisms into a liberal and managerial politics, including some "extreme" examples like the Concertación governments in Chile (1990–2010), Menem's administration in Argentina (1989–1999), or, in Bolivia, Víctor Paz Estenssoro's final term (1985–1989) and the governments of the Revolutionary Nationalist Movement (MNR), which invited the then-neoliberal American economist Jeffrey Sachs to restructure the economy in order to halt inflation. Nonetheless, if this perspective centered on building alternatives "from below" solely focused on the social level, the limits of such an approach soon enough became apparent to the militants who sought to defeat neoliberal hegemony. In short, the 2000s were the decade in which the "sociopolitical" came back to prominence. In these years, the movements became increasingly intertwined with party-political action that sought to reach government via the ballot box, in order to drive (more or less radical) social change. Some of these movements worked alongside parties that took part in local or national elections, while others even helped create such parties. Of course, this link between the space of popular movement and the political terrain operated according to very different temporalities in different countries: in Bolivia and Ecuador, for example, it was the product of a sudden rupture-acceleration "from below," whereas in cases like Brazil, Uruguay, or Nicaragua, it rather more expressed the long continuity in the left's and the movements' tradition of participation-institutionalization. There were also "in between" situations, such as the marriage of street insurrection and enduring Peronism in Argentina, or the rise of a "left-wing populist" military figure like Chávez in Venezuela.

Following their different "shortcuts," by the beginning of the new century the movements had thus opened the way to progressivisms, the return of political anti-imperialism, and the center-left. In this, they made use of what was all in all a rather favorable "structure of political opportunity."[36] These factors included the endurance of representative constitutional regimes and pluralist electoral systems (whatever their weaknesses); the end of the Cold War; a more favorable international economic context than in the past; and, lastly, a growing crisis of legitimacy among the traditional political leaders. This allowed growing sections of the population to align with the demands raised by the popular movements:

> These movements have contributed, in multiple ways, to the wave of victories that has led Latin America to become the only region in the world that has mostly been governed by the left and center-left for more than a decade. On the one hand, they did so through their powerful mobilizations against the established political regimes, parties and economic oligarchies—some of which were quasi-insurrections, like in Argentina, Bolivia and Ecuador in the early 2000s. On the other hand, through formulating demands and proposals that could inspire or define progressive candidates' programs—particularly in terms of remolding the rules of democratic life itself, and moreover in providing these candidates with organized social bases during their election campaigns. In some cases, the social movements drove the formation of parties, or largely contributed to this: for instance in Bolivia with the Movimiento al Socialismo (MAS); in Ecuador, where the creation of the Alianza País coalition benefited from the strong support of indigenous movements that had fought against the country's previous governments; and in Brazil, where the social movements participated in the foundation of the Workers' Party (PT).[37]

Among the more spectacular and explosive conjunctures in the plebeian moment of the last decades, we could mention what the Argentinian Marxist Claudio Katz aptly calls "four great popular rebellions."[38] Here we find "figures of revolt" with deep roots in the region's history. They burned their mark on the new century in one of those "temporalities of the gap" that for a moment seems able to shake up all the pieces and to reforge society itself: "for various types of reasons, the mechanisms of social and political control are overwhelmed or inadequate for a moment, and then for an initially indeterminate time there opens up another space-time, in which the hitherto prevalent codes and norms are as if suspended and cease to apply."[39] These momentary gaps are what Antonio Gramsci called "strategic conjunctures," concentrating numerous social contradictions with the potential to start (or end) transformative political cycles.

The first great revolt took place in the country that would—for a while, at least—embody the foremost anti-imperialist rupture in the region, namely Venezuela. The initial flame had in fact been lit in 1989 with the Caracazo (which we already mentioned above). After the fall of Marcos Pérez Jiménez's dictatorship and the sealing of the "Punto Fijo pact" in 1958—an alliance between the Christian-Social Party (COPEI) and the social-democratic Democratic Action (AD), excluding the Communist Party—Venezuela was presented as an example of "democratic stability." The Caracazo, in which the forgotten majorities of the population entered the stage, brought to light this political system's real underside. The revolt was subdued by fierce repression (with more than 1,000 deaths), but it continued in a certain sense "from above" with the (abortive) nationalist-progressive coup attempt mounted by the young lieutenant-colonel parachutist Hugo Chávez in 1992, supported by the Revolutionary Bolivarian Movement (MBR). This initial defeat ultimately led to a surprise electoral victory for Chávez at the 1998 presidential elections, alongside the Fifth Republic Movement and the left-wing parties that supported him as part of the "Patriotic Pole." The long experience of the "Bolivarian Revolution," a process that was both exceptional and contradictory, had now begun. Here we saw the collapse of the dominant party system and the Fourth Republic, and the rise of a charismatic mestizo military figure, a popular nationalist. Here was the symbolic, rhetorical, and bodily *incarnation* of "the people," in an oil-dependent rentier state with a weak tradition of mass movements and class independence.

The second was the indigenous-popular rebellion in Ecuador. We have already emphasized the role played by the CONAIE. In fact, no fewer than three governments were "beaten down" by the indigenous organizations and their allies. After the 1994 mobilizations "for life and agrarian reform" which paralyzed Quito for two weeks, the CONAIE brought down President Abdalá Bucaram in 1997 and allowed the creation of a National Development Fund for Indigenous Peoples. In the meantime—as further proof of the passage from the social to the political, working its way around the region—the CONAIE and peasant organizations created the Pachakutik party, which rapidly won numerous local and even parliamentary contests, but fell short at the presidential elections. Finally, in 2000, faced with a grave economic crisis, corruption, and the dollarization of the economy, Ecuador's neoliberal President Jamil Mahuad was deposed after six months of intense street clashes and growing dissent within the armed forces. The CONAIE leadership then "embarked" on a populist political project, supporting the former colonel Lucio Gutiérrez at the 2002 elections and even joining his government, with two ministers. This idyll would be short-lived, but the political cost of this participation in government would be longer-lasting (in part at least, this continues to be the case even today). However, indigenous people mobilizing alongside the rebellious movements of the urban middle classes did help bring down Gutiérrez, indirectly allowing for the formation of the Proud and Sovereign Alliance (PAIS Alliance) (though no agreement was ever reached with its leader) and the humanist Christian, heterodox economist, and former minister Rafael Correa's election as president. With these electoral victories and the calling of a National Constituent Assembly in January 2007,

> there began a political cycle characterized by the contradictory deployment of the most ambitious project for social transformation that had been attempted since the return of democracy in 1979. Change and conflict would continually intersect, across a decade marked by a dynamic that set face-to-face the populist and movementist logics of political understanding, the state and collective action, all of them immersed in a dizzying period of reforms.[40]

The third great "insurrection" of the anti-neoliberal period took place in Argentina. After decades in which the economy had been aligned to the dollar, Argentina faced a severe liquidity crisis, the drastic reduction of both public and private sector wages, privatization, and ballooning unemployment. At the end of 2001, with the imposition of the *corralito* (a measure taken at the initiative of the economy minister, Domingo Cavallo, which limited bank withdrawals and sought to save the big banks rather than middle-class savers), Argentina exploded. After a one-day general strike, the *cacerolazo* protests along with the riots (and the deaths) of December 20–21, 2001, would be engraved in Argentinians' memories.[41] This forced President De La Rua to flee the *casa rosada* (the presidential palace) by helicopter, and even his successor only lasted five days in power. The impoverished urban middle classes were particularly mobilized, as well as a part of the more precarious urban poor and working class, while the—timid—traditional trade union movement lagged behind. The following government under Eduardo Duhalde would also have to hand over the reins in May 2003, faced with the extent of the struggles and the popular outcry following the repression of the *piquetero* movement. In 2002 Argentina became a laboratory for new forms of collective action, noticeable in the mobilizations by unemployed workers' unions, the emergence of neighborhood assemblies, the recuperation of dozens of bankrupt factories—now under workers' control—and the proliferation of self-managed cultural centers, gardens, canteens, and daycare centers. Amidst the ferment of 2001–2002, the need for solidarity and cooperative experiments increasingly asserted itself. But at the beginning of 2003 the declining resistance, the fragmentation of the *piquetero* and trade union movement, and Peronist forces' attempts to channel the movements, all gradually fed hopes of a "return to order." For want of any coherent alternative (unlike in the Bolivian case) or an "outsiderish" charismatic leader (like those in Ecuador and Venezuela), it was one of the "progressive" elements of Peronism that made off with the electoral prizes, as Nestor Kirchner and the "Front for Victory" reached the heights of state power. The new Justicialist government put the motto "For a serious country, for a normal country" on the airwaves, even as it tried to make a partial response to the needs of the middle classes, to elaborate a discourse of regional integration, and to put an end to the "Full Stop Law" and impunity for the dictatorship's officials.[42]

Yet the plebeian explosion was most dramatic and radical in Bolivia.[43] This was also the country in which the relations between participation and *caudillismo* (big-man leadership) as well as the "jumps" from movement to party organization, from popular mobilization, and from the street to the halls of power were most spectacular.[44] Founded at the end of the 1990s, the MAS-ISP (Movement toward Socialism—Political Instrument for Peoples' Sovereignty) led by the Aymara-origin *cocalero* (coca grower) unionist Evo Morales stood exactly on the boundary between the social and the political. This "instrument" was wholly original, in that it presented itself as an "organic" representation of multiple unions that affiliated to the MAS *collectively*: they included, among others, the Bolivian Peasant Confederation (CSUTCB), the Peasant Women's Federation (FNMCB), and the Confederation of the Indigenous Peoples of the Bolivian East (CIDOB). Union organizations are the only door into the party, and the MAS is also a party in which rural union organization had a privileged role throughout the whole period from 1995 to 2006. In this period the MAS was considered an apparatus allowing access to financing and resources (in a corporatist and often clientelist logic). But the rapid transformation of the political panorama changed this situation. The Andean country would in fact see several years of peasant-indigenous (and also miners') uprisings—particularly centered on the strength of community organizations—that fought for control of natural resources and that led to the fall of presidents Gonzalo Sánchez de Lozada in October 2003 and

Carlos Mesa in June 2005. In 2000 the popular movements in Cochabamba, organized in the Coordinadora de Defensa del Agua y de la Vida (Coordination in Defense of Water and Life), mobilized against the spectacular rise in water prices that followed the signing of a forty-year concession contract with the US multinational Bechtel. After six months of struggles—and at the cost of fierce repression—the movement won the "water war" and expelled the company. In January 2005 a second "water war" broke out in El Alto, the self-built popular city standing over La Paz. This also succeeded in expelling the Suez subsidiary Aguas del Illimani and forced the new Bolivian government to reverse water privatization. Finally, the natural gas question provided the backdrop to Evo Morales's rise to power, with the mobilizations of 2003 and 2005—known as the "gas wars"—which ended with the deaths of several dozen people. On May 1, 2006, the freshly elected president, Evo Morales, announced the "nationalization" of hydrocarbons,[45] and he signaled to the world that "Bolivia no longer has masters, but partners." The indigenous and popular "multitudes" (of which the Marxist sociologist and Vice President Álvaro García Linera has spoken),[46] the subaltern "bloc for collective action," had ultimately been able to remove the old white, racist, neocolonial oligarchy from political power, opening the way for a project that declared itself national, inclusive, and decolonial, and that had adopted a position within the long history of resistance to oppression. This strategic "jump" from the streets to the halls of power was also the product of multiple forms of nonstate popular power such as the neighborhood *juntas* (councils) in El Alto and the various experiences accumulated by the networked subaltern organizations built by Aymara and urban communities.

> Deeply rooted in Bolivian history, this process combines the heritage of three "memories" of struggle: the "long memory" of the indigenous resistance against the Spanish colonial Empire and then the Republic over the eighteenth and nineteenth centuries, today expressed in the rural movements' will to call a Constituent Assembly: the "intermediate memory" of the National Revolution of 1952, which helped radically modernize the Bolivian state through the implementation of demands for the nationalization of the mines, agrarian reform and universal suffrage; and finally the "short memory" of a cycle of antiliberal mobilizations that emerged at the end of the 1990s. . . . Far from the Marxist reference points that once dominated the nation's left-wing political landscape this "democratic and cultural revolution"

brought to light an "insurgent Bolivia" with multiple faces, born from the debris of a workers' movement pulverized by the "shock therapy" implemented by a government that had been converted to the virtues of the free market. MAS's ideological syncretism, made up of nationalism, Indianism and anti-capitalism, is in large part the aleatory articulation of these different legacies of struggle.[47]

Venezuela, Ecuador, Argentina, Bolivia. Looking beyond these four popular rebellions and drawing up a regional balance sheet, we would find that it was essentially the most institutional, gradualist, and moderate versions of the political left that broke through in most countries. The most important in geopolitical terms is obviously Brazil—a country representing almost 50 percent of South America's GDP, and which had 180 million inhabitants in 2002 when Luiz Inácio "Lula" da Silva won the general election. The history of both the Workers' Party (PT) and Lula begins from the depths of the bastions of the working class and the engineering workers of the ABC (São André, São Bernardo, São Caetano), as well as the CUT union (founded in 1983). This was a party that announced in 1990 that "The socialism that we want to build can only be realized through the establishment of a genuine economic democracy." But the PT that took charge of the federal government in 2003 was no longer the same party: after three defeats in the presidential contests of 1988, 1994, and 1998, the party redefined itself considerably, moving to a more social-liberal and centrist position. This was particularly true of its leadership and its presidential candidate himself. Already before 2002, the party had won ground in important city halls around the country as well as in some of the federation's state governments, with an apparatus that was ever more professionalized and aloof from the party base. In his quest to win the presidency and then confront a structurally dispersed Congress dominated by conservative elements, Lula imposed a broad alliance policy that included some of the ruling-class parties. He went so far as to take an industrialist—José Alencar, leader of the right-wing Liberal Party—as his partner and vice-presidential candidate. The PT leader was elected in the second round of the 2002 contest with over 61 percent of the vote, defeating the Social-Democratic (PSDB) candidate José Serra. Lula had stood on what was already an openly social-liberal program. In his June 2002 "letter to the Brazilian people," the former trade unionist confirmed his metamorphosis before the whole nation (and, most important, the local and international elites). He had abandoned any talk of rejecting IMF interference; he promised that his government would respect existing international trade deals and that it would not declare any moratorium on its debts. His campaign slogan was "Peace and Love": he proposed to "teach Brazilians to be patient" and encouraged the arrival of foreign capital (especially in the agro-fuels sector), while also responding to the social emergency with the "zero hunger" plan and the reorientation of many of the programs that had been created under Fernando Henrique Cardoso. It was this logic of class alliances that dominated—with numerous notable twists and turns—Lula's presidency from 2003 to 2011, but also that of his successor, Dilma Rousseff, from 2011 to August 2016.[48] Experiences like the victory of the Broad Front in Uruguay (Tabaré Vázquez was elected in 2004, with 56.6 percent of the vote in the second round) and even that of the "new" *sandinismo* in Nicaragua—with the irreplaceable Daniel Ortega (elected at the first round in 2006) at its head—are rather more part of this institutional, center-left lineage than a product of a plebeian rupture.

Around the world—and especially in South America—the anti-neoliberal sociopolitical dynamic of the 1990s thus translated into the electoral arena in an uneven and differentiated way. There was a proliferation of executives captured by political organizations identifying with the left, the critique of neoliberalism, and sometimes even anti-imperialism. It is worth emphasizing that this progressive or anti-neoliberal tendency in the region was strengthened during the long electoral cycle—a series of twelve presidential elections, all won by the left—stretching from November 2005 to January 2007. Beyond the elections of Tabaré Vázquez, Evo Morales, Daniel Ortega, and Rafael Correa, we could mention the reelection of Chávez in 2006, Lula's second win in Brazil that same year, and in 2007 the election of Cristina Fernández de Kirchner in Argentina (who thus succeeded her husband). To this list we could add Michelle Bachelet's victory in Chile (2006) or even the former priest Fernando Lugo's win in the 2008 Paraguayan presidential race—and it is worth emphasizing the symbolic and democratic impact of women, former trade unionists, progressive Christians, and even former *guerrilleros* reaching high office in the region—a phenomenon that would have been unthinkable, in these proportions, only a few years previously. For Latin America, this series of elections marked a deep crisis of both neoliberal hegemony and the ruling classes' traditional forms of domination.[49] The fact that there was such talk of a "turn to the left" reflected the reality that many of these votes stood in contrast to the uniform right-wing successes of the 1990s, as mobilizations forced the authorities to accord greater importance to the social question, the return of the redistributive state, and to national sovereignty. Simón Bolívar's dream and attempts at an alternative integration of the region returned to the continental political imaginary, in the attempt to recover a space autonomous from the great powers of the global North and imperialism. To use Rafael Correa's expression, Latin America seemed to be embarking on what was less an "epoch of change" than a "change of epoch." Yet the progressive parties that won presidential elections during this period were, for the most part, moderate and center-left forces, standing far from anti-capitalist or revolutionary reference points or indeed identification with the Cuban model, which had been so able to stir forces on the left in the 1970s. Since 1990, an era that no one would confuse for an "age of reason" has translated into a clear process of social-liberalization, for many parties at least. This is notably true of what has become of Daniel Ortega's "Sandinista" government in Nicaragua (where authoritarianism intersects with clientelism and the use of the state as private property). This new path has logically translated into the reformist evolution of the "São Paulo Forum" (created in 1991), even if it includes organizations as different as the Cuban Communist Party and the Chilean Socialist Party.[50] A paradigmatic example of this phenomenon—which can also be seen worldwide—is the twenty years of neoliberal government by Chile's Concertación, a tendency largely continued during the rule of the "socialist" Michelle Bachelet (2006–2010; 2014–2018). This evolution has also taken hold of one of the world's biggest workers' parties, the Brazilian PT. It seems that what the liberation theologist Frei Betto—a man once very close to Lula—described as the "blue fly of power" has done its blood-sapping work, in the face of the demands and the constraints of realpolitik and its arrangements.[51] We detail these phenomena further in the lines that follow. Nonetheless, when these political and electoral triumphs took place, they appeared to large sections of the popular classes as a possible light at the end of the tunnel of authoritarianism, social regression, and neoliberalism, including its most violent forms (what Pablo González Casanova has called "war neoliberalism").[52]

The Institutionalization of Progressivisms, Redistributive Social Policies, and State Capitalism (2006–2013)

During the years that followed Chávez's reelection, the impression of a "turn to the left" in Latin America seemed to be confirmed. This generated great enthusiasm around the world, seeing the possible end of the famous TINA

("There Is No Alternative") snootily proclaimed by Margaret Thatcher back in her day. Was the region showing how the dynamic at the ballot box could be combined with the voices of struggle, in the construction of democratic or even "revolutionary" models? It is true that the euphoria of the moment and the proliferation of laudatory analyses (or, at least, ones with little critical perspective) tended to paint a monochrome portrait of what were in fact complex realities that had often been contradictory from the very outset. Taking an overall view, we see that there existed three different variants of Latin American regimes in the 2006–2013 period. Alongside the neoliberal-conservative and pro-US alternative represented by Colombia and Mexico, we find a second bloc of countries not fully aligned with the United States, based on parties with many decades of history that defended some autonomous positions for their local bourgeoisies and were more oriented to the center-left, whether in its social-liberal variants (Brazil, Uruguay) or in its left-wing populist ones (Argentina, Nicaragua). Finally, a third bloc emerged oscillating between popular-nationalism, anti-imperialism and neo-developmentalism, with governments that opposed Washington as well as local oligarchies on many issues and had emerged from political forces born of the debris of their countries' previous political systems. These latter governments (essentially meaning Venezuela, Bolivia, and Ecuador) had charismatic "outsider" leaders and fed high levels of citizen participation, though even this was controlled "from above" according to Caesarist and "Bonapartist" logics. Nonetheless, the position taken by governments or official parties on this or that subject could oscillate significantly between these three types of regimes, depending on the international relationship of forces, conflicts with the opposition, and internal class struggles.[53]

The only way to understand the "grammar of power" of these progressive governments is to pass them through the sieve of critique, taking as a central criterion not only their discourse but their real praxis—their relationship with popular movements, capital, and indeed the great powers. As the sociologist Immanuel Wallerstein emphasizes, it is particularly important to take into account their position and their actions toward Washington.[54] At this level, it is clear that the three experiences that have most had to confront US hostility and positioned themselves according to an anti-imperialist perspective are the same ones that have restored revolutionary symbolism to prominence: the "Bolivarian Revolution" and then "twenty-first century socialism" in Venezuela, the "Citizens' Revolution" and *buen vivir* in Ecuador, and the plurinational state and "communitarian socialism" in Bolivia. Beyond the rhetoric and the sharp contradictions between talk and realpolitik, it is undeniable that imperialism has tried to destabilize these three experiences, starting with *chavismo*, firstly because it has been the principal radical national-popular process in this period but also (and above all) because Venezuela owns the world's biggest oil reserves, a war chest that had hitherto been under US control. The April 2002 coup against Chávez, actively supported by the Central Intelligence Agency (CIA) and the local bosses' federation (Fedecamaras), along with the two-month oil company lockout starting later that year, reminded Venezuelans how much of an enemy of democracy Uncle Sam can be in Latin America. This destabilization was only thwarted thanks to an imposing popular mobilization and the support of the Bolivarian Armed Forces. Since then, various "soft power" techniques of civil-society and media interventionism, as well as reiterated threats of military invasion—made by various White House and Pentagon officials— have sought to present Venezuela as a "threat" to *yanqui* strategic security.[55] These American pressures were real, even if—in parallel to them—Caracas remained a very good trade and energy client for the giant of the North and its multinationals. The "Bolivarian Revolution" emerged strengthened from its clashes with imperialism in 2002–2003 and radicalized from 2004, at the same time as consolidating both its electoral bedrock and in particular its clearly civic-military character, given how vital the Bolivarian Armed Forces are to the central power mechanism of the regime.

In Bolivia, Evo Morales's government had to pass its own test of fire in 2008, and had to face down the secession threats—supported by US Ambassador Paul Goldberg—that were coming from the white and mestizo oligarchy in the *media luna* departments of Pando, Beni, Santa Cruz, and Tarija.[56] Indeed, even as the government was consolidating its new hegemony among peasant and indigenous populations—a phenomenon corroborated by Evo's 67 percent victory in the August 2008 recall referendum—the bourgeoisie of the large landholdings and agroindustry, alongside the opposition's departmental prefects (later called governors), defied the central government with a "civic strike" of racist, classist, and pro-imperialist tones. Here again, the defeat of these destabilization efforts was a result of the collective mobilization of the new ruling bloc's social base (in this case, thousands of peasants and indigenous Bolivians) as well as the government's own decisive action to subdue the reactionary revolt. Ultimately the US ambassador was expelled from the country, together with the American Drug Enforcement Agency (DEA). In 2013 it was the United States Agency for International

Development (USAID) that became persona non grata, condemned for its interference in Bolivia's internal affairs. Ecuador's Citizens' Revolution has also clashed with Washington—if to a lesser degree—especially when Correa decided not to renew the concession of the Manta military base to the US armed forces. Washington also came under attack (in 2007–2008) in a historical audit of Ecuador's debts, which resulted in a denunciation of the country's illegitimate debts and its unilateral suspension of the repayment of the commercial bonds due to mature in 2012 and 2030 (and then the repurchasing of these bonds at less than 35 percent of their value).[57] Ecuador did this to the great displeasure of the United States and the World Bank, whose permanent representative was expelled from the country.

These cases are emblematic of the upsetting of the relationship between North and South, which was restructured by new and autonomous forms of regional integration—the Bolivarian Alliance for the Peoples of Our America (ALBA), the South American Community of Nations (UNASUR), and the Community of Latin American and Caribbean States (CELAC). (The strengths and limits of these regional integration projects will be discussed further in chapter 2.) But it should be emphasized that there is no real homogeneity among the "progressivisms" that make up this regional process, or even in the public policies they have implemented. Instead, we can see more of a variety of convulsions in response to the crisis of the hegemonic model, with the emergence of governments that range from the "faded rose" to a keenly asserted opposition to liberalism, and from a social-neoliberal left (Bachelet in Chile) to more-radical nationalist-popular forces (*chavismo*), with established social-democratic parties (like Uruguay's Broad Front) in between. We also need to emphasize that while these processes took form in what are all strongly presidentialist political systems (and this is, in part, a legacy of the independence process), they do so within regimes that are stabilized and institutionalized to highly varied degrees: strongly so in Brazil or Uruguay and very weakly so in Venezuela and Nicaragua. Moreover, we should not forget that many strategically important countries continued to be governed by the right throughout the 2000s, starting with Colombia and Mexico. So, like most observers, we should significantly temper the simplistic image of a more or less homogenous "turn to the left." The same goes for the debate that has so energized intellectuals asking whether there exist "two kinds" of governmental lefts (as we will see in more detail in chapter 3): a "modern" or "social-liberal" left (depending on your perspective) as in Chile, Uruguay, or Brazil, combining the market with a few moderate social or societal reforms, and then another "populist and old-fashioned" or "radical and anti-imperialist" left (and again, the choice between these terms depends on the particular author's political orientation) led by Bolivarian Venezuela, Ecuador, and Bolivia.[58] Since 2006, some observers have criticized the "myth of the two lefts" in favor of a reading that emphasizes the multiplicity of left-wing forces and reflects the different national realities. Indeed, these different lefts are often apparent within a single movement, party, or government. The protean character of this phenomenon sometimes justifies the most contradictory analyses, ranging from a perception that the situation is pregnant with a wave of revolution, to a conclusion that it has already reached a social-liberal normalization consisting of pragmatism and retreat.[59]

Nonetheless, in most cases the first steps taken by the national-popular presidents and the progressive forces marked the return of the state and of redistributive public policy, surfing on very high raw-materials prices, export revenues, and a favorable economic context.[60] In this sense, we can rightly speak of a cycle with a post-neoliberal horizon. According to CEPAL, within only a decade more than 70 million people were lifted out of poverty, and if in 1990 some 22.6 percent of Latin Americans were considered destitute and 48.4 percent of them poor, by 2014 these figures were "just" 12 percent and 28 percent, respectively.[61] And it was precisely in the countries of the "left turn" that the results were most pronounced. In Bolivia, poverty fell from 66.4 percent in 2005 to 39.3 percent in 2014, while inequalities also decreased; the same was true in Ecuador (where the poverty rate fell from 37.6 percent of the population in 2006 to 22.5 percent in 2014). The results in Venezuela were also spectacular: in the 1998–2011 period it was the single country that did best in reducing inequality (the Gini coefficient fell from 0.486 to 0.390), as it reduced the poverty rate by 10 points and extreme poverty by 14.[62] During this period there was a constant increase in the state budget and public spending on social needs, while the GDP of each of these countries also increased (the most exceptional case being Bolivia, where it rose from $8bn in 2002 to $30bn in 2013). In addition to tighter state regulation on the products coming from extraction or the exploitation of natural resources, some governments have also carried out nationalizations in other fields (that had previously seen privatization). Of course, this is particularly true of the Bolivarian Revolution: from 2007 onward, Chávez introduced state control over a series of sectors considered strategic—for instance, the nationalization of the telecoms and electricity companies, the oil-producing area around the river Orinoco, the country's biggest steel producer, and three cement companies, in all of this relying on the decisive aid of the Bolivarian Armed Forces. In Argentina, Kirchner took the post and communications services back into state hands, as well as the airline Aerolíneas Argentinas, and even renationalized the pension and retirement funds (in 2008). These nationalizations were undertaken without breaking the law and within a market framework—that is, via negotiations that led to compensation, or via an international arbitration process. We could also mention the "water reform" in Uruguay, with the nationalization of the supply of drinking water (2011). The "progressive," neo-developmentalist state is a state that invests in a combination of social policies, with a priority focus on so-called "vulnerable" layers that in fact make up as much as 40 percent of the population, for instance in the case of Ecuador and its Citizens' Revolution. Thus, once Brazil's PT had reached national office, it fused earlier programs (the Schooling Allowance, the Food Card, Gas Aid, and the Food Allowance) into a single "Family Allowance," which benefited over a quarter of Brazilians (the poorest). Granted to citizens on incomes under $67 a month, this program was wholly in line with the World Bank's recommendations and, all in all, was not so different from those implemented by other governments, including those on the right (for example the Oportunidades program in Mexico). This Family Allowance is granted to mothers in exchange for the schooling of their children or involvement in healthcare programs. Between 2004 and 2014 it allowed more than 28 million Brazilians to escape extreme poverty (if not lesser degrees of poverty); 88 percent of these benefits were directly used for food. This program also explained the extremely solid electoral bedrock that the PT—and President Lula in particular—were able to build up among the more precarious layers of the population, especially in the northeast of the country. Indeed, the PT governments did so at very little cost to the central state, amounting to just 0.5 percent of GDP (some studies even show that the Family Allowance program generates more economic benefits than costs, given its effect in stimulating popular consumption and direct tax receipts).[63]

This type of conditional income transfers strongly took root across the entire region during the progressive golden age. Moreover, it has been combined with new public policies seeking to improve infrastructure (for instance, Ecuador's roads and airports) and also to provide increased access to free primary education, healthcare, and housing. In 2008 Bolivia became the third Latin American nation (after Cuba and Venezuela) to achieve one of the Millennium Development Goals indicated by the UN: the eradication of illiteracy. Another important element of the situation is that while progressive governments have organized a far superior fiscal pressure on the extraction of raw materials and drawn greater royalties from multinationals, they have not engaged in any ambitious project to increase taxes on the incomes and assets of the ruling classes. Yet these taxes are structurally low across the whole region, and revising them ought to be the very first initiative taken by the left once it reaches high office, however moderate.[64] Even when a government like Correa's conducted a far-reaching tax reform in 2015, notably affecting inheritance tax, he had to confront a major public opinion campaign waged by the country's economic elites, ultimately forcing him to retreat. The same was true of Fernández de Kirchner: in 2008 she had to endure a long (and politically very costly) conflict with the main agricultural bosses' unions when she proposed a bill taxing grain exports.

The third field of intervention for some of the progressive governments was workers' rights. Many authors have emphasized that this domain is essential for any prospect of structurally transforming situations that are defined by poverty and inequalities of income and wealth, in a way that goes beyond a simple (re)deployment of the welfare state.[65] In countries with strong traditions of trade unionism, in which movements of organized workers have accompanied the rising electoral weight of left-wing forces, several measures have been taken to this end, even if often in a quite timid fashion, in order to avoid frightening these countries' main capitalists. The minimum wage has been increased considerably in Brazil, Venezuela, Uruguay, and even Argentina (even if these measures have been undermined by inflation or, as in Venezuela, even totally destroyed by hyperinflation). We can also note examples of government support for the extension of insurance coverage and social security (Bolivia); and, in some countries, we see clear efforts to strengthen collective bargaining within particular economic sectors and to reaffirm the right to work, the right to strike, and trade union rights (unlike in Chile, where the Concertación governments instead operated with Augusto Pinochet's legacy and the neoliberal labor code of 1979). One of the clear limits of these real advances is the still-very-high proportion of the workforce who are employed informally—thus remaining beyond the reach of this progress—who often surpass 30 percent or even 50 percent of the economically active population. Venezuela's 2012 labor law has sometimes been cited as an example to follow, even as the sign of a real "transition to socialism." *On paper* this is an extremely bold piece of legislation, strengthening women workers' rights and equality with men; forbidding subcontracting; announcing the creation of "workers' councils" involved in company management; and even the right to workers' control in case of illegal or fraudulent closures. But again here, in the Bolivarian experience, a gulf exists between rhetoric and practical implementation: the few concrete experiences of workers' control or co-management have ultimately been thwarted in infancy by the Labor Ministry itself (notably in the case of the great steel plant in Guyana state).[66] As for real working conditions, they improved only in very relative terms, before dropping dramatically after 2012 with the crisis, as various forms of state and managerial repression against trade union leaders multiplied.

From 2003, amidst a context of strong sociopolitical polarization, the "Bolivarian Revolution" nonetheless attempted to propose original forms of social intervention, through the creation of the *misiones*. These included the "Mercal" mission for the distribution of subsidized food, "Barrio Adentro" (a first-response health service), "Robinson" (literacy programs, primary education), "Ribas" (secondary education), and "Sucre" (higher education), just to mention the most prominent. This policy most of all responded to a social emergency, even as it strengthened *chavismo*'s political and electoral base. These missions sought to draw on popular participation, in particular the "Barrio Adentro" program, a primary healthcare service covering numerous popular neighborhoods throughout the country. It relied on the arrival of thousands of Cuban doctors (in exchange for oil). In order to operate effectively, these missions required the backing of organized communities, and their rollout strengthened various forms of local grassroots organization. According to Edgardo Lander, the Barrio Adentro program "includes the community as a co-constituent" of the rollout of public policies seeking to deal with a social emergency.[67] The *misiones* allow the circumvention of the rentier state apparatus, with all its bureaucratic encrustations. But ultimately they depend very directly on the presidency, encumbered by clientelism and the various forms of Caesarist verticalism that go along with such a "bypassing" of state institutions. One of their failings is that they are not attached to any structural improvement in the existing public amenities, such as could be planned in the long term (for example, if we look at healthcare, the hospitals continue to fall apart in alarming fashion). Even so, these measures offered an urgent response to essential problems that the elites of the Fourth Republic (1958–1998) neglected. This social spending represented over 60 percent of the state budget during Chávez's presidency: many indicators of popular living standards increased immediately (for instance, the mortality rate or the size and weight of children). Sadly, these indicators turned for the worse with the economic collapse that began in 2012–2013, thus revealing the fragility of a weakly stabilized social policy poorly anchored in the country's institutions.

Clearly many other questions could help us distinguish between the nature of the various progressive administrations' policies. We cannot mention all of them in this short book. But even so, we will run through what we see as the most crucial ones.

First is the question of agrarian reform and the war on the *latifundio*. This was an important factor at the moment of the explosion of the agro-fuels market and the reactivation of peasant struggles, for it highlighted the need to implement bold policies that would allow producers to participate effectively in the organization of production and the consolidation of food sovereignty. The most recent studies show how far, also in this domain, the progressivisms have ended up allying with agribusiness more than with small peasants.[68] Seen in this light, it is clear that Lula's government reneged on its promises to carry out major land redistribution; during his two terms in office the Brazilian leader redistributed fewer hectares of land than the previous administration under Cardoso. In a country in which 1 percent of the population still possesses 46 percent of the cultivable land, the PT had promised to move 100,000 families each year onto a plot of land between 2003 and 2006. But as of 2006 only 40,000 had been settled. In 2010 the agrarian reform had, so to speak, been written off, an "omission" confirmed by Dilma Rousseff's government, whose agrarian policy was centered on the development of agribusiness, the softening of rules on GM crops and intensive farming for exports in the hands of consortiums like Monsanto. By way of consequence, the mighty MST issued growing criticisms of the PT, even as it reaffirmed its vote for a party still perceived (as it continues to be today) as a "lesser evil" compared to an arrogant and repressive right.

As a counterpoint, if we look at the Bolivian case, we are still waiting for the famous "agrarian, productive and community revolution" that had previously been announced, though advances have clearly been made in terms of redistributing property deeds, under the pressure of the peasant movement and despite the numerous tensions between the inhabitants of the lowlands and the Andean regions.[69] This process of "judicial consolidation" moreover emphasizes recognition of indigenous community land. Under Evo Morales's government, 32 million hectares have been officially recognized as collective property (out of a national total of 106 million), and this represents a leap forward compared to the previous period. Nonetheless—and it is here that we find the whole contradiction between rhetoric and practice—even in a country in which 87 percent of cultivable land is in the hands of a 7 percent minority of big landowners, there is no question of the MAS following the example set by the wave of *latifundio* expropriations during the 1952–1953 revolutionary period. Moreover, in July 2013 the Bolivian government signed an agreement with the agribusiness magnates of Santa Cruz, in which it committed to increase the cultivable area by a million hectares a year until 2025, the bicentenary of Bolivia's independence. Following straight in line with the neo-developmentalist course and the new social pact that "Evoism" has sealed with the dominant economic interests, agri-productivism and GM crops are favored in the name of "food sovereignty," even as the government also shored up small family-based agriculture in the Andes and existing community lands. This apparent dualism is in fact imbalanced: Santa Cruz soy crops represent some 66 percent of all hectares of cultivated land in Bolivia. As the director of the NGO Fundación Tierra (Land Foundation) has emphasized: "In truth the government wavers between a political rhetoric that speaks in favor of redistributive agrarian reform, and an economic policy that favors capitalist accumulation."[70] This also explains the criticisms of the government coming from former Deputy Minister of Land Alejandro Almaraz, who has attacked the strengthening of a productivist model of agriculture focused on exports.

A second essential theme is the control of raw materials and natural "resources" (oil, gas, mines, but also water and biodiversity). Venezuela's and Bolivia's policies in this field are much bolder than those of their neighbors, even though they ultimately conform to the laws of the market and are very moderate compared to real nationalizations (without compensation) as in, for example, Allende's nationalization of the copper mines in 1971. Nonetheless, whereas during her two terms in office the Chilean "socialist" Bachelet rooted her development policy in mining concessions to large private corporations (including what are considered strategically important ores like lithium), Evo Morales has compelled the multinationals to become Bolivia's "partners" rather than its "masters," imposing royalties at the level of 50–70 percent of their income on gas and hydrocarbon extraction. The same is true of Chávez, who took control of the petrol giant PDVSA (publicly owned since 1975) in order to make it a key player in his social, health, and educational policy, even as he signed a series of deals with foreign companies so as to diversify their origins (including companies from China, Russia, Europe, and elsewhere). But this also proceeded by way of the laying-off (called the "purge") of many thousands of the company's employees and managers blamed for participating in the 2003 oil lockout—a measure that disorganized the energy company in the long term. In some cases, governments claim that they have no choice but to compromise with multinationals that have major technological capacities and capital or distribution networks that are cruelly necessary if these governments are to be able to access fresh money and proceed with their promised social policies. In other situations, presidents open their doors to foreign capital with the enthusiasm of the convert, granting them all kinds of tax breaks and sweeteners to move into their countries.

Last, it is worth mentioning the question of "participatory democracy"—indigenous populations' rights and the decolonization of oligarchic political systems. We can, indeed, see "power in a new color" in the region, and can observe democratic innovations whether at the level of institutions, symbolism, or social status. Countries that had seen real political ruptures then engaged in a battle to set up innovative Constituent Assemblies and bring their work to a proper conclusion, allowing the creation of so-called "plurinational" states. These latter suppose the emergence of a new state model with an (at least symbolically) decolonial scope, including all the diversity of indigenous peoples-nations within the republic but also recognizing their rights, sanctified in a new kind of Magna Carta. Among others, these include: rights to prior consultation of indigenous communities for any project concerning their historic territories; the right to autonomy and the decentralization of powers (for want of real self-determination); respect for indigenous customs, including in terms of the justice system (albeit with several limits); and even joint official status for their languages (on the same footing as Spanish).

This plurinationality is combined with other legal innovations regarding participatory democracy, in constitutions approved by referendum and elaborated after very long debates including the participation of popular movements (but always in a way very much controlled by the official parties) and sharp clashes with conservative forces. Such new constitutions followed in quick succession in Venezuela (1999), Ecuador (2008), and Bolivia (2009).[71] In all three countries, referendums with the ability to "recall" the elected authorities became part of the political system, but so, too, did the idea of adopting a mixed economic model that would combine capitalist private property and state ownership but also "social" (cooperative/community) property. Moreover, a new generation of rights also made their appearance, in particular the notions of the Rights of Nature and "good living" (*buen vivir*, or *sumak kawsay* in Quechua). These latter are intended as the necessary establishment of new interrelations between all living things within the biosphere and, in theory, as a radical challenge to the traditional notions of progress and development (the Ecuadorian minister René Ramirez has even proposed the concept of "Biosocialism").[72] As for "protagonist democracy" and "people's power," it is without doubt the "Boliviarian Revolution" that has most emphasized this dimension, in particular following Chávez's victory in the 2004 recall referendum and his reelection as president in 2006 and then again in 2012. Most important, unlike the PT in Brazil—which allied with the center-right in order to forge parliamentary majorities (in a historically fragmented Congress)—the Bolivarian leader benefited from the leeway provided by his absolute control of parliament between 2005 and 2010, at the same time as he repeatedly confirmed his democratic legitimacy through the ballot box. His attempts to drive forward his proposals for "twenty-first century socialism" (inspired for a period by the controversial intellectual Heinz Dietrich) experienced a setback in 2007 with the referendum defeat for the "socialist" constitutional reform, after which Chávez sought to elaborate a "communal democracy." This first meant the creation of thousands of "communal councils"; in urban areas, each of these would bring together between 200 and 400 families (fewer in the countryside). These councils embodied the central government's will "to allow the organized people to exercise the direct management of public policies" (Communal Councils Law, 2006), and they were also an international showcase for *chavismo*. The councils were meant to handle a budget of several thousand dollars, granted by "presidential commissions," in order to deliver various community projects (street maintenance, health, culture, security, local services, and so on) which were discussed, voted on, and—at least normally—controlled by assemblies. Some authors define this as a "radicalization of democracy" and local experiences of people's power in practice.[73] However, these councils remain the prisoners of a dynamic that wavers between an original policy of territorial-level participation, based on partial self-organization, and a strong vertical subordination to presidential power, which ultimately controls the financing of the councils, their scope of operation, and even their subsistence. The popular power proclaimed in these councils "is, in reality, confronted with the inertia in the organization and functioning of the state apparatus, which seeks to maintain the old model of public administration, reproducing old clientelist and technocratic practices."[74] In this sense, as the historian Margarita López Maya remarks, under a cover of direct democracy the communal councils are also a means through which *chavismo* centralizes power in Miraflores (the presidential palace) without having to rely on the famous "intermediary bodies." The councils would be largely mothballed under Chávez's successor, Nicolás Maduro, as the economic and food crisis spread; they were replaced "from above" by supply bodies under civic-military control like that of the Local Committees for Food Supply and Production (CLAP).[75]

This difficult relationship among popular movements, parties, the state, and progressive governments is key to understanding this period. In general terms, we can see a moment in which numerous movements have been strongly institutionalized, and often a co-option and bureaucratization of a considerable part of their leaders. At the initiative of its vice president, the sociologist Álvaro García Linera, the Bolivian government under Evo Morales proclaimed itself a "government of the social movements." And if we looked at the makeup of its ministries, we could indeed see numerous trade union leaders and indigenous peasant women in their ranks. This political and socioethnic revolution would have been unthinkable only two decades ago, which explains the sense of dispossession felt among the traditional white oligarchy, which had been accustomed to controlling the state apparatus in its own preferred manner ever since independence. The base of the Morales government was made up of indigenous peasants, *cocaleros*, and tenant farmers, but also mining cooperativists and certain trade unionists (notably the oil workers); relations with the COB were, however, both more complex and more strained. Movements like the National Council of Ayllus and Markas of Qullasuyu (CONAMAQ), an organization of highland indigenous populations, or indeed the Confederation of Indigenous People of Bolivia, were also essential to understanding the promulgation of the new Constitution in 2009. Nonetheless, as these organizations became increasingly critical of MAS's economic model, they were gradually marginalized or even denounced by the central government. In 2007 a "National Council for Change" (CONALCAM) was created, in order to coordinate the political links between the executive and the popular movements supporting MAS's actions; some authors have described it as "the trade union arm of the ruling party." Evo Morales was himself the president of this organization, having been continually reelected leader of the Coordination of the six *cocaleros*' producers' federations in the tropics of the department of Cochabamba. He combined this with his function as president of the Republic, "which well illustrates the accumulation of posts."[76]

This mix between co-option, symbolic reward, and the institutionalization of movements is present to varying degrees in all the progressive experiences.

Often, it follows the multiple logics of "revolving doors," individual or collective calculations, and several intermediate "gray areas."[77] These processes come in exchange for movements' greater influence over the orientation of public policy and their cadres' and militants' greater access to state emoluments, various funds, or posts as ministerial advisers, MPs, and the like. For the leaders of trade unions or social movements, this newfound institutional influence is a movement conquest that needs to be maintained. But it also has follow-on effects in terms of demobilization, social control from above, and in many cases corruption. These have followed in crescendo over the last decade: to stick with the Bolivian case, we could mention the management of the Indigenous and Peasant Development Fund (administered by social organizations), which comes from the taxes on hydrocarbons, and from which $15 million have gone missing.[78] The question of large-scale corruption, embezzlement, and the treatment of the state as private property is evidently a theme central to explaining the disaffection that ever-wider layers of "popular *chavismo*" felt toward their leaders in the final Chávez years, and even more so under Maduro;[79] the same was true during the PT governments in Brazil. We will delve further into these questions in the next section. The tension between autonomy, co-option, and integration is also combined with another—the one linking marginalization to neutralization or even repression—for those organizations that do not align themselves with the progressive governments' agenda. We can clearly see this in the dislocation of the *piquetero* movement in Argentina, whose "autonomist" and radical wing was isolated by Kirchnerism, thanks to a targeted use of social plans and a permanent immobilization of their actions even at the local level. By contrast, a *piquetero* leader like Luís D'Elía became undersecretary of social housing during the first Kirchner government, while also remaining prepared to serve as leader of a "shock troop" in the streets, in service of the government. From 2009, D'Elía seemed to distance himself from Fernández de Kirchner, faced with what he termed the "ill-treatment" she was inflicting on the social movements. He was ultimately marginalized during the election campaigns of 2016–2017. The human rights movement has experienced something of the same dilemmas, beginning with the "Mothers of the Plaza de Mayo." Part of this movement enthusiastically supported both Nestor Kirchner's and Cristina Fernández de Kirchner's policy of an end to the impunity for the dictatorship's torturers (after years of struggle by the victims' families), while the rest wanted to maintain the movement's independence. This split the movement in two (Hebe de Bonafini, the legendary founder of the "Mothers of the Plaza de Mayo" movement and a fervent Kirchnerist, was moreover subject to judicial investigation for the illicit financing of the Justicialist Party's campaigns and the embezzlement of public funds).

The labor movement also experienced this type of divides-and-diversions during the progressive golden age.[80] In Brazil, for instance, the Unified Workers' Central (CUT) was at the origin of the rise of the PT and its electoral victories: in return, many of its leaders were integrated into the state apparatus, thus pushing the *central* itself toward a more moderate position, and creating a growing malaise among its mobilized grassroots militants, some of whom turned toward autonomous radical confederations like the Popular and Union Central (CSP-Conlutas) or Intersindical. In Argentina, the union confederations initially gave enthusiastic support to Nestor Kirchner, but during Cristina Fernández de Kirchner's first term the General Confederation of Labor (CGT) and Argentinian Workers' Central (CTA) split between factions supporting and opposed to the government, whereas a Peronist union leader like Hugo Moyano allied bureaucratic integration and criticisms of *justicialismo* in the media.[81] In Venezuela, the National Workers' Union of Venezuela (UNT) imploded over the divide between "autonomy" from the Bolivarian government or else "dependence"; it oscillated between economic demands and a priority on supporting the political process. The central government even created a new confederation, the Bolivarian Socialist Central of Urban, Farming and Fishing Workers (CBST-CCP). For Wills Rangel, president of this union, speaking in August 2013, this was "a political-trade union central designed to ensure continuity between the working class and the government."[82] In Ecuador, Correa promoted a United Workers' Central of Ecuador over the historic union confederation, the Workers' Unitary Front (FUT), which had mobilized against the executive's policies. Governments have thus initiated ad hoc parallel union organizations and divided workers' organizations according to their support (or otherwise) for the executive's own desiderata. We find the same thing in Nicaragua, where the extraneousness of the National Workers' Front (FNT) to the field of political power, corporatism, and Sandinista control has placed it in service of a government-controlled class alliance:

> Since Daniel Ortega's return to power, the revival in the state's productive and integrative role has translated into inclusive policies benefitting workers. Imbricated in the FSLN's party structures and blending into the state's institutional apparatus, the trade union movement is

active in the biannual re-evaluation of the minimum wage and the social protection of wage-earners. But this institutionalized trade unionism covers a whole repertoire of functions that come together in political backing for the government and support for the prevalent economic model through the pact between the state, the unions and employers.[83]

But since 2007–2008, certain elements of the indigenous and socioenvironmental movements have begun to reorganize above all on the basis of criticisms of the extractivist-productivist model (see chapter 2 on the political economy of extractive capitalism). This has marked the first major ruptures between, on the one hand, the hegemonic neo-developmentalist progressive or left-populist vision (based on the export of mineral ores, hydrocarbons, and products deriving from agribusiness) and, on the other hand, the (minoritarian) demands for a post-neoliberalism that would also be post-extractivist or even anti-capitalist, or in any case respectful of ecosystems and indigenous rights (such as those that the new constitutions of Ecuador, Bolivia, and Venezuela theoretically uphold).[84] Studying figures from the United Nations Economic Commission for Latin America and the Caribbean (ECLAC), Maristella Svampa counted some 226 conflicts between 2010 and 2013 linked to extractive megaprojects and resulting from struggles demanding respect for the environment or indigenous lands, which were often repressed by the state or private actors, thus accelerating the divorce between movements and governments.[85] This conclusion has been widely documented by NGOs like the Observatory of Latin American Environmental Conflicts (OLCA) in Chile and the Observatory of Natural Resource Conflicts (OCRN) in Argentina.[86] In many cases, local communities' right to prior public consultation has been frustrated or manipulated; in other situations, local authorities or whole territories are "coopted" and placed in service of these megaprojects in exchange for some financing for community services, the promise of jobs, or the payment of emoluments. The leaders of social, indigenous, and ecologist movements can even be criminalized and publicly denounced if they remain opposed to these implacable logics. This divorce was very much apparent in the terrible relations between a good part of the CONAIE's national leadership and President Correa in Ecuador; in December 2007 he proclaimed on national television, "Don't believe all the romantic environmentalists; whoever opposes the country's development is a terrorist." In Chile, the "socialist" president, Bachelet, has applied anti-terrorist legislation dating back to the Pinochet dictatorship against Mapuche struggles, despite the hunger strikes conducted by numerous indigenous political prisoners as well as the murder of militants by military police in recent years. The fact that the Inter-American Court of Human Rights has repeatedly invoked the right to fair trials for those who continue to demand the restitution of their usurped land and denounce the existence of the Chilean state as a racist and colonial endeavor does not seem to have troubled the center-left government, which has continued its practice of defending the interests of the big foresting companies over the interests of the Mapuche people.[87] In Bolivia and Ecuador, well-known environmentalist organizations close to indigenous organizations, and recognized internationally for their expertise, have been subject to persecution or even banned. García Linera has sought to discredit them by placing them on an even footing with the NGOs financed by the great powers, "in service of a green imperialism" that apparently wants to transform the global South into a "nature park warden."[88] This drift accelerated from 2013 onward (and we will return to this question). But social-territorial conflicts targeting mining, fracking, or major dams (like Belo Monte in Brazil, or the canal project in Nicaragua) have multiplied, as the precarious balances of state capitalism and neo-developmentalism have come to surface level, revealing all their limits.

The explicit objective of many Latin American progressive leaders on reaching government has been both to restore the role of the redistributive state and to modernize capitalism, in particular thanks to the income from raw materials. This is the "Andean-Amazonian" capitalism of García Linera, Nestor Kirchner's capitalism *"en serio,"* or the capitalism that Uruguay's former *guerrillero* leader José "Pepe" Mujica considered "an instrument of economic prosperity"—and this model entered into crisis from 2011 to 2012 under the blows of the great global crisis of capitalism, the fall in raw materials prices, and the more-aggressive reorganization of the neoliberal right and the regime in Washington itself.

Progressivism in the Labyrinth: The Crisis of the
"Bolivarian Revolution," the Authoritarian Drift, the Return of the
Neoliberal Right, and New Dynamics of Struggle (2013–2020)

The region's politics entered into a new period with the death of Hugo Chávez in March 2013 (and his replacement by Nicolás Maduro); the defeat of Kirchnerism in the Argentinian presidential election in November 2015; the Venezuelan opposition's victory in the parliamentary contest one month later; the institutional coup d'état against the Brazilian president Dilma Rousseff in August 2016, followed by her PT party's washout in the local elections that October; and Evo's defeat in the referendum on lifting term limits in Bolivia (February 2016). This political landscape was rooted in progressivism's extractivist economic model, which was profoundly affected by the global conjuncture; it cut from beneath these governments' feet the income they needed to finance social policies. This impact was all the greater in the absence of any fundamental transformation of the social relations of production and distribution, and in a context in which the ruling classes' media and economic power had been left largely untouched; in some regards that power had even been strengthened, notably in the financial and agro-extractive sectors. Big capital in general had been able to profit from the progressive golden age. Thus in Ecuador, in 2006, with a GDP of $46.8 billion, the country's 300 largest companies concentrated some 43.6 percent of GDP; by 2012 these companies accounted for 46.4 percent of GDP, and in the meantime the national wealth had almost doubled, confirming how far the dominant were able to profit from the neo-developmentalist administration![89] We could give similar figures for most countries concerned. The moment of reflux, the "end of the post-neoliberal cycle," in fact showed the extent to which, rather than concerning themselves with the implementation of post-capitalist strategies, many of these governments instead—using different repertoires of action—developed a cohabitation or even a fusion with big capital and the most dynamic elements of the bourgeoisie, even as they drove a redefinition of the state's role that favored a democratization of popular consumption and basic social services as well as a boom in the internal market.

This closeness, or "pact," with one or more ruling-class fractions obviously had certain evident vagaries and differences, according to different national contexts: we need only compare the regular clashes between Chávez and the Venezuelan oligarchy and the United States, and in Michelle Bachelet's constant accommodations in service of powerful moneyed interests and in the name of respect for free trade. But we can identify one phenomenon they have in common: an ever-greater separation between the president's party (or parties) and the rest of society, in a classic oligopolization process, such as Robert Michels studied in his day with regard to European social democracy and the birth of a techno-bureaucracy ever more assimilated into the various circles of economic power.[90] This was combined with a "hyper-presidentialism" and leaders' strong influence as "tribunes," whose charismatic presence overdetermined a number of questions of national policy orientations and decisions.

From 2005 to 2007 it became quite common in activist circles to say that while the Latin American progressives had reached government (through the ballot box), they were yet to win power, which remained in the hands of the capitalists, the main media concerns, the big landowners, the churches, and so on. There was also talk of "governments in dispute" that remained to be conquered—ones riven by authentic tendencies toward rupture or radical democratization and opportunist or reformist currents considered bourgeois or liable to corruption.[91] Nonetheless, it seems that the very facts of being at the head of a capitalist state (however much it was reformed by new constitutions), and of seeing all the country's problems through this prism, meant that power poisoned militants' actions, public policy, and worldviews, whether they had come from the left or from popular nationalism.

Thus we have seen electoral machines like the PSUV (United Socialist Party of Venezuela, founded in 2007) become enormous bureaucratic apparatuses that have millions of members but are governed by a handful of ministers and figures close to the president, without any internal debate or democracy, with election candidates appointed "from above" for each locality, and with any dissident in the critical-*chavista* milieu being kicked out. A militant like Gonzalo Gómez of the organization Socialist Tide would repeatedly pay the price for this, until finally breaking with the Maduro government, which he denounced as authoritarian and counterrevolutionary. Now a whole series of former ministers and even generals, who were comrades of Chávez's and are today very critical of *madurismo*, are treated as pariahs or even arrested under suspicion of collusion with "the enemy." This new oligarchy has produced a sui generis caste, or even new ruling-class fractions, sometimes in conflict with other "historic" sections of the bourgeoisie.

Hugo Chávez himself went some distance in criticizing this drift, even though as the main leader he was himself partly responsible for it. He did this in his public self-critiques and his attempts to "steer to the left," particularly after his October 2012 text *El golpe de timón*, in which the *Comandante* called for the deepening of the Bolivarian Revolution on the basis of the Communal State and denounced widespread corruption. A genuine "bolibourgeoisie" (others call them "lumpenbourgeoisie") began to benefit from the control of oil rents and the multiple subsidiary activities connected to the hydrocarbons and steel industries, including by means of the foreign currency controls introduced in 2003. Marxist analysts like Manuel Sutherland and Michael Roberts and the former minister of industry Víctor Alvarez (along with many others) have repeatedly shown how hundreds of millions of dollars have been "captured" and privatized by a minority of bureaucratic and military figures, but also by their allies, namely the new Bolivarian entrepreneurs and cadres in the armed forces and the upper ranks of the civil service. This regressive phenomenon is also combined with enormous capital flight, evaluated by Chávez's former planning and finance minister Jorge Giordani at more than $300 billion since 2003 (the equivalent of a year's national GDP!), directly benefiting the many entrepreneurs who choose an easy means of self-enrichment based on the overvaluation of the Bolívar and the possibility of defrauding both the exchange controls and the System of Transactions with Securities in Foreign Currency (SITME) on an industrial scale at the moment of declaring their imports.[92] The multiple corruption scandals linked to this have worsened under Maduro, as the foreign debt has exploded, the price of oil has collapsed, and the opposition Democratic Unity Roundtable (MUD) has sought to destabilize the executive through violent street action.

> Maduro principally favors the armed forces (or the officers, in any case), who create and take up positions in companies across all sectors of the economy, transport, energy, telecoms, investment funds, banks, etc. This policy has, since November 2014, been combined with Maduro's creation of Special Economic Zones, which allow companies—including, and especially, those controlled by members of the regime and those that have signed agreements with them—to abstain from respecting social and environmental rights, as well as the rights of indigenous peoples, in the name of the higher national interest. In order to participate more actively in this scramble for natural resources, in February 2016 the armed forces' high command created the Military PLC for the Mining, Oil and Gas Industries, thus allowing it to directly access these SEZs and extract resources.[93]

This reorientation takes place in the context of the foundation of the "Orinoco Mining Arc," a vast project in the south of the country on land that is, in part, protected due to its wealth of biodiversity and the presence of numerous indigenous communities, but which is also rich in gold, diamonds, iron, bauxite, and other ores (as well as oil shales). This initiative, launched by President Chávez in 2011, is officially designed to "impose order" in a region where thousands of small and highly polluting mining operations exist side-by-side with mafiosi and smugglers. In the end, a "National Strategic Development Zone" was created, based on the awarding of concessions covering a territory that will ultimately represent some 12 percent of national territory (an area equivalent to Cuba). The exploitation agreements signed between dozens of (especially Chinese and Russian) multinationals, companies controlled by army officers, and the bolibourgeoisie are supposed to allow Venezuela to raise its head above the waters of the economic tsunami it has been living through since 2014.

In this context, the Venezuelan opposition has been further emboldened, especially given the fervent support for their cause from Washington under Donald Trump. This shared purpose of the conservative opposition and the Trump administration was expressed, for example, in Washington's immediate recognition of a parallel government following Juan Guaidó's self-declaration as Venezuela's "interim president" in January 2019, followed by US support for his ill-conceived and ultimately unsuccessful coup attempt in April of the same year. This came on the heels of severe sanctions on Venezuela introduced by Trump in 2017 and hardened further in 2019.[94]

Some authors have also described such castes in power in other countries. Huascar Salazar Lohman portrays the reconstitution of a state capitalism and new forms of domination by way of Bolivia's MAS, indeed in opposition to anti-neoliberal community forces.[95] A new elite has favored the parallel emergence of indigenous (especially Aymara) commercial bourgeoisies and a middling layer of cooperative bosses at mines. This latter has gone so far as to bite the hand of the man that it had earlier brought to power: during the August 2016 riots against the executive's proposed measures to regulate the sector, the miners beat the deputy interior minister Rodolfo Illanes to death after the police murdered two demonstrators. Such contradictions of the Morales era opened up the possibilities for the right-wing opportunism of the October 2019 coup d'état. That coup lies somewhere between the "hard" military coup in Honduras in 2009 and the "soft" parliamentary coups against Fernando Lugo in Paraguay in 2012 and Dilma Rousseff in Brazil in 2016.

In the Bolivian case, the far-right managed to coopt and commandeer mass centrist protest by urban middle classes that preceded the coup, steering them on a violent trajectory. On Sunday, October 20, 2019, Morales sought a fourth mandate as president. For the first time since he came to office in 2006, the contest was relatively polarized, with a regionally and ideologically fragmented right-wing opposition cohering, in the main, behind center-right candidate Carlos Mesa, a former vice president under Gonzalo Sánchez de Lozada, and then his unelected presidential successor between 2003 and 2005. Morales's popularity had diminished significantly in the wake of the 2016 referendum loss. Through a series of legally dubious maneuvers, Morales ignored the results of the referendum and was approved to run in the October 2019 elections by the relevant state authority. The referendum became the fulcrum around which urban middle classes and regional civic committees gathered, hoping to unseat Morales, but unable to achieve these ends through democratic means. The official vote count eventually determined that Morales won 47.08 percent of the popular vote to Carlos Mesa's 36.41. The gap between the two being greater than 10 percent meant that no second round would be necessary, according to Bolivia's electoral rules. However, before the official count even came in, immediately after the unofficial "quick count," Mesa proclaimed that fraud had occurred and put his weight behind violent protests, which quickly eclipsed his leadership. The Organization of American States (OAS) applied fuel to the fire by calling into question the legitimacy of the electoral results, without providing evidence of fraud. The stage had been set for police mutiny, military collaboration, and the violent and unconstitutional assumption of the presidency by Jeanine Áñez.[96]

The picture of techno-bureaucratization from within a progressive government looks all the more cruel in Daniel Ortega's Nicaragua. In that country we are seeing the gradual entrenchment of a genuine ruling "mafia," under a presidential couple that controls several business conglomerates and almost half the media, while also maintaining a stranglehold over the executive, legislative, and judicial branches. Ortegismo now declares itself "neither left nor right": it is today in favor of a "corporatist alliance between the government, employers and trade unions," along with a free-trade deal with the United States and improbable alliances with the country's conservative Church and former counterrevolutionaries (including Eden Pastora).[97] In April-May 2018, the repression of demonstrations and riots in opposition to the counterreform of a social-security system on the brink of bankruptcy ended in over 135 deaths, most of them people killed by the police force or the Sandinista youth's paramilitary group: this mass political violence is without precedent since the dictatorship of Anastasio Somoza. The regime's partisans invoked the shadowy interference of the United States and plans for a "color revolution" as they sought to explain the destabilization in process, denying the extent of the repressive authoritarianism that is today in power.

Brazil is perhaps the case where we could identify the most stable (or stabilized) version of a fusion between cadres linked to the PT, the CUT, and the world of finance. In power, the PT not only integrated tens of thousands of its own cadres into political roles at the heart of the state apparatus:[98] this party of trade unionists also received millions of dollars from the country's major capitalist corporations in order to finance its campaigns and fill its own coffers. In 2010 it was the single party that received most donations from construction businesses ($15 million), including *multilatinas* (multinational corporations with headquarters in Latin American countries) like OAS or Odebrecht. These same firms were at the heart of massive corruption scandals linked to the semipublic oil giant Petrobras, not only in Brazil but throughout Latin America. These scandals ultimately heaped discredit on the PT at multiple levels, especially thanks to the many-tentacled "Car Wash" inquiry, which the right skillfully instrumentalized (notwithstanding the fact that its own leaders were far more deeply mired in this mass-scale corruption than the PT had been up to that point).[99] Over more than two decades the PT and its main ally the CUT also formed a genuine trade union "caste," which co-administered (together with the employers) the whole country's state and private pension funds. These funds counted among the biggest financial entities in Latin America, shifting many dozens of billions of dollars a year; the PT presented them as an excellent "complement" to workers' paltry pensions, but President Lula himself also considered them an instrument of economic development that ought to be encouraged. The ascent of this layer of trade unionists into the upper ranks of society has grown so out of proportion that some authors working on this phenomenon (Francisco de Oliveira, João Bernardo, Luciano Pereira, Maria Chávez Jardim) have even proposed the notion of a "trade union capitalism" or a "new social class."[100] And one of the consequences that has been observed with the expansion of this ruling elite was the strengthening of a trade union structure that became ever more dependent on state connections. In the more favorable conditions created by Lula's neo-developmentalist policy, the unions in fact made greater recourse to strike action during his period in office (2003–2013), but they did so by focusing on corporatist material claims. They thus abandoned more general political demands in favor of the growing moderation actively pushed by both CUT and PT leaders. We could even speak of a "PT-CUTist" model of integration, including the demobilization/depoliticization of workers' struggles.[101] This scenario has been termed a "perfect neoliberalism,"[102] for it combines policies favorable to local and global capital with a tendency to control the working class's trade union activity, even as it forms a very solid electoral base (or clientele) among the ranks of capitalism's main victims. Former prominent Lula advisers like André Singer confirm as much: Singer has rather acidly described a "conservative pact" that partly recalled the populist period under Getulio Vargas: namely, a project centered on the personalization of political power, class conciliation, nationalism, and the integration of the popular layers through access to mass consumption and the Brazilian market. With the election of Dilma Rousseff, this project built ever-more alliances with the right and increasingly tilted in a conservative direction. Rousseff now proposed to govern together with yesterday's enemies—the center-right Brazilian Democratic Movement Party (PMDB)—along with local notables and representatives of the banking sector, on the basis of an austerity project.

Ernesto Herrera highlights how a similar phenomenon has taken place, albeit on a very different scale, in much-smaller Uruguay. There, the Broad Front became an enthusiastic supporter of private investment, the IMF, and free trade, and an enemy of agrarian reform, relegating the question of poverty to a "personal problem" and championing the strengthening of the "punitive state." "Pepe" Mujica appeared on the world stage as the jovial embodiment of critical-humanist thinking, at the same time as he offered the bourgeoisie in his own country conditions it would never have dared to dream of.[103] The limits of the Mujica era laid the basis for the electoral defeat of the Broad Front's candidate, Daniel Martínez, in the 2019 general election to the conservative National Party's Luis Lacalle Pou.[104]

Also instructive in this regard is the example of Michelle Bachelet's second term in Chile (2014–2018). After the massive social explosion in 2011, demanding "free, public, and high-quality education" and fighting against the hated legacy of Pinochet's "Chicago Boys," the socialist leader first reacted by integrating promises of free education, constitutional reform, and fiscal reform into her campaign program. Through this progressive rhetoric of change, she was able to capture part of the energy that had been given off in the streets, as she brought the Communist Party into her coalition for the first time (alongside the Christian Democrats). This also allowed her to win the 2013 presidential election, defeating the right. But if we draw a balance sheet of the government that followed, we see that Bachelet's "New Majority" was in fact a social-liberal transformism (the concept of transformism is explored in chapter 3): hence, part of higher education was made free, but via a "voucher" system that financed private university fees using public funds; minimal reform was made of the constitution, thus burying millions of citizens' hopes for a Constituent Assembly; the fiscal reform turned out to be painless for the country's wealthiest families and the main multinationals; and so on. And while some important measures were indeed taken—for example, with regard to abortion rights—their significance was immediately undermined: legalized abortions would only be allowed in extreme cases (immediate danger to the mother's life, rape, or where the fetus was nonviable), while the doctors and the (numerous) Catholic healthcare institutions were forbidden to conduct abortions, for reasons of religious belief. Thus the major fissures in Chilean neoliberalism that had regularly opened up over the course of several years were once again "plugged" by progressivism and its allies: namely, a political caste that was deeply fused to and intermarried with the country's business, media, and financial elites.[105] This also explains the record level of abstention (surpassing 50 percent of the electorate) in national elections, the emergence of a force to the left carried by a new generation (with the Broad Front), and the multi-millionaire businessman Sebastián Piñera's victory in the 2017 presidential election. Faced with the original and a mere copy, voters turned back to the original.

Today, ten Chilean billionaires boast combined assets worth 16 percent of GDP. The Bello columnist for the British liberal magazine *The Economist* offered a telling observation late in 2019: "Some years ago your columnist attended a drinks party of about 60 people in Santiago. A friend whispered in his ear 'You realise that half of Chile's GDP is in this room.'"[106] Set apart from those in attendance at the cocktail festivities, the working and middle classes live off credit, putting themselves in debt to pay for the enormous cost of living associated with privatized education, healthcare, pensions, highways, and water services. Hidden taxes on the poor—and the burdens they bring—reach into every orifice of quotidian life; particular sources of discontent, as in Brazil in 2013, are the high fares on transit. Household debt in Chile is the highest in Latin America at 45.4 percent of GDP; personal indebtedness of the working classes is an enormous disciplinary whip in the hands of capital, one that keeps workers treading ever harder with the aim of staying above water. One of the bitterest ironies of the present scenario is that Piñera made much of his estimated $2.8 billion by introducing credit card debt to the plebeian substratum.[107]

In an interview that would come to haunt him, published in the *Financial Times* on October 17, 2019, Piñera captured the ethos of the Chilean model as seen from the perspective of the ruling class: "Look at Latin America," Piñera said. "Argentina and Paraguay are in recession, Mexico and Brazil in stagnation, Peru and Ecuador in deep political crisis and in this context Chile looks like an oasis because we have stable democracy, the economy is growing, we are creating jobs, we are improving salaries and we are keeping macroeconomic balance.... Is it easy? No, it's not. But it's worth fighting for."[108] The next day, the country exploded, with "oasis" becoming a popular meme ridiculing Piñera. The country became the site of one of the world's most insurgent antineoliberal rebellions. Few witnesses to the country's upheaval that October could avoid recalling earlier moments in Chilean history. In the participatory assemblies and pitched street battles late that year, the stirrings were visible of a renewed fidelity to those who fought and were defeated in 1973 (in the overthrow of the Popular Unity government of Salvador Allende).

The spark was a fare increase on Santiago's public subway system. Santiago has one of the most expensive public transit systems in the world, with an accumulated 40 percent increase in fares between 2010 and 2015 in real terms. Building on an infrastructural bed of militancy first established through the high school rebellions in 2006 and university uprisings in 2011, the first actor set in motion was the student movement, which organized a "mass evasion." Demonstrators would not pay the subway fare in a collective act of resistance. Police responded with gratuitous violence, stoking far-flung contempt for their actions among the public and correspondent levels of support for the evaders. The president declared a state of emergency, suspending constitutional rights and introducing a curfew, first in Santiago and then later in many of the country's other cities. The military was sent into the streets with heavily armored vehicles for the first time since the end of the Pinochet era. Piñera announced that his regime was "at war" with a powerful internal enemy. Masses of people responded with violations of the curfew and assemblies throughout the night all around the country. The revolt far transcended a 30-peso fare increase. As one viral slogan put it: "It's not about 30 pesos, it's about 30 years!" The recent revival of popular feminism in Chile—as in much of the rest of Latin America—converged with the combativeness of students, indigenous movements, and labor (especially dockworkers). While protests subsided in November 2019, it is clear that Piñera's rule had been destabilized to the core. The fissures of neoliberalism in Chile seem no longer capable of plugging.

Post-neoliberalism thus often appears to stand in continuity with logics inherited from the previous period; in what political scientists call "path dependence," it is supposed that the political costs of a change of trajectory are too high. And the paths of productivism, foreign debt, financial deregulation, and changes from above "within the limits of the possible" are returning at breakneck speed. This also helps explain the metamorphoses of the discourse of the "palace intellectuals."[109] Of course, in seeking to explain the retreats, the contradictions, and the tensions, leaders have foregrounded the immense obstacles that dependent economies have to overcome; the weight of economic, cultural, and institutional inertia; the "creative tensions" (García Linera's term) that have to be tamed;[110] the power of the imperialist offensive; or even, in Rafael Correa's words, the "perfect storm" that these executives face. In the Ecuadorian case, this meant a combination of extremely powerful external factors resulting from the global crisis, the weaknesses of a still-dollarized economy, the fall in hydrocarbon prices, and the violent earthquake of April 2016. But the imperialist ogre's maneuvers or the vagaries of the global economy cannot hide the fact that the reflux of progressive hegemony in the region and the rapid rise of right-wing forces is fueled by the retreats and the conservative metamorphoses of the left in government. This is a much-needed debate that is all too often sidestepped within the activist circles that identify with "left-populism."

Here we will not detail the history of the institutional coup d'état against Dilma Rousseff in Brazil in 2016 or the subsequent 2018 election to the presidency of the far-right outsider Jair Bolsonaro; the victory of Mauricio Macri's new-look "new right" in the Argentinian elections of 2015 (defeated after one term in the 2019 general election, with the return of the Peronists, with Alberto Fernández as president and Cristina Fernández de Kirchner [no relation] as vice president); the conservative Venezuelan Democratic Round Table's (MUD) electoral rise in the popular neighborhoods of Caracas that were historically the heartlands of *chavismo*; or the character of the Jeanine Áñez post-coup presidency in Bolivia. Without doubt, this offensive will try to exploit all the space that the various faces of progressivism have left open or abandoned, in the right's own attempts to win back control of the state by violent or electoral means. It is not that the fundamental interests of the ruling classes were trampled on during the progressive golden age; in fact, we have seen that the opposite was the case. But that matters little: for this oligarchy has always believed that the national-popular or center-left experiences could only be parentheses, and that they must be as brief as possible. This oligarchy considers the republican state *its own property*—a creature at its own service and under its own exclusive control, whether it takes authoritarian or liberal-democratic forms. The fact that various charismatic leaders, former trade unionists, progressive women, or even indigenous presidents and their adepts became involved in their own "business," was thus seen as a heresy, an offense that had to be challenged, at whatever cost. The end of this "cycle" is a series of institutional coups d'état, more or less directly backed by

Washington. This offensive began in the weak links of progressivism, with the coups against the liberal Manuel Zelaya in Honduras in 2009 and Lugo in Paraguay in 2012. Once these victories were consummated, it could turn to a country central to global geopolitics: Brazil. As Michael Löwy notes, the attack on Brazilian democracy represented by the removal of Rousseff was deeply reactionary, as if emerging from the country's darkest past:

> a tragi-comic affair in which we see a clique of reactionary and notoriously corrupt parliamentarians overthrow a President who was democratically elected by 54 million Brazilians, in the name of "accounting irregularities." The main component of this alliance of right-wing parties is the (non-party) parliamentary bloc known as the "three Bs": "Bullet"—the MPs linked to the Military Police, the death squads and other private militias—"Beef"—the big landowners who own the cattle ranches—and "Bible"—the fundamentalist, homophobic and misogynist neo-Pentecostals. Distinguishing himself as one of the most enthusiastic champions of Dilma's removal was the MP Jair Bolsonaro, who dedicated his vote to the officials of the military dictatorship and in particular Colonel Ustra, a notorious torturer. Among Ustra's victims was one Dilma Rousseff.[111]

All this led to the courts taking an increasingly direct political role, with then-federal-judge Sérgio Moro in the lead of attempts to block Lula standing again in 2018. But here, too, it was the PT's unnatural alliances and decisions in favor of austerity that recoiled against it: the interim president following Rousseff's ouster from power was Michel Temer, none other than her own vice president.

The limits and contradictions of the PT's project opened opportunities for right-wing rearticulation in the country. Bolsonaro's astonishing ascent to the highest seat of authority in Latin America's largest economy, in the fifth largest country in the world by area and population, was all the more discombobulating, coming as it did in the wake of thirteen years of rule by arguably the twenty-first century's most stable and institutionalized social-democratic party. This was yet another instance of the unraveling of the political center in the rolling tsunami of global capitalist crisis. Bolsonaro's government was inaugurated on January 1, 2019. A former army captain and marginal congressperson, he won the second round of the presidential elections in October 2018 with 55 percent of the popular vote, defeating Fernando Haddad of the PT, who garnered 45 percent. In early June 2019, investigative journalists at *The Intercept* unveiled incontrovertible evidence of ex-federal judge and current minister of justice Sérgio Moro's clandestine collaboration with state prosecutors in the conviction and incarceration of Lula, just as the former president and PT presidential candidate was leading the polls and looked set to beat Bolsonaro in the 2018 elections by a landslide.[112] Haddad, Lula's replacement as PT candidate, was unable to make up lost ground at the last minute. Following a late surge in the polls, representative bodies of domestic and international capital abandoned their traditional party home—the Brazilian Social Democratic Party (PSDB)—and rallied behind Bolsonaro, who they saw as the only way out, on their terms, of the country's protracted economic and political crisis and a means of thwarting any return to office by the PT. Bolsonaro captured all the country, outside of PT strongholds in the northeast, and secured votes across the range of social strata, apart from the very poorest, who remained loyal to the PT.[113]

According to Claudio Katz, the essential difference between the PT's attitude faced with the abrupt return of the right and Nicolás Maduro's response in Venezuela is that this latter chose to resist at all cost, while *lulismo* surrendered along with its weapons even before the decisive battle had been fought.[114] It is true that for many militants and intellectuals close to the Bolivarian process, in the present conjuncture the "battle of Caracas" would be the mother of all battles with imperialism, or even a real Latin American "Stalingrad" (*sic!*), to adopt the Argentinian Atilio Borón's expression. The warlike statements that came from the Trump administration only fueled the flames. It is worth recognizing that since 2014 the "hard" sectors of the opposition have unleashed a wave of violence, openly backed by the CIA, with the aim of overthrowing Maduro. In the forefront were the *guarimbas* (barricades, roadblocks) identifying with leaders like Leopoldo López and Antonio Ledezma.[115] This *"salida"* strategy (seeking a "way out" from the current government) resulted in the deaths of forty-three people and left more than 800 wounded, sparking memories of the Venezuelan radical right's responsibilities in the 2002 coup d'état attempt. This street violence broke out again in 2017 and prompted a hardening of the established authorities, demonstrations, counterdemonstrations, the active state repression of far-right shock troops, armed parades by various *chavista* motorized "collectives," and calls for immediate US military intervention by various choice actors in the global and Yankee Right (especially those clustered around the "Lima Group"). All of this culminated, as mentioned above, in Juan Guaidó's failed coup attempt in April 2019. The Venezuelan situation is, indeed, catastrophic, due to the violent polarization, the constant attempts at destabilization coming from the outside, but also the government's own rapidly accelerating authoritarianism. As well, the problems of corruption and the lack of a diversification of production—in a context of almost total economic breakdown—are also an important part of this picture, as mass shortages, four-figure inflation, and the crisis of the healthcare system mean that a large proportion of the social advances of the Chávez period now look like an image from the past: since 2015, three-quarters of the population has been living in poverty. The process that incarnated the hope of "twenty-first century socialism" in the eyes of millions of people—or, at least, the dignity of defending national sovereignty from Uncle Sam's repeated interference—is merely a shadow of its former self.[116] Rather than help kick-start (either public or private) national industry, the government has preferred to respond to the various pressing needs by way of massive imports. For example, the public sector increased its imports by a gigantic 1,033 percent between 2003 and 2017, with annual increases as high as 51 percent (2007), rather than invest in the creation of its own companies:

> We can see that Bolivarian economic policy has nothing to do with a revolutionary, anti-capitalist change or even a metamorphosis of social production relations. The Bolivarian process has been nothing but another variant of the economic policies proper to the 'oil rentism' experienced during the first Carlos Andrés Pérez government (1974–79). The ideological, anti-imperialist and anti-business elements of various speeches confuse most analysts, who prefer to study presidential rhetoric rather than policies on the ground. Even if the Bolivarian government has increased social spending, nationalized companies, developed policies for direct transfers to the poorest, and subsidized public services, the main orientation of its economic policy has been nothing more than to pursue the parasitic appropriation of oil rent and then waste it through an escalation of controlling policies whose only result has been to accelerate the destruction of agriculture, industry and trade—to the benefit of financial and importer capitalism and the fattening of a highly corrupt bureaucratic and military caste that freely pillages the country, to the point of impoverishing it to levels never previously reached in this part of the world.[117]

This critical conjuncture also explains the extent to which intellectuals and militants have polarized into opposite camps, as crystalized in two international appeals (to which we will return in chapter 3). First, in May 2017, came the "Urgent International Call to Stop the Escalation of Violence in Venezuela—Looking at Venezuela beyond Polarization," which attacked Maduro's concentration of powers and lack of respect for the 1999 Constitution, insisting "we do not believe, as certain sectors of the Latin American left affirm, that we should a-critically defend what is presented as an 'anti-imperialist and popular government.' The unconditional support offered by certain activists and intellectuals not only reveals an ideological blindness, but is detrimental, as it—regrettably—contributes to the consolidation of an authoritarian regime."[118] Then came the response from the "The Network of Intellectuals and Artists in Defense of Humanity" (REDH) entitled "Who Will Accuse the Accusers?" One of its central arguments was the observation that the Venezuelan crisis is above all the product of imperialist aggression and an armed uprising organized by the neoliberal right, as well as an "economic war." This statement insisted that amid a regional context marked by the resurgence of right-wing forces, the left is obliged to close ranks behind the existing governments and leave "secondary contradictions" aside.[119]

For the critical sociologist Edgardo Lander, who does not in any way deny the extent of imperialist aggression, the return of this argument invoking "secondary contradictions"—an argument used widely in the age of Stalinism and the Cold War—displays a mounting regressive tendency, which seeks to avoid any debate on the internal tensions within the Venezuelan process. And this is especially important at a moment when the Constituent Assembly is being used as an avatar of the executive, designed to neutralize the National Assembly:

> The holding of the presidential recall referendum in 2016 was blocked, the gubernatorial elections that December were unconstitutionally postponed, and the National Assembly's prerogatives have been thwarted and usurped by the executive and the Supreme Tribunal of Justice. Starting in February 2016 the president began to govern on the basis of a state of exception—the 'economic emergency'—and in so doing expressly violated the conditions and time limits fixed in the 1999 Constitution. Assuming prerogatives which the Constitution instead grants to the sovereign people, Maduro called a National Constituent Assembly; the mechanisms of its election were designed to guarantee his total control over this assembly. A monochrome National Constituent Assembly was elected, with all 545 members identifying with the government. Once established, this assembly proclaimed itself plenipotentiary and

above the constitution. The majority of its decisions are adopted by acclamation or unanimously, without any debate.[120]

The end of the progressive cycle, or its reflux, has not always unfolded in such a radical or definitive manner as it has in the Brazilian or Venezuelan examples. In several countries, we instead see a social-liberal stabilization of the situation (as in Uruguay), or an election that leads to a change of government and a fresh neoliberal offensive (Argentina, Chile), or a "continuity" popular-nationalism that assumes a "degraded" or even regressive form. In Ecuador the victory of Rafael Correa's successor, Lenín Moreno, in the 2017 elections led to a war among the leaders of Alianza País (the movement supporting the president). There were fratricidal accusations in which Correa loyalists accused Moreno of planning to pull apart the post-neoliberal legacy, while Moreno's own followers accused Correa of authoritarianism, corruption, and bureaucratic inefficiency. According to Franklin Ramirez, Lenín Moreno's moves to relieve tensions with the CONAIE and certain social movements, while also sealing alliances with media magnates and top employers, represented an attempt to "de-Correa-ize" national politics, in a perspective of "post-populist pacification" and normalization, which would above all confirm the exhaustion of the earlier populist rhetoric.[121] Nonetheless, it seems that Moreno's efforts to distance himself from Correa are also a step away from the perspectives of social transformation that initially animated Alianza País itself: his agenda now seems to be determined by a pro-market turn dictated by business elites (from Guayaquil, in particular) and embodied in a team of ministers who are much more devotees of free trade than they are admirers of Marx.[122]

The existing schism between popular movements and the Moreno government broke wide open in 2019. In March of that year the International Monetary Fund agreed to lend Ecuador $4.2 billion as part of an expansion $10.2 billion "package" in which the Latin American Development Bank (CAF) also coughed up $1.8 billion, the World Bank $1.7 billion, and the Inter-American Development Bank $1.7 billion, with the remainder covered by a collection of smaller multilateral organizations.[123] As is usual in these arrangements, the loans came attached to conditional "structural reforms," focused mainly on reducing the fiscal deficit, reforming labor, increasing foreign reserves, and making conditions even more attractive for transnational corporate investment in the extractive sectors of Ecuador's economy. While the IMF has fixated on the deficit, in the most immediate sense the real problem is the dollarization of Ecuador's economy, which has deprived the country of any normal monetary policy capacity, and which has made imports exaggeratedly cheap and the production of industrial goods for export impossibly expensive to sustain.

On October 1, 2019, Moreno announced the accompanying adjustment package. Instantaneously, a popular uprising began. The immediate catalyst was a reduction to subsidies of gasoline and diesel, leading to a sharp rise in gasoline prices and a doubling of diesel prices overnight. This triggered the highest levels of social unrest in the country since the late 1990s and early 2000s. Beginning on October 3, eleven days of nationwide protests exposed the repressive, weak, and inept character of the Moreno regime. While transport drivers led the initial call, the leading edge of the protests was assumed by the rejuvenated CONAIE. Militant indigenous marches converged on Quito from some of the most impoverished and most indigenous provinces, such as Esmeraldas, Napo, Chimborazo, and Morona. Indigenous protests converged on Quito and were joined by students, the unemployed, precarious workers, and labor activists in running clashes with the armed forces and police. The seat of government had to be temporarily moved to the coastal city of Guayaquil. Moreno declared a state of emergency, suspending constitutional rights to mobility and association, and a 3:00 P.M. curfew was declared in Quito with thirty minutes' notice. At least five people were killed over the course of the protests, and 2,000 arrested.[124]

In Bolivia, after Evo Morales lost a 2016 referendum on a measure that would have allowed him to stand again for election, he was no longer troubled by keeping up appearances and secured the constitutional court's agreement that he could run for a fourth term anyway. The right took advantage of this dynamic in staging the successful coup d'état that ousted Morales in 2019.

It is true that throughout Latin America—as elsewhere in the world—the authoritarian state or even the "state of exception" seems to be strengthening, and even becoming normalized and constitutional. And the return of the forces of the right clearly confirms that these latter have, indeed, maintained their political influence, their capacity to adapt and to exploit the numerous weaknesses of the left, and even their ability to occupy the streets through mass mobilizations lasting several days. This is also the return to strength of conservative churches—particularly evangelist ones—that are now capable of conquering local governments (for instance, the mayoralty of Rio de Janeiro), of bringing governments to power, or of even bringing them down (again in Brazil, organized evangelists were key in the fall of Rousseff's government and the rise to office of Bolsonaro at the national level). In many areas, these religious movements have become the sole "mass organizations" rooted in civil society; and their most reactionary currents are dogged enemies of any emancipatory vision, even if it is projected into the medium or long term.[125] This turn to the right also sees the resurgence of a "combat neoliberalism"— particularly in Temer's and then Bolsonaro's Brazil, Macri's term in office in Argentina, and Áñez's Bolivia—but also a strengthening of its repressive face. The murder of the young pro-Mapuche demonstrator Santiago Maldonado in southern Argentina in August 2017, that of the Brazilian lesbian and feminist militant Marielle Franco in March 2018, and the massacres of at least nineteen mostly indigenous protesters in late 2019 in Bolivia, all have symbolized this repression that is hitting thousands of militants. This, at a time when countries like Colombia are sinking ever further into barbarism, with more than 80,000 official accumulated cases of "disappeared" people. The repression of social movement and trade union activists continues into the present under the right-wing presidency of Iván Duque. Reporting from Medellín for the *London Review of Books* in mid-July 2020, Forrest Hylton wrote:

> The gang rape of a teenage Emberá girl by Colombian soldiers in late June; the murders of the Afro-Colombian leaders Carmen Mena Ortiz and Armando Suárez Rodríguez on 6 July; the murder of the Indigenous leader Wilson Eduardo Baicue Quiguanas on 11 July (which makes 37 confirmed murders of movement leaders in 2020, with 49 cases still under investigation); the murder on 13 July of the ex-Farc combatant José Antonio Rivera (which makes 218 since 2016, and 34 in 2020)—these are not glitches. They are design features of the national security state and the narco-paramilitary organisations to which it gave birth (with consistent, decisive support from the US).[126]

The same could be said about Mexico, at least until the election of center-leftist Andrés Manuel López Obrador as president in 2018. It is still too early to determine how effective his administration will be at quelling the violence associated with the "War on Drugs" in that country, but early signs are not promising. The period of the initial consolidation of progressive governments saw a notable drop in all forms of state repression; but in these countries, too, from 2012 to 2013 we can see a growing recourse to the *mano dura* (iron fist), contradicting these left-wing governments' "friendly" international image.[127] For example, the Ecuadorian government of Correa passed anti-terrorist legislation in opposition to the demands of the Shuar peoples and protests against mining operations in the south of the country. Moreover, the murders of environmentalist figures opposed to extractivism like José Tendetza, Freddy Taish, and Bosco Wisuma remain marked with the stamp of impunity. In Brazil, while the current Bolsonaro government is sharply increasing the militarization of the *favelas* (poor urban neighborhoods), this logic of racialized social "cleansing," which first of all targets these neighborhoods' black inhabitants, was already very much present before the coup, especially after the passing of a new anti-terrorism law under Dilma Rousseff. We could also mention, in this same vein, the criminalization of struggles in 2013 or during the football World Cup in 2014, and indeed during the Rio Olympics of summer 2016. Similarly, the lack of condemnation of the crimes against trade unionists and criminalization of trade union struggles in Venezuela, and even the postponement of union elections at state oil company PDVSA and in the nationalized steel plants (with the Labor Minister's backing), make up part of this same picture. This is not to mention the explosion in the number of violent deaths in Caracas and many other major cities, along with a government response based on militarizing the poorest urban areas through a national plan cynically named Operation Liberation of the People (OLP). In Chile, Michelle Bachelet maintained and even extended the repression against the Mapuche people in the south of the country. She continued to apply the anti-terrorism law dating back to the Pinochet dictatorship, and if for some she embodied a friendly face as "mother" of the nation, numerous expressions of social movement, trade union, and student demands were met with extremely violent repression.

With the deployment of the "right hand" of the progressive or left-populist state, this latter becomes increasingly distant from the popular movements, or even directly confronts them. There were long multiple signs portending such a divorce between the social and governmental left. We might note that this was expressed in the extended conflict in Bolivia in 2011 over the plans to build a road through the TIPNIS" (Isiboro Sécure National Park and Indigenous Territory).[128] This normally protected space is home to between 7,000 and 12,000 indigenous natives, but also to thousands of settler-farmers, who support the executive's project. This road was meant to make this territory more accessible and help open up national capitalist development to Brazil. The government's authoritarianism, its refusal of any advance consultation, and its refusal to negotiate the route the road would take, all prompted indigenous people and unions to mount a sixty-six-day protest march to La Paz.

In September 2011 these marchers (around a thousand in number) were stopped at the foot of the Andes and violently repressed by the police. This prompted the resignation of the deputy minister of rural development and stirred a strong emotional response in both Bolivian and international public opinion. The workers' central, the COB, also rose up in a strong mobilization. Ultimately, Evo had to abandon these plans, at least momentarily; the project would not resurface again until 2017. Ultimately, it was approved.

> Bolivia seems caught in its own contradictions: the contradiction between the ecologist and indigenous stance it has taken and the reality of its domestic politics; the contradiction between the protection of its eastern spaces and its desire to participate fully in continental integration; finally, the contradiction between the promises of socio-political change and the reality of the return of a centralized state.[129]

As for Ecuador's Citizens' Revolution, it was Rafael Correa's abandonment of the Yasuni ITT (Ishpingo-Tambococha-Tiputini) project in August 2013 that accelerated the divorce with ecologists and indigenous communities. The idea had been to leave 20 percent of Ecuador's oil, situated beneath the Yasuni national park, underground—this being a region containing many of the world's most important biodiversity reserves and that is home to two indigenous groups living in voluntary isolation (the Tagaeri and the Taromenane). The originality of this project had won international renown for Correa. In exchange for this, Ecuador was expecting partial financial compensation from the international community, in the name of the "right not to emit greenhouse gases." But, faced with the selfishness of the "great powers" (more than $3 billion had been expected, whereas not much more than $10 million was collected), the president threw in the towel. For many activists, and even figures once close to Correa like Alberto Acosta, the project was still viable, despite everything. Correa, an economist with a productivist and extractivist vision, would never have believed in this. From the outset this unprecedented initiative was balanced between green capitalism and ecosocialism;[130] its ultimate abandonment opened up Amazonia to the mining companies a little further. When the "Yasunidos" collective submitted a petition to the National Electoral Commission (CNE), signed by no fewer than 757,636 Ecuadorian citizens, in hopes of sparking a popular-initiative referendum, it had no impact. The year 2014 would end with an attempt to evict the CONAIE from its historic headquarters, in a move that received international condemnation.[131]

Popular discontent or growing disappointment with the diverse varieties of progressivism also translated into a resurgence of struggles, a certain reactivation of the repertoires of mobilization, and sometimes even the appearance of new generations of activists, born in the late 1990s. Many examples of this can be seen, and many different types of actors were involved: peasants, urban youth, student and trade unionists, women, indigenous people, and so on. We can again see the plurality of plebeian forces that were mobilized in the 1990s. By way of example we could point to the growing revitalization of trade unionism in Chile, and indeed its politicization, despite the extreme spread of precarity. We should also mention the rediscovered strength of a radical, dynamic, popular, mass, and clearly internationalist feminist movement, with the rise of "Ni una menos" ("Not one less").[132] This movement against the killing of women, violence against women, and patriarchy itself first began in Argentina in 2015, bringing together hundreds of thousands of demonstrators. It then spread across the whole of Latin America and far beyond. The "feminist revolution" in Chile in May–June 2018, with the occupation of more than twenty universities and several weeks of youth mobilizations against gender violence and for equality, showed that this movement was a real groundswell. Popular feminism was also at the forefront of the late 2019 and early 2020 uprisings in Chile. In Brazil, these new resistances translated—among other things—into the growing strength of movements like the Homeless Workers' Movement (MTST), which protests against problems in accessing housing (especially in São Paulo state) or indeed ones like the Movement of People Affected by Dams (MAB). But without doubt, the great mobilizations of urban youth in June 2013 represented the first major confrontation between the PT and a mass movement. This in turn opened the way to a reconfiguration of social struggles, a different relationship with the state, as well as a new protest cycle that broke through the demobilization and the conservative pact that the "PT-CUTist" model of control or integration had been able to entrench in previous years:

> Like all movements of this type, the days of protest action in June mixed together different voices, actors and demands. They took root in a highly contemporary grammar of mobilization, whether in terms of their slogans, their forms of organization or the link that was created between individuals, the movement and society. The launching of these massive demonstrations did not owe to big civil-society organizations but to a relatively modest network of young 'alter-activists':

the 'Passe livre' movement, which fights for free public transport. Protesting against the bus companies' price hikes (and in Brazil these services are largely privatized), it opened up a vast field of conflicts around urban transport, which gradually extended to include other public services (education, healthcare, police abuses, etc.) and then the relationship between society and the state, to the point that it became the space for the expression of an indignation that had previously been latent and yet relatively generalized among Brazilians as a whole. The viral spread of the movement, its networked forms of organization, and the mainstreaming of its agenda ultimately rallied millions of citizens.[133]

These diverse, largely urban protests now opened the way to the expression of the discontentment that had built up against the PT, as well as of more particular demands—which were sometimes quite varied, or even sharply opposed among themselves. The June protests mobilized militants on the anti-capitalist left who challenged the government from its left, but so, too, from the right and even the far-right. These latter forces also rushed into the fissure that had opened up, as they sought to build their own mass mobilizations and thus prepare the destabilization of Dilma Rousseff and the sidelining of Lula. This is one of the paradoxes, and the difficulties of the era that comes at the "end of the progressive cycle": clearly, it does not automatically benefit the radical or revolutionary left. Quite the contrary: their forces have often proven too minoritarian, dispersed, dogmatic, or lacking in credibility to be able to embody a concrete alternative for government, not least in a situation in which the "populist" incorporation of the popular classes is mostly carried out by means of welfare provision and the extension of access to credit—that is, through consumption and the market rather than through politicization, the building of class consciousness and of community, or self-managed organization. Cristina Fernández de Kirchner's comment in this regard has become famous: "You know what there is to my left? Nothing but the wall" (2014). This phrase was all the more provocative in a country in which—like it or not—a "Left and Workers' Front" (FIT) has been built over recent years, bringing together three small historic Trotskyist organizations, and which managed in the 2017 parliamentary elections to win more than 1.3 million votes, to gain three MP, and most importantly to sink strong roots in several bastions of combative trade unionism. However, in the presidential elections, FIT-U—the successor of FIT—won only 600,000 votes, having been electorally marginalized and weakened by both sectarianism and the internal controversies of some of its constitutive organizations.[134]

A similar dynamic is true of the Socialism and Liberty Party (PSOL) in Brazil, which has remained fairly marginal in electoral terms, but, most importantly, seeks to animate an anti-capitalist, feminist, and ecosocialist space to the left of the PT, while also standing Guilherme Boulos, a MTST leader with a background in popular struggles, as a presidential candidate. Nonetheless, in each case these forces very much appear marginal faced with the wider retreat of the progressivisms and the steamroller being driven by the right and the dominant media. This is all the more so, given that they seem immersed in the most utter confusion. For instance, the heteroclite left-wing coalition that stood against Correa's successor in the 2017 presidential election was led by the social-democratic retired general Paco Moncayo; its candidate as well as a section of its supporters (including several indigenous leaders) ended up calling for a second-round vote for the neoliberal banker Lasso out of hatred of the "dictator Correa," thus losing both any credibility and any political compass. In many cases, then, the fall in the popularity of the existing leaders does not translate—in the short term, at least—into the rebuilding of a radical or revolutionary left-political perspective. This phenomenon is aggravated by the systematic obstacles placed in front of those treated as "dissidents" and "traitors" or considered "sham revolutionaries" in service of the right, or even as enemies, by the governmental left. Thus in Bolivarian Venezuela the independent candidates representing a "critical" *chavismo*—anarchist and Trotskyist milieus, or even some former allies of *chavismo* who are today opposed to Maduro, given the electoral manipulations and the overlapping of powers—are treated as enemies, intimidated, or even persecuted and arrested. Former interior minister Miguel Rodríguez Torres can bear witness to this. At a deeper level, the fracture between the Bolivarian government and the popular categories has grown in tandem with the economic crisis and the cycle of violence (fueled by the "hard" sections of the right). For if Maduro has succeeded in showing that he was indeed capable of grasping the political process by the scruff of the neck and securing new legitimacy at the ballot box—indeed, repeatedly so (starting with the 2018 presidential elections)—and by neutralizing a large part of the opposition and driving it out of office, then some of the historic bastions of *chavismo* have now gone adrift. The fact that a Caracas neighborhood with such a historic record of popular resistance as 23 de Enero is no longer won for the government is itself highly symbolic, all the more so given that this same district was the site of violent demonstrations against the National Electoral Council proclaiming the PSUV candidates alone as having been elected to the National Constituent Assembly, to the detriment of the independent candidates on the *chavista* left.[135] Moreover, it is worth underlining that according to the estimate of the United Nations, roughly 5 million people had fled Venezuela by the end of 2019, mainly to neighboring Colombia, but also in significant numbers to Peru, Chile, Ecuador, Brazil, and Argentina.[136] This is above all an economic exile, consisting mainly of Venezuelans from the poor and middle classes.

Overall, whether we are faced with a more or less violent return of the pro-imperialist right or a regressive reflux of the initial left-populist or progressive impulse, without these latter forces yet being defeated at the ballot box, this period again seems to be characterized by the search "for the left from below," as the necessary basis of any emancipatory perspective that seeks to overcome the limits and contradictions of the progressive cycle, without thereby aligning with conservative and oligarchic forces. The return of forms of popular- and working-class resistance, each with its own agenda, augurs possibly rapid recompositions of the class struggle. One indicator of all this is the massive general strike that Brazil saw in late April 2017, faced with the illegitimate Temer government's counterreform of the labor market, which sparked uproar far behind the ranks of the CUT and PT leaderships, followed by another massive general strike against the Bolsonaro administration in late June 2019. On this same register, there were massive demonstrations against Mauricio Macri's pension reform in December 2017; the government response was a level of repression not seen since December 2001. This was followed by a fall in Macri's popularity, as confirmed in the parliamentary elections, and his defeat in the 2019 presidential contest. In addition to the uprisings in Ecuador and Chile in 2019 mentioned above, that same year witnessed impressive popular revolts in both Puerto Rico and Colombia.[137] *Contra* the left-populist interpretations inspired by Ernesto Laclau,[138] this is also a matter of going beyond a state-centric vision of processes of rupture that are hyper-dependent on the leader-*caudillo* figure, already very well-established on account of the presidentialist traditions of Latin America's political system. Rather than eulogize populism, the important thing is to build on popular movements' capacities of self-organization and self-management and then to put the questions of antagonisms of class, races, and genders in society back at the heart of the ecosocialist emancipatory project. Indeed, making the universe of class explicit is vitally important in the current Latin American conjuncture, because the different projects being debated—neoliberal, neo-developmentalist, radically anti-imperialist—express class interests that need to be clarified. These ideas in turn sustain very different projects, from the renewal of the existing plutocracies to the construction of a new political system.[139]

Another part of the present challenge is to draw on the vitality of Latin American critical thinking—all of it that refuses to bend to the injunctions of the established authorities and seeks to contribute to popular resistance, despite a difficult context in which neoliberal forces are winning back control of government or the authoritarian state is becoming increasingly powerful.[140] The crisis of the progressive experiences indicates, above all, that a project of social transformation can never be limited to "reforms from above" along with a redeployment of the state based on a redistribution of raw materials revenues, the intensification of extractivism, and the embrace of destructive models of consumption. The end of this cycle also confirms that there are gigantic obstacles and difficulties to overcome. These first include the historic weight of the legacies of colonialism and imperialism; next, the structural dependence of economies and elites; and, as well, the impossibility of a long-term rupture in a single country, without integration into solidarity encompassing the regional level. (The difficulties of the Cuban Revolution are another kind of confirmation of this.)[141] The end of this cycle, moreover, illustrates the resilience of the dynamics of capitalism and neoliberal institutions, as well as the depth of the power of the ruling class and of its ideological and media apparatuses to thwart any attempt at change, however tiny or moderate. Finally, it shows the contradictions and tensions within the popular camp, when it is thinking through the possibilities of other worlds beyond capitalism and extractivism, and does so in conditions dominated by corporatist and conservative reflexes, as well as by the divisions between organizations, everyday violence and organized crime, careerism (for some), and precarious individual situations (for the majority).

Nonetheless, the politics of emancipation in "Our America" are constantly being built and elaborated anew, and, despite the present disenchantment throughout the world, the paths to a democratic, ecosocial, feminist, and internationalist anti-capitalism remain open. The eclipse of the period that began in the early 1990s is pregnant with dangers, but also with potential, *if* critical lessons are drawn from these recent experiences and *if* the rising far-right and neoliberal forces are resolutely confronted in the streets and at the ballot box. Faced with the generalized corruption, authoritarianism, maldevelopment and malaise, patriarchy, and the destruction of ecosystems, finding ways out of the "capitalist labyrinth" is not only possible but indispensable.[142] The task now is not only to think in terms of "post-neoliberalism": more broadly, the end of the present crisis makes up part of the global crisis of capitalist civilization. This obliges us to rethink from the ground up the possibilities of ecosocialist alternatives, a society of the commons and *buen vivir*[143]—not only in *opposition* to the existing dominant order, but *for* the restoration of the "principle of hope," in service of future generations of humanity.

The specific political-economic hurdles any such project would face in Latin America are revealed in the next chapter's extended analysis of this component of the experience of Latin American progressive governments' attempts at reform in the twenty-first century in a context of shifting winds in the world market and the pressures of imperialism.

2. WORLD MARKET, PATTERNS OF ACCUMULATION, AND IMPERIAL DOMINATION THE POLITICAL ECONOMY OF THE LATIN AMERICAN LEFT

Politics and economics, according to the Argentinian political economist Claudio Katz, have been out of synch in twenty-first century Latin American politics. While the two dimensions are closely related, with mutations in one always impinging on the other, they do not always proceed at the same rhythm, or even move in the same direction.[1] As we outlined in the previous chapter, politically, the left turn—or "pink tide"—that began at the turn of the millennium disrupted elitist citizenship regimes associated with the preceding neoliberal model of economic development.[2] There were important democratic conquests, such as the constituent assemblies and new constitutions in Bolivia, Ecuador, and Venezuela.[3] Laws granting impunity to leading figures of the Argentinian dictatorship (1976–1983) were overturned as unconstitutional.[4] Progressive governments have also allowed for maneuver room—albeit sometimes reluctantly—for social movements from below. Even a cursory comparison with the repressive right-wing regimes of Colombia, Peru, Honduras, and Mexico on this score is instantly revealing. In many countries where the left has made advances, there has been an ideological recovery of anti-imperialist traditions, as well as the revival of more thoroughgoing conceptions of popular sovereignty.[5] In a few countries, the question of what socialism might look like in the contemporary world was at least raised, if not actualized. Important experiments were also conducted in alternative regional integration projects to counter US dominance in the region.[6]

And yet, as this chapter's stress on economic dynamics reveals, these political and ideological advances failed to translate into either a transformation of class structures or an alteration of Latin America's subordinate insertion into the international division of labor. Right-wing governments, such as those in Colombia (under both Álvaro Uribe and Juan Manuel Santos) and Peru (under Alejandro Toledo, Alan García, and Ollanta Humala), utilized the commodities boom (2003–2011) to further consolidate neoliberal pillars of their economies. Center-left governments, like Luiz Inácio Lula da Silva's and Dilma Rousseff's in Brazil and Nestor Kirchner's and Cristina Fernández de Kirchner's in Argentina, entered into modest confrontation with some neoliberal precepts, while leaving others intact. In more-radical processes, such as those in Bolivia and Venezuela, under Hugo Chávez and Evo Morales respectively, greater breaches of the inherited order were put on the agenda, but rarely—and then, only partially—realized. The desynchronization of politics and economics is an expression, in this instance, of popular rebellions mitigating the frenzy of neoliberal torment, without uprooting its groundwork. They were uprisings strong enough to prevent their own routing, but too weak to mature into triumphant anti-capitalist revolution, or even deep structural reformation.[7]

In the boom years, South America, in particular, achieved relatively high average annual aggregate rates of real per capita income growth—between 2003 and 2011, 4.1 percent. This translates into a 78 percent improvement on the 2.3 percent rate of the high-neoliberal era (1990–2002).[8] Export revenues—whether from mining minerals, agro-industrial commodities, or natural gas and oil—were used by progressive governments to fund targeted social policies for pauperized strata, to increase and sustain employment rates (albeit typically in insecure and low-paid jobs), and to spike domestic consumption. Measurable improvements were seen in living conditions for popular sectors of society. Poverty was reduced while income inequality was slightly reduced (though this was also true of some countries in the region led by right-wing governments, and the region remains the most unequal in the world).[9] The pace of privatizations slowed and was even reversed in some economic sectors in a few countries. Increases in spending on basic social services and infrastructure in poor urban neighborhoods and marginalized rural areas mitigated some of the residual social damage of the neoliberal period. Access to basic free education was expanded, and in some cases access to university was democratized.[10] These social gains, limited as they were, have been endangered since the end of the commodities boom, with the fallout from the global economic crisis affecting Latin America sharply since 2012, and issuing in a new era of low growth and state austerity.

This chapter analyzes the political economy of Latin American progressivism through an examination of regional trends, while linking these trends to the wider dynamics of the world market, including the geopolitics of imperialism. The discussion is divided into six parts. First, the chapter provides a survey of the rise and decline of neoliberal orthodoxy (1980–2000) in the region, in order to situate the Latin American left turn in the twenty-first century as quintessentially a response to the specific crisis that regional capitalism entered into at the close of its high-neoliberal phase. Second, the chapter explores the political-economic consequences of the coincidence of center-left and left parties' assuming office in much of South America and parts of Central America at precisely the same moment as a nascent international commodities boom (2003–2011). This section examines the specific dynamics of the intensification of extractive capitalism under progressive governments in the areas of mining, natural gas and oil, and agro-industry. Third, it maps the political-economic limits of the break with neoliberalism attempted by a variety of progressive governments in the region; that is, it highlights neoliberal continuities into twenty-first century Latin America. Fourth, the chapter explores the delayed effects of the global economic crisis of 2008 in Latin America. Fifth, it situates the broad patterns of accumulation in the region discussed in previous sections within the influencing dynamics of imperialism, and in particular the dominant trends in foreign direct investment, along with the imperial strategies of the United States and China vis-à-vis Latin America. Sixth and finally, it explores the attempts made by Latin American progressivism in the twenty-first century to forge novel projects of regional integration as a counterweight to imperial domination in general, and US domination in particular.

Neoliberalism

In assessing the political-economic limits of the recent rise and decline of progressivism in Latin America, it is helpful to begin with the dynamics of the preceding neoliberal period. Continuities and breaks across the last four decades, as well as breaks in continuity, can thus be established. The orthodox neoliberal period in the region stretched from the early 1980s debt crisis to the steep recession of the late 1990s and early 2000s. The erratic economic performance over this tumultuous period commences with a deep recession of 1982–1983, and traverses a short-lived recovery in positive per capita growth from 1984 to 1987, a period of widening and deepening reforms between 1988 and 1991, and a series of consolidation measures— "second generation reforms"—over the course of the 1990s and early 2000s, amidst a sequence of sharp financial crises in Mexico in 1994, Brazil in 1998, and Argentina in 2001.[11]

Growth was poor in the neoliberal era relative to the preceding decades of import substitution industrialization (1930–1980). If between 1933 and 1980 the average annual rate of economic growth of Brazil and Mexico was 6.3 and 6.4 percent, respectively, between 1981 and 2000 these rates fell to 2.1 and 2.7 percent.[12] The period 1990–2001 is sometimes considered another "lost decade" for Latin America, after the entirety of the 1980s was lost to the debt crisis. Average growth in the second lost decade was only 1.6 percent, relative to 0.8 percent between 1980 and 1990.[13] The region's total debt by 2002, sitting at $US 725 billion, was twice what it had been at the onset of the debt crisis in the early 1980s. Financial resources—net debt flows, foreign direct investment (FDI), bonds, and equity capital—flowing into Latin America between 1990 and 2001 reached $US 1.0 trillion. However, outflows—debt service, interest payments, and profit remittances—simultaneously increased, meaning that net inflows ultimately amounted to only $US 108.3 billion. This figure was unable to cover the deficit in investment catalyzed by the acute diminution in public spending and the savings rate, both prescribed by advocates of neoliberal structural adjustment policy across the 1980s and 1990s.[14] As growth faltered, the proportion of the region's population in poverty shot up from 40.5 percent in 1980 to 44 percent in 2002.[15] In absolute terms, this meant that 84 million additional people entered poverty in the region between 1980 and 2002. Still the most unequal region in the world, in 2003 the top 10 percent of its population captured 48 percent of all income.[16]

By the end of the 1990s, neoliberalism entered into a severe economic crisis, which soon ushered in a parallel crisis of political rule. There were medium and short-term dynamics to this dual impasse of neoliberal economics and politics. The underlying medium-run dynamic was associated with the socioeconomic fallout from two decades of neoliberal restructuring— low growth, sharp financial instability, and skyrocketing inequality. This set of factors underpinned and made more dramatic the short-term problem of steep economic recession between 1998 and 2002. In aggregate terms, the region as a whole suffered negative per capita growth over this four-year interregnum. On the back of two decades of worsening social conditions, poverty and unemployment spiked still further in the context of recession. Symptoms of the growing politicization of the economic downturn started to become visible everywhere—declining support for (mainly right-wing, pro-market) incumbent ruling parties throughout the region; a dramatic resurgence in extra-parliamentary social movements contesting neoliberalism through riots, strikes, road blocks, factory takeovers, land occupations, and myriad additional repertoires of collective action; and a general decline in the legitimacy of neoliberalism in public opinion, as indicated in a major 2004 Latinobarómetro poll that showed that 70 percent of the Latin American population was dissatisfied with the performance of the market economy.[17]

Within a couple of years of the close of the 1998–2002 recession, the early, extra-parliamentary social movement militancy that was gaining ground throughout much of the region started to find at least muted political translation on the terrain of formal electoral cycles. Center-left and left governments began to replace right and center-right governments throughout South America and into parts of Central America, such that the electoral map by the mid-2000s had been fundamentally reconfigured. Only a few residual, conservative hangovers from the 1990s remained intact—the regimes of Mexico, Colombia, Peru, and Chile standing out among them.

Commodities Boom and Extractive Capitalism

In terms of political economy, the most significant feature of the new period of progressive electoral ascent was the fact that it coincided with renewed capitalist growth in the region. The period 2001–2008 registered the highest regional growth (3.7 percent) since the 1970–1980 period (3.2 percent).[18] An international commodities boom, driven above all by Chinese industrial demand, began in 2003 and persisted until 2011. This boom accounts for much of the upturn in economic growth. Chinese demand as a proportion of world consumption across a range of commodities—from aluminum, to oil, to soybeans—increased dramatically between 2002 and 2012. As a result, throughout South America, and to a lesser degree in parts of Central America, and even parts of Mexico, there was a significant intensification of agro-industrial mono-cropping (particularly soy), mining, and natural gas and oil extraction.[19]

The fact that this deepening of extractive capitalism was being driven primarily by Chinese demand had an important impact on aggregate trade patterns, particularly in South America. China became the principal destination for South America's main exports, replacing the United States, even if the latter remained the dominant destination for Latin American and Caribbean exports as a whole. Central America and, especially, Mexico remained deeply intertwined with the US economy, affecting aggregate trends for Latin America and the Caribbean.[20]

Latin America and the Caribbean were uniquely positioned for the provision of many of the commodities that China required. The region contains 25 percent of the world's forests and 40 percent of its biodiversity. It is also home to 85 percent of all known reserves of lithium, and a third of copper, bauxite, and silver reserves. Latin America and the Caribbean are similarly rich in coal, oil, gas, and uranium, with 27, 25, 8, and 5 percent respectively of all discovered deposits in the world currently being exploited. New underwater oil reserves, meanwhile, are regularly being discovered along the region's vast coast lines. Finally, the region contains 35 percent of the globe's potential hydroelectricity and the biggest reserves of freshwater under its soil.[21]

Even before the latest commodities boom, the transition to neoliberalism, and away from import-substitution industrialization (ISI), had already involved a strong reorientation of agricultural production toward exports and a refocusing of governmental minds on mining and natural gas and oil extraction.[22] Ironically, the latest cycle of progressive governments has consolidated this trajectory in a context of high prices. While the contribution of primary commodities to Latin America's GDP rose in the twenty-first century, the contribution of the industrial sector declined from 12.7 percent in 1970–1974 to 6.4 percent in 2002–2006. Simultaneously, Latin America's productivity, technological innovation, pace of patent registrations, and levels of investment and development in industry weakened relative to accelerations across these areas in East Asia.[23]

For Maristella Svampa, one of the keenest observers of this "new extractivism," the subregional shift in South America toward primary commodity exports destined for China should be characterized as a turn away from the "Washington Consensus" of neoliberalism in the 1980s and 1990s, to the "Commodities Consensus" of the present.[24] The renewed focus on primary commodity exports witnessed the expansion of megaprojects across mining, oil exploitation, and capital-intensive agro-industry—including supportive energy infrastructure such as hydroelectric megadams—designed to extract and export natural resources with little value added. Open-pit mining projects proliferated, oil exploitation advanced in tropical areas, hydraulic fracturing ("fracking") was introduced, and the surface area dedicated to monocropping exploded.[25]

The common extractive logic across these distinct areas are their expansive scale, export orientation, monopolization of land and territory, predominance of transnational capital, and absence of democratic control from below. Furthermore, they are characterized by growing ecological devastation and negative social and health consequences.²⁶ The granting of concessions to private capital for resource exploitation of minerals and hydrocarbons transforms territories and landscapes, both in terms of the immediate projects being put into motion, as well as in their adjacent energy infrastructures. The extension of agricultural frontiers likewise reconfigures ecologically fragile territories for the fleeting pursuit of profits by capital.²⁷ The extension of the mining, agro-industrial, and natural gas and oil frontiers has involved "a deepening dynamic of dispossession or plunder of lands, resources, and territories, and produces new forms of dependency and domination."²⁸ It has also been accompanied by the contamination of soil, the loss of biodiversity, and the pollution of waterways used for peasant and indigenous socioeconomic practices and social-reproductive strategies.²⁹

Extractivism as a model of accumulation has also meant a reconfiguration of ideological worldviews, in which a fetishistic productivism now reigns again throughout Latin America, regardless of important political differences between progressive and conservative governments. Shared axiomatic premises across otherwise distinct political genealogies include a commitment to productively utilizing natural resources to take advantage of conjuncturally high global commodity prices. As the monetization of natural resources is held up as the overarching aim of state management, there is a simultaneous "disqualification of other logics of valorizing territories," territories that are considered by state managers and private investors alike to be "socially empty" until they have been made "useful" by the metrics of exchange-value, or profit.³⁰

Abundant resource rents were utilized by progressive governments to establish a variety of "compensatory states" in different countries, in which political legitimacy was predicated on the modest redistributive outcomes achieved in part through targeted cash transfer programs to the poorest sectors of society, while underlying class structures and social-property relations remained predominantly intact.³¹ Relatively high social spending, in the context of high growth, lubricated consensus politics in these new compensatory states, despite the fact that cash transfer programs were never designed to confront the structural causes of the reproduction of poverty and inequality in Latin American societies.³² Compensatory states, therefore, broke with specific elements of the orthodox neoliberal policy toolkit in terms of the scale of social spending, but largely left intact the structural bases of the economy. While social spending on the poor, together with improved employment opportunities generated through relatively high economic growth, alleviated poverty to a certain degree in many countries, such modest improvements for the popular classes coexisted with unprecedented net profits for foreign and domestic private capital investing in natural resource sectors.[33] The coincidence of high export prices and volumes, on the one hand, and low borrowing rates and high international liquidity, on the other hand, facilitated higher rates of national production and credit expansion, which in turn fueled domestic demand via household consumption, capital investment, and public spending on social services and public infrastructure.[34] The cases of Venezuela and Brazil are useful exemplars of two opposite poles along the political-economic continuum of compensatory states. Venezuela is the compensatory state that broke most thoroughly with neoliberalism, while Brazil is the one that most minimally modified the preceding political-economic order. Despite their differences, however, stark structural similarities can be found in each case that highlight the limits of Latin America's latest left turn in transforming inherited social-property relations and the region's subordinate insertion into the international division of labor.

Neoliberal Continuities in the Twenty-First Century

With hindsight, what is perhaps most striking are the significant underlying structural continuities—regarding the region's position in the world market and its internal class structures—across the orthodox neoliberal period and the era of the compensatory state. One basic set of observations, as we have seen, has to do with the velocious turn to primary commodity exports already by the 1980s, during the heyday of orthodox neoliberalism.[35] In agriculture, the renewed focus on exporting basic commodities transformed not only the crops being cultivated, but also the social relations underlying rural life in the region. Agribusiness corporations became the chieftains of agrarian counterreform, leading a conversion to capital-intensive mono-cropping. Older landed oligarchies were transformed into allies through close economic association with the new entrants—transnational agribusiness corporations.[36] Soy fields—ultimately for cooking oil and animal feed—now dominate the landscapes of Argentina, Brazil, Paraguay, and Uruguay. Monsanto and other multinational giants predominate in these huge operations, which generate on average just one job for every 100–150 hectares under production.[37] If agro-industrial capital was the game-changer in the elaboration of the new dynamic, small producers were its disposable by-product. Dispossession of peasants manifested itself through increased input costs, competitive pressures, and risks associated with bumps and dips in the international market. Attempting to adapt to the novel imperatives of agro-chemical inputs, refrigeration, and rapid transportation, small producers frequently became indebted, lost their lands, and migrated to the cities, joining a growing reserve of unemployed and underemployed informal proletarians.

Growth of the agro-mining complex is closely related to the relative decline of industry. As noted, the weight of manufacturing in Latin American GDP in 2002–2006 was approximately half of what it had been in 1970–1974, and the directionality did not change under progressive governments; indeed, it often worsened. But rather than industry disappearing altogether, it has been restructured in a subordinate way to the latest cycle of dependent reproduction.[38] In Brazil, productivity has decelerated, costs have jumped, and there is scarce industrial investment in a context of rapidly deteriorating energy and transportation infrastructure. Similarly, in Argentina, in spite of small reversals in the last decade, regression of industry continues, with a move from 23 to 17 percent of GDP since the 1980s, concentration of foreign ownership, and weak links to national production of component parts.[39] The progressive political cycle of the early twenty-first century across much of the region has not modified Latin America's vulnerability in the face of twists in the world market. This fragility persists, in part, because of the relative decline of industry and expansion of primary exports, as well as the lack of productive diversification.[40]

In smaller countries in the region, remittances and tourism have become ever more important in terms of generating foreign exchange. Latin America has been transformed into the biggest regional recipient of remittances, with at least eight countries counting them as their first source of foreign exchange—the Dominican Republic, El Salvador, Guatemala, Guyana, Haiti, Honduras, Jamaica, and Nicaragua—and a number of others, their second source—Belize, Bolivia, Colombia, Ecuador, Paraguay, and Surinam.[41] Much of this flows from the United States, of course, where roughly 30 million documented and undocumented Latin American migrants reside.[42]

Transformations in agriculture, mining, industry, remittances, and tourism have had an impact on class formation, from above and below. The more-successful Latin American capitalist groups have become more concentrated and internationalized, establishing regional clusters called *multilatinas*.[43] These multilatinas emerged from wealthy families with familiar surnames—Slim (Mexico); Cisneros (Venezuela); Noboa (Ecuador); Santo Domingo (Colombia); Andrónico Lucski (Chile); Bulgheroni and Rocca (Argentina);

Lemann, Safra, and Moraer (Brazil)—and have tied themselves to global management, extending their priorities to a regional scale. Brazil and Mexican multilatinas are leading the pack, followed by Argentinian and Chilean enterprises.[44] Although these entities are more powerful than Latin American corporations of the past, the regional capitalist class remains secondary on a global scale, and has lost significant ground to competitors in Asia.[45]

Urban labor markets, meanwhile, have deteriorated with the privatization of state-owned enterprises, the decline of public sector employment, and the relative decline of industry. Precarity, a normal feature of capitalism historically, is extending its purview in the present phase. In a number of countries, marginalized youth have sought refuge in the burgeoning narco-economy, where they often end up contributing—in one sense or another—to soaring homicide statistics.[46] The extractive model of accumulation—agro-industry, mining, natural gas and oil—creates few jobs, and what industrial jobs remain are increasingly "informalized," through the spreading use of flexible, nonunion, female workers.[47]

Under most left administrations, there has been an extension of social assistance to temper the worst of impoverishment. But the priming of cash transfers to the extreme poor was only ever a transitory stopgap, offering no solution to the root causes of the problem. Crucially, these programs persist alongside precarity in, and informalization of, the world of work along neoliberal lines.[48] While there has been a diminution in income inequality in the twenty-first century, the aggregate Gini coefficient of the region (51.6) remains well above the global average (39.5), and is double that of the average in advanced economies.[49]

Global Crisis Reaches Latin America

The worst crisis of world capitalism since the 1930s was always bound to have an impact on Latin American politics and economics, even if its initial epicenter in 2007–2008 was the United States and, slightly later, the Eurozone.[50] Indeed, the crisis did pinch the region, severely, but it took almost four years for this to begin in earnest.[51] Initially, aggregate growth in Latin America and the Caribbean continued at a relatively high rate of 4.8 percent in 2008, followed by a dip to 1.9 percent in 2009 and a steady resumption of growth at 5.9 percent in 2010 and 4.3 percent in 2011.[52] The fact that commodity prices remained steady due to continued dynamism in China was critically important. Additionally, elevated international liquidity and low borrowing rates (due in part to an external context marked by the expansive monetary policies of the Federal Reserve and the European Central Bank), an increase in FDI flowing into the natural resource sectors of Latin America, and countercyclical spending on the part of many governments in the region—tapping into foreign reserves accumulated during the boom—helped initially to mitigate the effects of the world crisis in the region.[53] Of course, this general summary conceals heterogeneity across subregions and particular countries, which will become clearer below. For the moment, it is sufficient to note that although the initial impact of the crisis in South America was muted, mainly because of the shift in the first decade of the twenty-first century toward deeper trading relationships with China, and away from the US market, the country of Mexico and the regions of both Central America and the Caribbean remained deeply integrated with the American economy. From the outset of the crisis in the United States, then, these latter subregions were much more dramatically affected than South America. Simultaneously, they suffered a collapse in their principal export destination, and a slowdown in remittances from migrant laborers, as well as a return from some migrant laborers who had been laid off in the United States, adding pressure to domestic labor markets.[54]

Countercyclical spending efforts in several countries could not withstand the impact of the winding down of the commodities boom, with a drop in mining mineral and agro-industrial commodities beginning in 2011, and, slightly later, a plunge in oil and natural gas prices in mid-2014.[55] Growth in China began to falter significantly in 2011, even if the country remained one of the zones of highest growth in the world. At the same time, the lack of recovery in the United States and the Eurozone meant that there were no dynamic areas of accumulation in the world market to pick up the slack induced by deceleration in China. The enormous fall in China's average annual growth between the periods of 2003–2008 and 2010–2016, from 9.4 to 6.6 percent (a total decline of 29.8 percent), was accompanied by proportionally bigger contractions in the Eurozone, from 1.5 to 0.9 percent (a total drop of 43.2 percent), and the United States, from 2.4 to 1.5 percent (a total hit of 38.4 percent).[56]

The sustained deterioration of the external environment did not affect all subregions equally. The end of the commodities boom had a devastating impact on South America, and a negative effect on Mexico, while net importers of oil and natural gas in much of the Caribbean and Central America benefited from the downturn in prices in this respect. The slowdown in China struck exports in South America particularly hard, whereas the downtrend in the United States was much more serious for Mexico, Central America, and the Caribbean.[57] If the key mechanism for the transmission of the crisis to South America was a fall in commodity prices driven by slackening Chinese demand, the mechanisms into Mexico, Central America, and the Caribbean were a fall in remittances from documented and undocumented labor in the United States, and a decline in exports to their main export destination, as the economy of the United States withered on the vine.

The effects of the ongoing global slump became ever more clearly discernible in Latin America as time passed. While annual aggregate growth across Latin America and throughout the Caribbean had been 3.9 percent in the 2003–2008 period, it was only 2.8 percent between 2010 and 2016. Although most regions of the world grew more slowly in the latter period, the downturn in Latin America and the Caribbean was notably sharper than elsewhere.[58]

Whereas in 2011 aggregate growth in Latin America and the Caribbean reached 4.7 percent, this was followed by a downturn to 2.9 percent in both 2012 and 2013, with a sharp plunge to 1.1 percent in 2014, the lowest rate of growth since 2009. Finally, in 2015 and 2016 there were negative growth rates in the region as a whole, at −0.4 and −1.0 percent, respectively, with Argentina, Brazil, and Venezuela being the most affected of the large economies. The subregion of South American contracted by 1.2 and 2.9 percent in 2015 and 2016, respectively.[59] There was a weak recovery of growth in 2017 and 2018 to 1.3 percent and 1.2 percent, respectively, in Latin America and the Caribbean.[60] In 2019, eighteen of twenty Latin American countries (twenty-three of thirty-three Latin American and Caribbean countries) experienced a slowdown in growth of economic activity, as global recessionary dynamics returned. The world economy grew by only 2.5 percent, which was the lowest growth rate since the global crisis of 2008.[61] Commodity prices experienced an average decline of 5.0 percent in 2019, contributing significantly to Latin American economic trends.[62] Over the first half of 2019, Latin America's GDP fell from 1.34 percent in 2018 to 0 percent. Only Colombia and Guatemala escaped an economic slowdown relative to the previous year.[63] In the first half of 2019, South American economies contracted on average by 0.26 percent from 1 percent growth in 2018. Central America grew at a rate of 2.8 percent growth over the same period, a 1.5 percent contraction relative to growth in 2018. Central American and Mexican growth in the first half of 2019 was a combined 0.6 percent, a sharp fall from 2.2 percent the previous year.[64]

Between 2009 and 2016, as exports and investments fell in importance, government spending and credit-driven private consumption drove what little economic growth there was.[65] Financial liberalization, initiated in preceding decades, continues to allow for financial resources to flow into the region even as FDI diminishes. In particular, such inwardly flowing resources are taking the form of credit to the private sector. On the one hand, there has been a concerted expansion of household debt. On the other hand, the nonfinancial corporate sector in Latin America is seizing on the escalating role of international bond markets and has increased its borrowing levels substantially.[66] In an analysis of the ratio of private credit to GDP across the periods of 1995–2008 and 2010–2015, what is most evident is that the growth of credit to the private sector and rising household borrowing levels are increasing most significantly in South America; particularly notable is how these trends are playing out most resolutely "in some of the economies whose production structures are most vulnerable to external shocks."[67] In Brazil, for example, average household debt rose dramatically in just a decade, from 21 percent in 2006 to 42 percent, with service of household debt growing on average from 15 to 22 percent of disposable income 2016.[68] In terms of indebtedness of the nonfinancial corporate sector, between 2009 and 2016, Latin American bond issues increased from roughly $US 20 billion to $US 90 billion, after cresting at $US 150 billion in 2015. External debt liabilities for Latin America and the Caribbean in the first quarter of 2016 amounted to $716 billion, compared to an approximate figure of $US 300 billion between 2000 and 2009.[69]

Imperialism

Thus far, an argument has been made that varieties of political-economic development, patterns of accumulation, and specificities of state formation in Latin America are determined both by the processes of uneven and hierarchical accumulation of capital on a global scale, and also by shifting balances of class forces and struggle internal to specific countries. It is important now to add to these components the issue of imperialism.

In *Bajo el imperio del capital*, perhaps the most important recent theorization of imperialism to have come out of Latin America, Claudio Katz offers a careful periodization and characterization of the distinct phases of imperialism since the late nineteenth century—classical (1880–1914); postwar (1945–1975); and neoliberal (1980s–present).[70] The great advantage of

Katz's framework is the attentiveness it affords to the underlying character of shifting epochs of capitalist development globally, alongside a careful defense against crude economic determinism. Capitalist dynamics in the world system in various historical periods are never reduced to empty abstractions, as though they mechanically determined political outcomes. Katz, following Karl Marx in this sense, descends from the abstract to the concrete as he introduces new, specific determinations and mediations across capitalist phases, as these determinations and mediations arise in different regions of the world, in specific ways. Class struggle—from above, and from below, and within both dominant and dominated countries—lies at the heart of Katz's historical narrative and theoretical premises. Thus, history is open, if not wide open.

Following Ellen Meiksins Wood's *Empire of Capital*, Katz stresses the analogous relationship between specific forms of domestic social relations and various forms of imperial rule.[71] History suggests that there has been a close association between both capitalist and noncapitalist societies, on the one hand, and their imperialisms, on the other. Noncapitalist colonial empires of the past—such as the feudal Portuguese and Spanish Empires in Latin America between the late fifteenth and early nineteenth centuries—were ruled by feudal lords in their relations with peasants, lords who dominated their territory and subjects through military conquest, and often by direct political rule, and therefore employed extensive extra-economic coercion; in contrast, capitalist imperialism "can exercise its rule by economic means, by manipulating the forces of the market, including the weapon of debt."[72] It is obvious, all the same, that capitalist imperialism continues to require coercive force. As Colin Mooers suggests, "*force* remains indispensable both to the achievement of market 'openness' where it does not yet exist and to securing ongoing compliance with the rights of capital."[73]

Neoliberal capitalism, Katz stresses, witnessed the transformation of the old international division of labor through the internationalization of production and the modularization of global value chains. The systematic transfer of manufacturing activities toward Asia intensified competition and reduced production costs.[74] Massive multinational corporations emerged as key agents in this process. However, contra theses of monopoly capital,[75] the augmentation in size of companies is not synonymous with either monopoly control or suppression of competition. Instead, capitalism systematically re-creates competition and oligopoly in complementary forms through reciprocal recycling. At certain moments of intense interfirm rivalry, specific companies introduce transitory forms of supremacy, but these cannot be maintained in the face of new competitive battles just around the corner. This dynamic, Katz insists, is constitutive of capitalism and will persist so long as this particular mode of production survives.[76]

Technologically, an information revolution has facilitated the various neoliberal mutations of capitalism, with the generalization of the use of computers in manufacturing and the financial and commercial management of mega-corporations. Radical innovation has increased productivity, cheapened transportation, and enlarged communications networks.[77] However, the internationalization of capital has also enabled more-rapid and total transmission of disequilibria in the global system—witness Japan in 1993, Mexico in 1994, Southeast Asia in 1997, Russia in 1998, the so-called dot-com bubble in 2000 in the United States, and Argentina in 2001. This list of regional precursors to the 2008 Great Recession is hardly exhaustive.[78]

The present system of imperialism is sustained, in part, through American military intervention. With a network of military bases (between 700 and 1,000) across 130 countries, the United States enjoys a historically unprecedented global military presence and attendant capabilities.[79] The shift to China as the fulcrum of dynamism in global capitalism constitutes a novel feature of the neoliberal imperial system. But for Katz it would be premature to offer confident statements regarding its rivalrous potential vis-à-vis American power.[80] The United States retains primacy of the dollar in trade and finance; 62 percent of the world's reserves and 85 percent of global transactions are in US currency. In spite of elevated debt and trade deficit, the dollar has been maintained as the preferred refuge of capitalists at critical moments, such as the period following the 2008 crisis.[81] Another sign of ongoing US power is the fact that this country has been able, in the wake of the 2008 global crisis, to rehabilitate the International Monetary Fund (IMF) as a key auditor of national economies and supervisor of adjustments. Only a short time ago, the IMF was a deeply discredited institution, yet it has recovered its earlier high stature in international financial affairs at the behest of US pressure. Although the United States contributes relatively little money to the institution, it maintains the predominant influence in its directorship.[82]

At the same time, US hegemony in the twenty-first century is much reduced, relative to its near-absolute dominance in the first half of the twentieth century. The effectiveness of its military superiority is increasingly in doubt, however, as the fallout from wars in Afghanistan and Iraq partially demonstrates.[83] Part of the explanation for US military belligerence in the neoliberal period, generally, and the temporally and geographically indefinite character of the "war on terror," specifically, can be understood as a compensation for declining industrial competitiveness and productivity. In the present moment, US military power is employed in part to redress economic deterioration.[84] The United States must constantly reaffirm its global leadership through new wars, Katz insists, though the results of each war are impossible to anticipate, and the instrumentalization of each bloody conflict has become more difficult with the absence of compulsory conscription.[85]

Those foreign policy analysts, like Leo Panitch and Sam Gindin, or Perry Anderson, who argue for relatively unmitigated and continuous US preponderance, are therefore too simplistic and one-sided in their portrayals of the contemporary world order.[86] Such an unmitigated US power perspective, observes Tony Norfield, "implicitly assumes that the capitalist global economy is managed in an orderly way, rather than being an anarchic system in which rival countries vie for position. A dominant state such as the US is indeed more able to influence events in its favor. But as the shambles in the Middle East and North Africa shows, that is not the same thing as managing the world."[87] Norfield proposes, instead, measuring the most powerful states along a five-dimensional index of power, turning in particular on "the size of a country's economy, its ownership of foreign assets, the international prominence of its banking sector, the status of its currency in foreign exchange trading, and its level of military spending."[88] According to Norfield's index, which considers each of the five dimensions as being of equal importance, the United States does indeed top the chart in four of the five indicators, falling behind the United Kingdom only in terms of international banking. In total, across all five dimensions, the United States leads, followed distantly by the United Kingdom, with China positioned in third place yet exhibiting the most forward momentum of any powerful state.[89] Of the roughly 200 countries in the world, Norfield suggests, only twenty, or thereabouts, have significant power and influence beyond their borders. These select countries, he writes, "play an important role in world trade and finance and are home to the world's largest companies. Some of them also send their warships, bombers, missiles, drones, soldiers, 'advisors,' military aid and private mercenaries to threaten or kill people in other countries, so this sort of power is far from being only economy-related."[90]

In what follows, the focus turns to imperialism in Latin America in particular, discussing, initially, that particular dimension of Norfield's power index related to control of foreign assets, as measured by FDI, and next discussing the specific strategies in Latin America of Norfield's first and third-most-important world powers: the United States and China—the United Kingdom, the second world power in Norfield's schema, being a relatively minor player in the region.

TRENDS IN FOREIGN DIRECT INVESTMENT

While trade has increased as an element of growing interconnectedness of the global economy since the 1980s, the most important feature of increasing interpenetration of economies has actually been the surge in FDI.[91] The central agents facilitating FDI, in turn, are the multinational corporations (MNCs) that emerged on a new scale and with a new scope from the 1960s forward, as the new international division of labor solidified. While these novel behemoths operate transnationally, across multiple countries, they retain headquarters in specific countries and depend on their home states to promote and defend their interests domestically and internationally. Imperialist states in the contemporary period seek to reproduce secure markets at home, while establishing or maintaining unimpeded access to new and old markets abroad.[92]

In Latin America, key elements of the dynamics of economic imperialism can be discerned through an assessment of the concentration of the leading FDI investor states with accumulating assets in the region. A snapshot of 2016 figures is revealing on this score. Of overall FDI into Latin America that year, the United States led investor countries of origin with 20 percent of the total, although the agglomeration of countries constituting the European Union collectively accounted for 53 percent. In disaggregated terms, the Netherlands led the EU contingent with 12 percent of total FDI in the region, followed by Luxembourg and Spain, each with 8 percent. Because the Netherlands and Luxembourg have been restructured into tax havens, figures of outwardly flowing FDI from these countries are opaque. They are used as launching pads by MNCs headquartered in third-party countries, and thus what appears as Dutch or Luxembourgian FDI should not always be considered as such. As one moves down the hierarchy further, Canada and the United Kingdom accounted for 5 percent of FDI in Latin America, Italy and France 4 percent, and Japan 3 percent. China was responsible for only 1.1 percent of total FDI in Latin America in 2016.[93] These official figures are somewhat misleading in the case of China, however, as analysis from the United Nations Economic Commission for Latin America and the Caribbean has pointed out. The official statistics underestimate the flow of Chinese capital because they exclude the role of mergers and acquisitions. With mergers and acquisitions included, China rises to the fourth largest investor in the region, on the tails of the United States, the European Union, and Canada, and is the country with the most forward momentum, as we will see in more detail below.[94] Regarding cross-border mergers and acquisitions in Latin America in 2016, more than half of the total were concluded by firms from the United States and countries of the European Union, 29 and 24 percent respectively. Canada was next, with 15 percent, followed by China at 12 percent.[95] Chinese firms were responsible for three of the top twenty transactions, with a concentration of purchases in the Brazilian energy and mining sectors, "thus cementing its role as a leading investor in Latin America and the Caribbean in recent years."[96]

US IMPERIAL STRATEGY

During the 1980s and 1990s, US foreign interests in Latin America were largely pursued around three axes: first, through structural adjustment policies enforced by the International Monetary Fund, World Bank, and Inter-American Development Bank to secure the transition to and consolidation of neoliberalism in the region; second, through the guise of "democracy promotion," especially via the financing of allied political parties and civil society organizations through the channels of the National Endowment for Democracy (NED), in an effort to contain new Latin American democracies within the perimeters of liberalism, and particularly elite competition between virtually indistinguishable pro-market parties;[97] and, third, through the "War on Drugs," a pretext for intervention almost as flexible as the war against Communism had been during the Cold War.[98]

It is evident that, during much of the twenty-first century, US imperial overextension in the Middle East, under the mantle of the War on Terror, meant that Latin America receded from the center to the periphery of American geopolitical strategy. More recently, under Barack Obama, there was a reorientation of security doctrine, including military priorities. The redesign involved a reduction in military presence in the Middle East, in order to increase the military power available to apply pressure on China. In the Middle East, this has meant the winding down of US wars, and the ceding of governance to local clients, with the Central Intelligence Agency (CIA) left behind to preserve control over secret operations, to coordinate information, and to selectively provide arms to allies as necessary.[99] In the Asia-Pacific, the Pentagon is elevating the number of troops located throughout the region, enforcing the siege of North Korea, and monitoring territorial disputes between Japan and China. Elsewhere, the United States continues to train allied military personnel in thirty-four African countries, and sustains its tensions with Russia via allied bordering states, especially those that have been incorporated into the North Atlantic Treaty Organization (NATO).[100] However, the rise of progressivism to office in much of South America in the mid-2000s, together with the pivot in strategy to Asia and the Pacific under Barack Obama and the importance of the western coast of Latin America in this turn, revived US interest in containment in Latin America and the Caribbean; through the mechanisms of free trade initiatives, opposition to "radical populism," and the ongoing wars on drugs and terror, Latin America has resumed its former position at the heart of American geopolitical doctrine.

At the beginning of this century, the principal economic initiative of the United States in the region was the promotion of the Free Trade Area of the Americas (FTAA), which envisioned a trading and investment bloc linking every country from Canada in the north to Chile in the south, with the exception of Cuba.[101] When the FTAA was put to rest at the Summit of the Americas in Mar del Plata, Argentina, in 2005, as a result of popular opposition of social movements and some left-wing Latin American governments (most notably, Venezuela, but also Brazil and Argentina), the United States shifted to a strategy of bilateral trade agreements with allied countries—Peru, Chile, and Colombia, for example, with NAFTA already having incorporated Mexico in 1994.[102]

These agreements forged the basis for the so-called Pacific Alliance, which became a part of the Trans-Pacific Partnership (TPP) plan. The Pacific Alliance initiative was first formalized at the behest of the Peruvian President Alan García, who convened a meeting with the heads of state of Chile, Colombia, and Mexico in Lima in April 2011.[103] The aim, according to the Declaration of Lima that came out of this gathering, was to "progressively advance toward free circulation of goods, services, capital and people" among the member states of the alliance.[104] However, the initiative was quickly linked to grander US strategy, particularly because the central players of the initial Pacific Alliance initiatives—Peru, Chile, and Colombia—were already signatories to bilateral trade agreements with the United States. Panama, Costa Rica, Uruguay, and Paraguay later signed on to the alliance as observers. Under US guidance, these countries would link with eleven Asian countries in a commercial and geopolitical encirclement of China. The TPP was to run alongside the US initiative to bind its ties with the European Union, via the Transatlantic Trade and Investment Partnership (TTIP).[105] On the geopolitical terrain, the Pacific Alliance was intended to concretize political ties between the United States and right-wing governments in the region so as to better thwart leftist initiatives to develop counter-hegemonic regional alliances, based on sovereignty and autonomy.[106]

In April 2009, shortly after he first assumed office, President Obama attended the fifth Summit of the Americas in Puerto España, Trinidad and Tobago. He signaled then that the US relationship with Latin America would be redirected toward an alliance of equals.[107] It is abundantly clear, with hindsight, that this symbolic gesture had no relationship with the actual geopolitical orientation of the US state vis-à-vis Latin America under Obama. Luis Suárez Salazar has provided a more realistic and grounded survey of the six main priorities that in fact drove Obama's policy in Latin America.[108] First, there was an effort to destabilize, and where possible defeat, through institutional means where possible, and other means where necessary, those governments in the region identified as being in conflict with US interests. Witness, for example, US support for the "parliamentary coup" in Paraguay in 2012, which removed the democratically elected president, Fernando Lugo, from power, or the military coup in Honduras in 2009, which ousted the democratically elected president, Manuel Zelaya, from office. Particular threats identified by the United States were those member nations of the most radical initiative of counter-hegemonic regional integration, the Alianza Bolivariana para los Pueblos de Nuestra América (Bolivarian Alliance for the Peoples of Our Americas, or ALBA), one of the motivations of overthrowing Zelaya, who had ushered Honduras into ALBA.[109] Despite objections raised in Congress over violations of human rights in the country, the Obama administration provided $US 338.2 million in economic, military, and police aid to the regime of Porfirio Lobo between 2009 and 2013.[110]

Second, an effort was made to strengthen and deepen multifaceted American control over Mexico, Central America, and the Caribbean. Third, as indicated above with regard to the Pacific Alliance, Obama sought to extend the geopolitical interests of the United States along the "Pacific arc," forging or consolidating diplomatic ties with Canada, Mexico, Guatemala, El Salvador, Honduras, Costa Rica, Panama, Peru, and Chile. Fourth, Obama sought to counteract threats posed to US hegemony in the hemisphere both by the growing regional power of Brazil, as well as by the "radical populist" regimes of Bolivia, Ecuador, and Venezuela. Fifth, the United States sought to impede any further growth of the Mercádo Común del Sur (Common Market of the South, or MERCOSUR), as well as the consolidation of Unión de Naciones Suramericanas (Union of South American Nations, or UNASUR), insofar as these represented potential counterweights to US influence in South America. Sixth, and finally, there was an effort under Obama to impede the foundation, and then functioning, of the Comunidad de Estados Latinoamericanos y Caribeños (Community of Latin American and Caribbean States, or CELAC), and, relatedly, an effort to defend the centrality of the Organization of American States (OAS), and its diverse commissions—particularly the Inter-American Court of Human Rights and the Inter-American Defence Board.[111]

The United States has accentuated its military presence in Central America quite dramatically, while retaining a presence in South America. Much of this militarization is carried out under the umbrella of the War on Drugs.[112] "More than 40 years after the 'war on drugs' was declared," a recent report highlights, "consumption of illicit drugs continues to rise, cultivation of coca, marijuana, and opium poppies remains high, violence and organized crime continue to spread, and imprisonment rates have skyrocketed. Since 2000, the United States has spent approximately $US 12.5 billion in Latin America to stop drugs at the 'source.'"[113] Under Obama, "counternarcotics strategy has continued largely unchanged. In fact, over the past few years the United States has expanded its military intelligence, and law enforcement agencies' direct involvement in counternarcotics operations in the Western Hemisphere. This has been particularly true in Central America, where it has had disturbing human rights impacts."[114]

The Southern Command, based in Miami, supervises military operations throughout Latin America and the Caribbean, and has more personnel dedicated to Latin American issues than all Washington departments assigned to the same region combined.[115] The persistence of the Pentagon within US Latin American strategy is indicated in the recent installation of seven military bases in Colombia, for many decades the closest ally of the United States in all of South America.[116] The US Fourth Fleet, having been dissolved in 1950, was reinstated in 2008, under the US Navy command, to patrol the Caribbean. More Latin American military personnel were trained between 1999 and 2011 (a total of 195,807) than in previous decades. Meanwhile, roughly 4,000 uniformed US military personnel are operative in the region through permanent emergency actions, while US drones operate extensively throughout the entire hemisphere.[117]

Atilio Borón offers a useful cartography of ongoing American military activities in the region. In addition to the aforementioned construction of new military bases in Colombia and the vigilant patrolling of the Caribbean basin by US forces through the rehabilitation of the Fourth Fleet, Borón points out the broad encircling of Venezuela with US military outposts—in the north, in Colombia and the Dutch Antilles (Aruba and Curaçao); in the south, on bases in Paraguay; in the west, on bases in Peru; in the east, on bases in Guyana, Surinam, and French Guyana.[118] Borón demonstrates how military expansion and joint military exercises with local armed forces have been enabled successively through Plan Colombia, Plan Puebla-Panama, and Plan Mérida, among other initiatives.[119] He also points out the difficulties in enumerating US military bases in recent decades with the move by the US Southern Command toward "forward operating locations," which are little more than specialized landing strips and crude accompanying infrastructures. Because the local communications facilities around these strips can be quickly enabled by the monumental network of US satellites around the world, and because of the availability of enormous C-17 Globemaster transport planes, what appear to be more or less empty sites can be retrofitted, Borón contends, with operational US troops and tanks within hours in most parts of Latin America and the Caribbean.[120]

While direct US aid to Latin American countries has declined in the years of American austerity following the 2008 economic crisis, Colombia remained in 2014 the principal destination of "military and police assistance," assistance designed to "consolidate" the presumed successes of the previous years of containing "subversion," "narco-trafficking," and "narco-terrorism."[121] In the general trajectory of military and police assistance flowing from the United States to Latin America and the Caribbean between 2008 and 2014, Colombia remained at the top of the hierarchy, followed by Mexico, the Caribbean, and Central America. Interestingly, there was a major boost to spending in Mexico in 2010, briefly elevating it to first place, while Central America is the only subregion to have received increasing amounts of spending on military and police assistance steadily over the entire timeline.[122]

The CIA, Drug Enforcement Agency (DEA), and other US state agencies participate directly in the devastatingly violent War on Drugs in Mexico, inaugurated in earnest under Felipe Calderón in 2006, with the militarization of counternarcotics strategies in the country.[123] The War on Drugs persists, despite its evident failure to reduce the flow of narcotics, and despite the transparent hypocrisy of the United States, given the latter's role as principal source of demand and financial refuge for narco-trafficking. By some accounts, American banks launder roughly 70 percent of the finances generated from narcotics in the Americas.[124] "As the State Department's security assistance programs turn their focus from expensive equipment transfers to security capacity-building programs, partnerships between US agents and local US-trained and vetted special units will likely increase," one recent analysis highlights. "State Department International Narcotics and Law Enforcement (INCLE) funds, military trainers, and DEA agents have helped to set up specialized military and police units and other elite, 'vetted' bodies that operate in some isolation from the rest of their forces. They are supported by at least half a dozen small Guatemalan, Honduran, Nicaraguan and Panamanian bases built, or renovated, with Defense Department funds."[125] The "War on Gangs" in Central America relies on similar dynamics, facilitating the militarization of much of the isthmus that runs between Mexico in the north and Colombia in the south. Meanwhile, American military bases proliferate in its colonial holdings, such as the Virgin Islands and Puerto Rico, and in Curazao, with the assistance of the Netherlands, and in Martinique, with the assistance of France.[126]

Under Donald Trump, Venezuela, in particular, has been of pivotal importance to the American imperium's calculus in Latin America, as evidenced by the US-led recognition of Juan Guaidó's self-declaration as Venezuela's "interim president" in January 2019, and by direct US support for this conservative opposition politician's spectacularly ill-conceived coup attempt at the end of April 2019. US sanctions imposed on Venezuela by presidential decree in August 2017 and January 2019 remain in place, as do de facto economic constraints confronting the administration of Nicolás Maduro in the wake of US recognition of a parallel government led by Guaidó. According to a detailed report for the Center for Economic and Policy Research in Washington by economists Mark Weisbrot and Jeffrey Sachs, the sanctions have gravely affected the Venezuelan population's caloric intake, the country's disease and mortality rates, the migrant exodus, oil production, power outages, and the government's ability to deal with the economic crisis more generally. According to the report, US economic sanctions made a "substantial contribution" to a 31 percent increase in general mortality in the country from 2017 to 2018, or more than 40,000 deaths.[127] Weisbrot and Sachs convincingly demonstrate that US sanctions have worsened the already massive dimensions of the economic crisis in Venezuela. They have done so by cutting off the country from international financial markets and preventing a restructuring of its debt. The sanctions have also restricted Venezuela's access to foreign exchange—used to import food, medicine, medical equipment, and other basic necessities—by further undercutting its levels of oil production and the capacity to sell its oil abroad. The United States has seized billions of dollars worth of Venezuela's foreign assets, such as the majority state-owned oil refinery and transport company CITGO, which is based in the United States. With the help of allied institutions like the Bank of England, the US initiative has also frozen much of Venezuela's $9 billion in foreign reserves, a significant portion of which are held in gold. Projections for 2019 suggest a fall in real GDP of 37.4 percent.[128]

CHINESE IMPERIAL STRATEGY

If the patterns of US imperial strategy are fairly consistent with the recent past, this is not true of the new role that China has assumed in the region. As Claudio Katz suggests, there is little evidence that China represents now, or will represent in the near future, a political-military rival to the United States in Latin America.[129] However, over the course of the early twenty-first century, the dominant Asian power has become a principal market for Latin America's primary material exports, absorbing 40 percent of such sales.[130] Prior to the twenty-first century, China had not been an important point of destination for Latin American exports, nor an important source of imports into Latin America. Therefore, it was quite a dramatic development that in 2013 China occupied first position as provider of imports for Brazil, Paraguay, and Uruguay; second position for Argentina, Chile, Colombia, Costa Rica, Ecuador, Honduras, Mexico, Panama, Peru, and Venezuela; and third position for Bolivia, Nicaragua, El Salvador, and Guatemala. Regarding exports, in 2015, China was the first destination point for Brazilian and Chilean exports, and second for Argentinian, Colombian, Peruvian, Uruguayan, and Venezuelan exports.[131]

China is also an investor of growing importance, with aggregate investment rising from a mere $US 15 billion in 2000 to an estimated $US 400 billion in 2017. Parallel to its roles as primary commodity importer and foreign direct investor, China has transformed itself into a critical line of credit to Latin American countries. Between 2005 and 2011, it lent more than $US 75 billion to Latin America, surpassing the sums advanced by the United States and the World Bank. While the conditions of Chinese loans are better than those on offer from the United States and the World Bank, it is also true that they are linked to projects of mining, energy, and other raw material provision, which threaten to lock Latin America into its dependent reproduction within the world system.[132]

One limit of the political turn to the left in the region has been the failure of several countries to work in unison through regional forums to forge more propitious relations with China. The opportunity to establish intelligent linkages with the Asian power, in an effort to counterbalance the influence of the United States, was missed, and in its place bilateral agreements in areas of credit and investment have been needlessly asymmetrical, with Latin America reinforcing its position as primary commodity producer, with increasing debt obligations.[133] While 84 percent of exports from Latin American countries to China are primary commodities, 63.4 percent of Chinese exports flowing into the region are manufactured goods.[134] Estimates for 2017 suggest that the value of commercial exchange between China and Latin America and the Caribbean reached $US 266 billion, very near to the 2013 high of $US 268 billion.[135] For the same year, estimates indicate that China was the destination for 10 percent of total exports from the region (and 18 percent of its imports), inching closer to the impending displacement of the European Union as the second most important destination for regional exports, after the United States.[136] The proliferation of bilateral trade agreements between China and several Latin American governments in recent years underlines the limits of recent attempts to build counter-hegemonic regionalism in Latin America. Rather than consolidating Latin American integration through the establishment of relative autonomy vis-à-vis US power, bilateral deals with China have tended to strengthen interstate competition in Latin America between primary commodity producers for a share of the same export market, while new relations of bilateral dependence on China are formally institutionalized for decades to come.[137]

Only a decade ago, outwardly flowing FDI from China represented only 1.3 percent of total global flows, compared to 16.5 percent for the United States, the biggest investor in the world. In 2016, China's share of total outwardly flowing FDI grew to 12.6 percent, and the country moved to second place in the world, behind the United States, which accounted for 20.6 percent of total FDI flows that year.[138] Asia was the most important region for Chinese mergers and acquisitions between 2015 and 2016, accounting for 23 percent of the total value of Chinese acquisitions. Europe and the United States together accounted for 16 percent of the value of Chinese acquisitions that year, while acquisitions in Latin America and the Caribbean accounted for only 4 percent of the Chinese total.[139]

Although this percentage is low, Chinese acquisitions have had a significant impact in the natural resource sectors in which they are concentrated. For example, 88 percent of Chinese acquisitions in Latin America and the Caribbean between 2015 and 2016 were concentrated in the energy and mining sectors, indicating that the region is viewed strategically as a pivotal future source of key natural resources for industrial and geopolitical purposes.[140] In late 2014, Mexican President Enrique Peña Nieto reached a series of investment agreements with his Chinese counterpart, Xi Jinping. If these are carried out according to plan, "China will invest US$14 billion in Mexico's infrastructure and energy sectors. Of that amount, US$5 billion is destined for PEMEX, the Mexican petroleum company, which earlier in the year had been privatized. China is the fourth-most-important recipient of Mexican exports, following the United States, Canada, and Spain. Until the 2014 announcement China had invested only US$83 million in Mexico since 2010–2012, only 0.25 percent of its total direct investment."[141] Nonetheless, other signals indicate that such sectoral investment concentration in mining and fossil fuels is diminishing, to a significant degree. While 42 and 18 percent of planned Chinese investments between 2004 and 2010 targeted the metals and fossil fuels sectors, respectively, the respective figures for the 2011–2017 period were only 20 and 6 percent. In the latter interval, there was an offsetting uptick in Chinese planned investments in telecommunications, real estate, food, and renewable energies.[142]

In the 2005–2016 period, Chinese FDI into Latin America and the Caribbean reached the modest figure of $US 90 billion, representing roughly 5 percent of inwardly flowing FDI in the region over that period. There was a notable uptick in 2017, however, with the estimated figures for Chinese FDI that year alone reaching $US 25 billion, or about 15 percent of the total entering the region that year.[143] In addition to sectoral concentration in natural resources, most of Chinese investment is received by a small number of countries. For example, between 2005 and 2017, 81 percent of all Chinese FDI into Latin America and the Caribbean flowed into Brazil, Peru, and Argentina, with Brazil leading by a wide margin at 55 percent of the total, followed by Peru and Argentina, with 17 and 9 percent, respectively.[144]

While the trend in Chinese FDI into Latin America and the Caribbean is one suggestive barometer of the scope and momentum of Beijing's imperial strategies, alone this information provides only a partial picture. A further examination of China's emergent role as creditor to the region is of equal importance, and illuminates a broader spectrum for Chinese imperialism. While official information from Chinese development banks—particularly the Development Bank of China and the Import-Export Bank of China—is difficult to disaggregate in any degree of detail, estimates of the total loan commitments to the governments of Latin America and the Caribbean between 2005 and 2006 surpass $US 141 billion. This exceeds the total loan figures to the region from each of the major financial institutions of the United States: the Inter-American Development Bank ($US 117 billion), the World Bank ($US 85.5 billion), and the Development Bank of Latin America ($US 55.1 billion).[145]

Crucially, the main recipients of Chinese loans have been countries with important hydrocarbon sectors. Between 2005 and 2016, the vast majority (93 percent) of Chinese loans were allotted to Venezuela, with Brazil (26 percent), Ecuador (12 percent), and Argentina (11 percent) trailing some distance behind.[146] As proportions of loans from Chinese development banks in the region, over half are loans linked to infrastructure projects, a third to hydrocarbons and related energy sectors, and the remainder to trade, overall financial aid, and a variety of mixed projects.[147] Apart from traditional loans, the Chinese state also utilizes "loans for oil," which account for roughly 50 percent of total Chinese lending to the region. Via loans for oil, Chinese development banks ensure that loans are repaid in kind, through shipments of oil.[148] The value of such loans amounted to $US 74 billion since 2008; Venezuela's six oil loans over this period reached $US 44 billion, Brazil's one loan to $US 10 billion, and Ecuador's four loans to $US 5 billion.[149] Oil loans in Latin America and the Caribbean constitute an important tactical maneuver allowing China to secure decades of control over important deposits of the most important commodity of modern industrial and military power.

Finally, there is the issue of construction contracts linked to Chinese development lending. As noted, over 50 percent of Chinese loans in the region are linked to infrastructure projects. In many cases, such loans stipulate that the construction contracts flowing out of the loans be awarded to a Chinese enterprise. As a consequence, between 2011 and 2016, an array of Chinese firms were awarded construction contracts valued at $US 40 billion. These construction contracts are concentrated, unsurprisingly, in the energy (including, crucially, hydroelectric projects) and transport sectors.[150] This is a classically imperial contrivance for the redirection of ostensible development assistance to the preferred private capitals of the imperial power in question.

In sum, China does not yet constitute a political-military rival to the United States in Latin America and the Caribbean. However, it has significant and expanding flows of FDI into the region, well-solidified and asymmetrical trading relations with the region in its favor, and loan connections that increase Latin American indebtedness to China, afford China long-term control over hydrocarbon deposits, and funnel Chinese development loans to Chinese private enterprises. Pronouncements made by China at the First Forum of CELAC and China in 2015 suggest that this relationship will heighten in importance in the near to medium term future. By 2025, China expects that trade with the region will be valued at $US 500 billion, while accumulated Chinese investments, particularly in infrastructure projects, will amount to $US 250 billion.[151]

Counter-Regionalism

One complex set of dynamics flowing out of the progressive turn in Latin America has been the variegated attempts to forge deeper ties of Latin American integration as a counterweight to imperial forms of domination in the region. Perhaps the most significant single event of the contradictory processes of constructing counter-regionalism in recent years was the defeat of the FTAA at Mar del Plata, Argentina, in 2005, forcing the United States to retreat temporarily to a much more modest imperial strategy of bilateral trade agreements, until eventually moving to the Pacific Alliance stratagem.[152]

A snapshot of the Sixth Summit of the Americas, held in Cartagena, Colombia, in April 2012, provides a useful sense of the intensifying polarization of competing regional projects in the twenty-first century, with two radically opposing camps, and one oscillating grouping in the center. On the one polar side, the Summit witnessed unified stances assumed by a bloc of countries allied with Washington—Mexico, Honduras, Colombia, Chile, and Costa Rica. This bloc is united by intimate diplomatic ties with the United States, an adherence to the basic axioms of neoliberal policy, and a commitment to advancing the conservative agenda of the Pacific Alliance.[153]

Antipodal to the reactionary bloc, another group of countries—Venezuela, Cuba, Ecuador, Bolivia, and Nicaragua—cohered around their commitment to the Alianza Bolivariana para los Pueblos de Nuestra América (Bolivarian Alliance for the Peoples of Our America, or ALBA), which was first forged in 2004.[154] This bloc, animated principally by the leadership of Venezuela under Chávez, was explicitly anti-imperialist from the outset, with far-reaching ambitions, including the creation of unitary currency across the region (the Sucre), the formation of a Bank of the South, and trade agreements between member countries rooted in principles of solidarity rather than market imperatives.[155] Inspired by a novel understanding of Bolivarianism—named after the independence figure Simón Bolívar—the ALBA countries sought to recover and renew a radical conception of Latin

American integration, vindicating once again the principles of sovereignty, self-determination, solidarity, and cooperation among peoples.[156]

A third group—the oscillating center—was made up of the countries of the Mercádo Común del Sur (Southern Common Market, or MERCOSUR), with Brazil at the head. They were in favor of integration, through initiatives such as the Unión de Naciones Suramericanas (Union of South American Nations, or UNASUR) and the Comunidad de Estados Latinoamerianos y Caribeños (Community of Latin American and Caribbean States, or CELAC), but were uninterested in open alignment against the United States.[157] MERCOSUR was established in 1991 as a typical multilateral trade agreement, at the height of the neoliberal period. Its core members include Argentina, Brazil, Paraguay, Uruguay, and, most recently, Venezuela, with associate membership status extended to Bolivia, Chile, Colombia, Ecuador, Peru, and Suriname. With Brazil, and to a lesser degree Argentina, as its central players, MERCOSUR was from the start designed to work as a free trade area with a key role for foreign investors, but with shared tariff structures and a common bloc for negotiations with external parties to boost the bargaining power of the individual member nations. These ambitions have failed to congeal into coherent integration, however, as indicated by the fact that almost two decades into the twenty-first century, the organization "has not taken any steps toward macroeconomic coordination," as Katz has pointed out. "The differences in currency, types of exchange, and fiscal policies among its members are enormous. Proposals to reduce the asymmetries between countries do not exist, and as industry declines there are no plans for manufacturing coordination or shared use of export profits."[158]

UNASUR, initiated in 2008 and finalized in 2011, brought together twelve South American countries, while CELAC, initiated in 2010 and concretized in 2011, is made up of thirty-three constituent member countries across the Americas, with the notable exclusion of Canada, the United States, and the overseas territories of France, the Netherlands, Denmark, and the United Kingdom, while ostentatiously including Cuba.[159] While profoundly heterogeneous in its political composition—Cuba and Venezuela alongside Mexico and Colombia—CELAC, and to some extent UNASUR, represented, at a minimum, a symbolic and diplomatic blow to the United States and Canada insofar as they rivaled the Organization of American States (OAS), long understood on the Latin American left to be little more than an extension of the American state's institutional apparatus.[160] While UNASUR and CELAC represented a symbolic blow to US hegemony vis-à-vis the decline of the authority of the US-dominated OAS, among other mechanisms, the extreme internal political fragmentation between the eclectic member states was a limitation to the depth of counter-regionalism that they would represent from the outset. Inside both regional projects were contending perspectives from those governments seeking genuine alternative expressions of regional power free from American domination, as well as from those seeking precisely to expedite novel forms of subordination to Washington.[161]

This geopolitical map of Latin America has changed substantively in recent years. Crucially, with the election of the conservative Mauricio Macri in Argentina in 2015 and the far-right politician Jair Bolsonaro in Brazil in 2018, these two countries were once again decisively aligned with US strategy under Donald Trump (though Macri's defeat in the 2019 elections to Alberto Fernández once again altered the equation in Argentina). In 2019, the Argentinian and Brazilian presidents, when Macri was still in charge of Argentina, were important backers, together with Chilean president Sebastián Piñera and Colombian president Iván Duque, of the initiative to replace UNASUR with the right-wing and US-aligned Foro para el Progreso y Desarrollo de América del Sur (Forum for the Progress and Development of South America, or PROSUR). By contrast, with the election of center-left Andrés Manuel López Obrador in Mexico in 2018, the United States could no longer rely on an entirely compliant ally immediately to its south.

For Darío Salinas Figueredo, the rise of the left and center-left in the first two decades of this century in Latin America marked an epoch of bifurcation for these competing regional ideals. On the one hand, the Bolivarian axis has represented a stress on self-determination and national sovereignty—especially in Venezuela, Bolivia, and Ecuador—while, on the other hand, Washington's Latin American allies have sought to recompose conservative political forces in the region to counter-regional efforts of asserting relative autonomy from the United States. These regional contestations are one expression of the fact that while neoliberalism and its system of domination entered into structural crisis in Latin America, anti-neoliberal forces were not sufficiently coherent at a regional level to articulate an alternative.[162]

With greater political coherence than CELAC or UNASUR, but burdened with serious structural limitations, ALBA represented a more-assertive bid for anti-imperialist unity. The incipient institutions of ALBA were conceived as a sharper rupture with, and critique of, US power, and were oriented toward the promotion of a multipolar world order. ALBA led experimentations with trade agreements and economic associations among member states based on principles of reciprocity rather than free-market norms of comparative advantage and ruthless competition. During the height of the oil boom, ALBA key economic projects, Petrocaribe and Petrosur, as well as its communications enterprise, Telesur, expanded rapidly, with registered impact in their relevant domains. More ambitious initiatives, such as the Bank of the South and the common currency, Sucre, never really got off the ground, and are today more or less moribund. Behind ALBA's near total implosion in recent years looms the proximate collapse of the international price of crude in 2014; but the deeper cause was the fact that of all the member states—Venezuela, Cuba, Bolivia, Nicaragua, Ecuador, Honduras (withdrew 2009), Antigua and Barbuda, Dominica, Saint Vincent and the Grenadines, and Saint Lucia—only Venezuela had any serious material resources to guarantee its reproduction. Even the Venezuelan economy, though, was not comparable to relatively industrialized economies in the region—Brazil, Argentina, and Mexico—and was thus extremely vulnerable to the delayed arrival of the global crisis of capitalism that erupted in 2008. The central mechanism delivering the global slump to Venezuela was, clearly, the fall of the oil price—the pillar of both its domestic social programs and its principal geopolitical endeavor, ALBA.[163]

Perhaps the most significant obstacle to a more thoroughgoing formation of counter-regionalism, however, has been the sub-imperial role assumed by the region's largest power, Brazil.[164] The most powerful South American state by a great degree, Brazil has acted as a vital intermediary between anti-imperialist and imperialist machinations in the region, a veritable sub-imperial arbitrator in South America. Since it need not submit to every whimsy of Washington—the place of Brazil in the international division of labor is closer to that of Spain than Nicaragua or Ecuador—it has sometimes charted an independent political course. Yet the moderate leadership of the Workers Party (PT) government from 2003 to 2016 also sought to play broadly within the accepted parameters vis-à-vis the United States. In its relative autonomy, for example, Brazil sought to defend the expansion of its fifteen largest capitalist enterprises operating throughout the region, often through the channels of its strategic integration project (Initiative for the Integration of the Regional Infrastructure of South America, or IIRSA) and its massive development bank, BNDES. Brazilian energies behind BNDES very quickly eclipsed any previous notions of a robust, region-wide Bank of the South.[165] The loan portfolio of BNDES has increased by 3,000 percent since Luiz Inácio Lula da Silva ("Lula") of the Workers' Party (PT) first took office in 2003.

IIRSA's infrastructure projects, underwritten by BNDES, continue to have as their priority "the export of commodities, rather than any sort of productive complementarity" across unevenly developed Latin American states.[166]

Regional economic data for the period 1985–2009 demonstrate that close to 80 percent of Brazil's exports to other South American countries are industrialized products of high or (mainly) medium grade technology, while other South American countries, insofar as they export to Brazil, tend to concentrate on primary products and natural resources, reproducing entrenched patterns of heightened uneven development.[167] Under both Lula and his successor, Dilma Rousseff, large Brazilian firms were backed by the state, and state managers in effect became their ambassadors abroad. Brazilian foreign investment proliferated throughout the region, and the geopolitical role of the Brazilian state assumed a typically sub-imperial position in the region, promoting an independent project of its own in Latin America, sometimes in competition with US and other imperialisms, but subordinating itself simultaneously to the greater power of the United States when necessary.

Brazilian state managers modernized the country's armed forces; attempted to mediate major conflicts in the Middle East, Iran, and Africa; and pursued a permanent seat on the UN Security Council. There is no other Latin American state operating with this level of regional and international power. At the same time, Workers' Party governments in Brazil in the twenty-first century harmonized with US foreign policy insofar as they allowed American military bases to operate in strategic Amazonian junctures, and they also played a leading role in the collective occupation of Haiti. Meanwhile, even in areas where Brazil's foreign policy was relatively independent of, and in potential conflict with, the United States on one level—IIRSA, BNDES—it often had the unintended effect of strengthening the US position on another level. The clearest example in this regard is the way in which the Brazilian sub-imperial pursuit of the interests of its own biggest capitals has frequently meant the undermining of more-radical integration projects, such as the Venezuelan-led ALBA.[168] Since the parliamentary coup that ousted the democratically elected Rousseff government in 2016, Brazil has been explicitly realigned in its foreign policy with the United States, first under the interim presidency of Michel Temer, and subsequently and more vociferously under the presidency of Bolsonaro since January 2019.[169]

As Maristella Svampa has argued, in the current conjuncture, despite early signs of progress with ALBA and its related projects, optimistic proclamations about the advances of a defiant regionalism seem to amount to little more than wishful thinking.[170] It is certainly true that US hegemony in the region was weakened in the early stages of this century. However, the limits and internal contradictions of the competing regionalisms highlighted above always made it unlikely that any one of the competing blocs would see its project come to full fruition. In the mid-2000s, against formidable odds, there was some momentum for the most radical counter-regional initiative expressed by ALBA. There is no longer wind in that sail, however, as the reverberations of the global economic crisis have undermined the Venezuelan economy and have put the political left in a weaker position throughout much of South America.

Conclusion

This chapter advanced five principal lines of argumentation.

First, it highlighted how, from a perspective of political economy, perhaps the most salient feature of the latest period of left-wing electoral success was its coincidence with a Chinese-driven world commodities boom. The dynamics of the boom accelerated agro-industrial mono-cropping, mining, and natural gas and oil extraction across a number of countries governed by center-left or left administrations, particularly in South America. The biggest actors in this intensified extractive capitalism continued to be multinational corporations, even if they were made to pay higher taxes and royalties.

Second, the resource rents made available by the commodities boom provided the material basis for the formation of "compensatory states" in a number of countries governed by the left. Political legitimacy of these governments was achieved, in part, through modest redistributive programs funded largely by contingently high resource rents. While relatively high social spending in a context of capitalist dynamism reduced poverty in a number of countries, such improvements were always vulnerable to a collapse in commodity prices. At the same time, the general political-economic programs of compensatory states in the region did not challenge social-property relations or inherited productive economic structures. The structural bases of these economies were left fundamentally intact.

Third, the structural susceptibility of much of Latin America to a downturn in commodity prices became plainly evident by 2012 in the delayed regional fallout from the worst global crisis of capitalism since the Great Depression. Because China slowed down, beginning in 2011, and because neither the Eurozone nor the United States provided alternative zones of dynamism in the world market, commodity prices have remained low, despite a small recovery in 2017 and 2018. The effect on South American economies, where the Latin American left was strongest, has been severe. Major recent recessions in Argentina, Brazil, and Venezuela are manifestations of this delayed arrival of the global crisis in Latin America. The economic crisis in the region has weakened the material bases of compensatory states and opened up political opportunities for right-wing renewal.

Fourth, the uneven and hierarchical dynamics of the global capitalism and the international division of labor are not explicable solely with reference to the unfolding of capitalism's laws of motion. While these laws produce unintended unevenness and hierarchy, both patterns are also reproduced and exacerbated by the intentional actions of powerful capitalist states as they seek to defend both their positions at the top of the world hierarchy as well as the positions of their specific national capitals. When they do so, they engage in imperialism. Patterns of foreign direct investment flowing into Latin America, one of the key indicators of imperial strength, were traced in detail, as were the particular imperial strategies in the region taken up by the American and Chinese states.

Fifth, the chapter surveyed the emergence of a series of regional formations that emerged in the twenty-first century as part of the broad left's project of asserting relative autonomy for Latin America and the Caribbean from US domination. More-radical expressions of such counter-regionalism included ALBA, the Bank of the South, and the Sucre currency. These existed alongside more moderate projects, such as MERCOSUR, UNASUR, and CELAC. As was demonstrated, US hegemony was weakened in the early twenty-first century in Latin America, in part due to the advances of counter-regionalism. At the same time, the momentum of the more-radical initiatives has faltered alongside the collapse of the commodity boom and the rise of new formations of the political right. Slowly but decisively, the imperial powers of both the United States and China are seizing this opportunity to exert their influence through traditional as well as novel paths.

TRANSLATED BY ANNE FREELAND

3. LATIN AMERICAN PROGRESSIVISM
AN EPOCHAL DEBATE

The emergence of popular social movements in the 1990s and the progressive governments of the 2000s (in Argentina, Bolivia, Brazil, Ecuador, El Salvador, Nicaragua, Uruguay, and Venezuela), in addition to altering the neoliberal relationship between state, market, and society—the subjects of the first two chapters—transformed the political and ideological landscape and opened up important debates in the field of Latin American critical thought.[1] However, while broad consensus has emerged around the principle of anti-neoliberalism, the question of progressivism has been a point of disagreement that continues to generate controversy, and this question has defined this moment in the intellectual history of the region. It is therefore worth trying, despite the inevitable distortions that result from proximity in time, to give a tentative overview of the coordinates and the contours of a debate on this period that is making history.

If in chapter 1 we focused on the politics of social movement-state relations in the era of progressivism, and in chapter 2 on the era's economic and imperial dynamics, in this chapter we turn to the intellectual history of critical thought over the relevant period, and offer our own preferred interpretive framework of passive revolution, drawing on the work of Antonio Gramsci. The chapter is divided into two principal sections. First, we survey the evolution of theoretical debates on the Latin American left ranging from the 1990s consensus around anti-neoliberalism to the myriad internal divisions that emerge with the rise of progressive governments, and, finally, to explanations for the decline of the progressive era and the rise of new rights in the region. We focus on a select number of representative authors, positions, concepts, and arguments in an effort to delineate the lines of demarcation between those intellectual discourses that are more or less aligned with progressive governments, on the one hand, and a broad spectrum of independent and critical left discourses, on the other. Second, we argue that the era of progressivism is best understood through Gramsci's theoretical concept of passive revolution, demonstrating its utility for understanding the phenomena of neo-developmentalism, statism, popular demobilization, and the eventual close of the progressive period.

Coordinates and Interpretative Framework of the Debate

FROM ANTI-NEOLIBERAL CONSENSUS TO DIVISION
ON THE QUESTION OF PROGRESSIVISM

In this chapter we propose only to survey the main coordinates of the debate in the intellectual sphere of the left, not only for the sake of reducing a vast field to more manageable proportions, but also because it is there that the shift mentioned above occurred; it is in this field that ruptures were produced and divergent positions emerged from a foundation of shared cultures, traditions, and discourses.[2] It is, therefore, a true debate and not a dialogue of the deaf or between people who do not speak the same language. For the same reason, it is a process that fractured a space that, without being exactly communitarian, was one of comradery and companionship in the struggles of past decades, in particular in the social movements of the 1990s—that is, the movements that generated or fostered this change of era.[3]

We must not forget that the term *neoliberalism* appeared in the middle of the decade and became a rallying point at a gathering titled "In Defense of Humanity and Against Neoliberalism," organized by the Zapatista Army of National Liberation (EZLN) in Chiapas in 1996, which brought together an array of popular struggles that, from then on, would be called *anti-neoliberal*. Over the course of the same decade, an intellectual field of the left was restructured around the opposition between neoliberalism and anti-neoliberalism, that is, the critical conception of neoliberalism and birth of anti-neoliberalism as an antagonistic and alternative option, taking up and continuing a tradition of Latin American critical thought.[4] This field, made up of various, hybrid activist and student groups, promoted and sustained a critique of neoliberalism as an economic model and of the transitions to democracy as its political correlate and became an important and influential pole within the Latin American intellectual universe as a whole, reconstituting or simply revitalizing an intellectual sphere that had retreated, fragmented, or dispersed following the defeat of the 1970s. Within this reconfiguration that constitutes a critical moment as well as an eloquent chapter in the intellectual history of Latin America, and amid various individual and collective trajectories, of particular importance were the authors and positions affiliated with the Latin American Council of Social Sciences (CLACSO), which became a point of reference for an anti-neoliberal critique under the successive directorships of the Argentinian philosopher Atilio Borón and the Brazilian sociologist Emir Sader.

It should be noted that the convergence around anti-neoliberalism happened in the defensive context of the 1980s, when the left was demoralized following the defeat of the 1970s, in an environment that was very different from the previous one, in which the debates were centered on the orientation and content of the coming revolution. In this earlier phase, different revolutionary movements and Marxist traditions—a multiplicity of socialist lefts with stronger or weaker anti-imperialist and national-popular tendencies—vied with one another for the role of vanguard and clashed over the form of the revolutionary event, the subject who would lead it, and the content of the socialism that it would inaugurate. It is not insignificant that precisely in the context of a resurgence and a new opportunity for the consolidation of an alternative—on the border between anti-neoliberalism and anti-capitalism—divisions erupted that, to a certain extent, recalled those old rifts of the 1960s and 1970s. Other divisions are clearly produced either by new cleavages—such as ecoterritorial, autonomist, or postcolonial currents—or by the return, in new forms, of old issues like those of indigenous and peasant sectors that had been subsumed and proletarianized at the altar of the historical subject of the worker who was destined to realize socialism in the name of all humanity.

As we have noted above, and as we affirmed in the first chapter of this book, the historical significance of the debate within the various traditions of the Latin American left at the beginning of the twenty-first century has to do with the horizon of the era and with a passage within it from anti-neoliberalism to post-neoliberalism, and from social movements to governments as the subjects of historical processes and political dynamics. These questions define the era—Latin America's present moment—just as the past century was defined by the questions of development and dependency, revolution and democracy, and popular and class subjects.

The debate as to the meaning of progressivism is situated within a historical and political process led by subjects on the left—social movements, parties, and governments, in order of appearance on the scene—in which the question of ideological definition and differentiation is important. A reconstruction of this debate, even a fragmentary and partial one, will therefore necessarily refer to a dispute between subjects directly involved or influential in a political process still under way. In other words, there is a relatively high degree of correspondence between a constellation of intellectual positions and the configuration of political forces, including parties or social movements.

Because of the temporal proximity and the scope of the phenomenon of the progressive governments, there are few historical-processual studies or histories of the present on a regional scale that account for the synchrony and transversality of the phenomenon. We will consider those that do exist, as well as those studies of national cases that are particularly relevant or influential. By contrast, we must recognize that the most important hypotheses about the nature of the phenomenon must tread the border between a discursive mode of intervention or public opinion and scholarly literature; as a result of the political affiliations of a large part of the Latin American intellectual sphere, there are a number of authors who privilege incursion into a strictly political debate, though many successfully combine this kind of intervention with analytical and interpretative rigor. Of particular importance, at the center of the most public and consequential conversations on the subject, are the interventions by the organic intellectuals of the progressive governments and movements themselves, as well as those formulated by other intellectuals of the left from a critical perspective. Amid these are a series of interventions that purport to be balanced, though they are always in lighter or darker shades of gray or, in some cases, suffused with academicism and detached from the ongoing processes and public debates. In this detachment the basic questions emerge as to the role and tasks of committed intellectuals and their relation to truth, critique, and instituted power—a series of questions that were always in the background, but that gained prominence as the political struggle intensified.

What we propose, rather than to contribute to a particular genre, is to trace the contours of the debate, its fundamental divisions and points of tension, and to bring into relief its most important and original propositions. In order to present the debate in the simplest way possible, we will categorize the several positions as either favorable or critical, rather than according to the principal themes that have emerged over the course of its development, including the socioeconomic question (post-neoliberalism, neo-developmentalism, anti-capitalism), the economic-environmental question (extractivism and dependency), the question of the state and democracy (populism, clientelism, transformism, and passive revolution), and the question of cultural diversity (plurinationalism and postcoloniality).

Since these points tend to intersect and overlap in different ways, rather than attempting a concise summary of each of them, it seems more constructive to present the arguments of the principal positions as expressed by some of the influential and representative authors who have intervened in the debate and have already taken it upon themselves to provide such overviews of the relevant questions.[5]

PROGRESSIVISM AND ITS INTELLECTUAL CONTEXT

Arguments in favor of the post-neoliberal turn have circulated widely, since they correspond to the discourse elaborated and disseminated by the many governments of the region under the banners of the Bolivarian Revolution, socialism for the twenty-first century, communitarian socialism, the Citizens' Revolution, the process of change, progressivism, or simply Chavismo (Venezuela), Kirchnerismo (Argentina), Evismo (Bolivia), Lulismo (Brazil), Correismo (Ecuador), and Orteguismo (Nicaragua). At the same time, it is worth looking at those texts that seek to synthesize them and, thus, provide a positive definition at the regional scale of what has been called a "change of era."

In the first place, we should point out that Chavismo has occupied a central and dynamic place within the sphere of Latin American progressivism because it gave rise to the first anti-neoliberal Latin American government, because of the geopolitical and ideological linkages that it built, and because of its radicality. On the terrain of the Marxian "battle of ideas," the Network of Intellectuals and Artists in Defense of Humanity was founded by Hugo Chávez in 2004. Its principal objectives are "to stand in solidarity with the processes of change" and "to resist imperialism"; it was an attempt to create a *think tank* to counter the powerful media campaigns of the right and to sustain the Bolivarian Chavista movement, but it also served to nudge the progressive governments toward the left.[6] In addition to its various meetings and declarations, the network's website is an important showcase of resources to support the progressive governments, and in particular that of Venezuela. Other Latin American websites that tended to favor these governments—such as rebelion.org or alai.net—fulfilled the same role in offering support, but they also opened up spaces for critical positions. Obviously, in the traditional media, but also on the internet, forums that disseminated more or less belligerent positions of the Latin American and US right proliferated.[7]

Among the many voices that are sympathetic to the progressive governments, a few stand out as plainly taking on the role of intellectual mouthpiece and trying to systematize and legitimate the official discourse in a leftist key: the Bolivian vice president Álvaro García Linera and the two aforementioned ex-secretary generals of CLACSO, the Brazilian Emir Sader and the Argentinian Atilio Borón.[8]

The official discourse, which these authors translated into a higher level of intellectual sophistication, has the same logical and argumentative structure that is premised on a fundamental and overdetermined opposition between imperialism and anti-imperialism. Thus, the principal enemy is the United States. Domestic right-wing sectors of each country are enemies in a secondary or derivative sense, portrayed as an extension of the United States, its accomplices, or its allies. The *national* is detached from the *popular*, that is, from the question of social justice that is the other pillar of post-neoliberal discourse, brandishing an old, familiar argument: no development is possible without first solving the problem of dependency. Both the national question and the social question, according to the progressive position, must be tackled through state intervention in defense of national sovereignty and in the service of the redistribution of wealth. The assumption of state power and the use of the state apparatus as a bulwark of sovereignty as well as an instrument of economic and social intervention becomes the heart and engine of the progressive strategy. On this point there is absolute consensus, nuanced only by quantitative differences. On the other hand, the urgency of the task, according to this line of argument, privileges the use of the state apparatus over its transformation, which meant putting the project of the substantial reform of the state—a cornerstone of the anti-neoliberal movements from which the new governments emerged or were even constitutionally sanctioned by them—on a back burner, or sacrificing this task altogether.[9]

This privileging of the state, generally accompanied by an exaltation of statism—of *statolatry*, to use Gramsci's term—that characterized the performance of the progressive governments is a problematic subject and one that has provoked criticism not only from the liberal right but also from positions on the left in relation to the question of populism. This question has haunted the debate since the emergence of what has been called left populism—or national-popular populism—that is, an explicit vindication of the virtues and efficacy of "populist reason" as theoretically formulated by Ernesto Laclau[10] and implicitly or explicitly sustained in the context of various governments (in particular the Kirchnerist government in Argentina) and in certain adjacent intellectual spheres.[11]

At the same time, without an explicit wink to the theorization of populism or to Laclauian language, but taking up national-popular or national-liberation traditions of the socialist left, some of the basic elements of a populist project that combines familiar and innovative features are in broad circulation, fashioned from a theoretical framework that reaches back to national-popular and Marxist traditions with variations according to their origins and the political and ideological formation of their subjects, their political forces, and their organic intellectuals.

In particular, the return in a statist key to Vladimir Lenin's thought is more surprising in García Linera, who came from an autonomist Marxist tradition than in Borón and Sader, who belong to an earlier generation and who were formed in a more orthodox Marxist environment.[12] Obviously, this Marxist-Leninist progressivism not only is in conflict with the concerns of the autonomist and libertarian lefts but also contradicts the idea of the withering of the state that Lenin himself imagined on the eve of the Bolshevik Revolution. García Linera's official discourse is focused on a passionate defense of statism, along with the primacy of the economy—that is, of development and growth as decisive concerns—and he goes so far as to claim that the expansion of the state includes the participation of civil society to the extent that it has been incorporated into the "integral state."[13]

The state appears, in these analyses, not merely as a tool for the development of the forces of production that would ultimately pave the way for a socialist future, but also as a catalyst of development, a guarantor of social equilibrium, the expression of universalism and affirmation of the nation. Progressive anti-imperialism is formulated, first, in a nationalist key, and second, on the regional level, following a tradition of thought that has deep roots in Latin America, in particular in Cuba at the intersection of José Martí's thought and Fidel Castro's.[14] Still, we must not forget that this was the ideological site of a historic encounter between the communist left and the popular nationalist currents since the 1930s, which gained momentum in the 1940s and stretched into the late 1950s, when the Cuban Revolution marked a turning point in this relation in which the socialist element came to predominate, in the name of national liberation.

This same evocation and renovation of arguments proper to the nationalist and Latin Americanist Marxist tradition, along with their attenuated, populist, and social-democratic variants, is reflected in another crucial aspect of this discourse, one that concerns development and social justice— that is, development and social justice translated into productivism and redistributionism. The development of the forces of production facilitates a gradual reduction of dependency, which justifies resorting to extractivism as a necessary evil. Extractivism could sustain the level of accumulation of resources required for either a system of direct redistribution (via wages or vouchers paid directly by the state) or indirect measures (social and labor rights) that would strengthen the internal market, stimulate consumption, and, therefore, spur production, following the classic Keynesian formula, in accordance with the version of Keynesianism advanced by the United Nations Economic Commission for Latin America and the Caribbean (ECLAC). Citing evidence of economic and social gains, in particular before the global crisis of 2008 and the attendant drop in commodity prices, the fundamental argument in support of the progressive governments has to do with social policy: the fight against poverty and improved material conditions of life for the popular classes, which has generally meant access to consumption of goods and services and increased upward social mobility.

If some are content with the gains of capitalist development with a more or less sensible redistribution of wealth—Nestor Kirchner's "serious capitalism"—for the governments further to the left, this is only a phase that should lead to a transition to socialism. This hypothesis is supported based on the experiences and declarations of the governments of Venezuela and Bolivia, in the first case the process under way (socialism of the twenty-first century) and in the second case as a future horizon (the communitarian socialism that would follow Andean-Amazonian capitalism).

From this standpoint, García Linera recites a classic stagist argument:[15]

> We are not yet talking about postcapitalist projects, since these will only be able to succeed on a universal scale; we are referring to post-neoliberal projects that allow the state to reclaim a central role in the production of wealth and the administration of the economy, prioritizing national interests and the popular classes.[16]

As both his apologists and his critics recognize, then, the public policies of the progressive governments, as a whole, remain within a neo-developmentalist horizon.[17]

Now that these common coordinates in relation to the statist-developmentalist framework that characterizes Latin American progressivism have been established, we must note some differences and interpretative nuances that emerged over the course of the debate.

In the first place, there is the argument that we must make distinctions and not overgeneralize. Beyond the obvious specificities that characterize each national case, distinctions have been made in reference to conventional antinomies and typologies: revolutionary/reformist; radical/moderate; left/center-left. At the center of every taxonomy is the singularity of the Venezuelan case as the vanguard of the progressive and anti-imperialist bloc, as the first anti-neoliberal government of the region (1998), because Hugo Chávez, with his intensely charismatic presence,[18] built and launched a regional movement and backed the subsequent governments; because it was Venezuela that went the farthest in pursuing an anti-neoliberal, anticapitalist, and socialist program; and because Venezuela, at least in intent, transcended the structure of the liberal state, stimulating—but also channeling—popular participation through the framework of Communal Power. After Venezuela, Bolivia and Ecuador came closest to this epicenter, more for the virulence of their anti-imperialist stance than for their socialist orientation or their commitment to participation from below, which is not a true feature of either.

This defense of the governments that were labeled revolutionary is not directly dependent on ideological affiliations, since there were important differences between Rafael Correa's Christian socialism and Chávez's Bolivarian socialism (though there is also a strong Catholic element in Chávez), but on a certain anti-neoliberal radicality attributed to the process of social transformation promoted by the state and on an anti-imperialist geopolitical alignment.[19]

This strictly ideological line of demarcation divides the intellectual field, since many Marxist intellectuals applaud Chavismo as revolutionary yet criticize the other progressive governments as reformist, whether social-democratic, as in the case of Lula's Workers' Party in Brazil or of the Uruguayan Broad Front, or populist and national-popular, as with Kirchnerismo.

The Venezuelan political-economic crisis, beginning in 2013 and later intensifying in scope and depth, increased this tension in the intellectual field of the left and exacerbated the tendency toward polarization that already characterized the debate. At its height, there was a confrontation of two opposing statements signed by a number of intellectuals—as noted in chapter 1—and, in the heat of the crisis, a highly nuanced debate was simplified so that on one side there were signatories with nuanced positions together with sworn enemies of the Bolivarian Revolution and, on the other side, with some of its unconditional and uncritical apologists.[20]

In the cases of Argentina and Brazil, the debate was less complicated, because among the intellectual left, with the exception of some long-term ideologues of the Workers' Party who refused to jump ship and of a certain Peronist intelligentsia from the 1970s (*setentistas*) affiliated with the Carta Abierta (Open Letter) group, the critical position quickly garnered consensus. In

Uruguay, in particular during the presidency of the ex-Montonero guerrilla José "Pepe" Mujica, the governments of the Broad Front, which included both Montoneros and communists, retained a certain appeal for the intellectual and student left.

The question with which the Cuban political theorist Francisco López Segrera opens his book assessing Latin American progressivism summarizes the confusion of the supporters of the progressive governments: "How is it possible that, with the social policies of popular empowerment carried out by the progressive forces of the left through the post-neoliberal governments, there is a return to the new right?"[21]

The stock answer to this question was formulated, once again, by García Linera, who was concerned with justifying from the left, in conventional Marxist terms, not only the actions of his own government in Bolivia but also those of progressive governments as a whole.[22]

While celebrating the gains in economic terms, in social justice, in sovereignty, and in the strength of the state, the Bolivian vice president, García Linera, tried to neutralize critical positions by incorporating them, translating them as "creative tensions" and objectively recognizing limits and contradictions but without assuming any direct political responsibility. Thus, he emphasizes that redistributive policies have effectively expanded the middle class in terms of power of consumption, but, at the same time, he recognizes and laments the problem of "redistribution of wealth without social politicization," which means that conservatism persists as the "dominant common sense." On the other hand, in relation to another thorny issue, he insists that the subaltern classes have seized the state, becoming "delegates, assemblypersons, and senators," and exercising "plebeian power." But also—and this point is more easily disputed—he maintains that there was a "strengthening of civil society," within and outside what he calls the "integral state."[23] In this sense, assuming that the popular struggles and participation would inevitably slip into corporativism, he defends a top-down process, promoting inclusion of the popular sectors within the state and the institutionalization of their struggles through the fulfillment of their demands, without recognizing that this itself contributed to demobilizing these sectors.

Finally, the impasse is resolved through a cyclical conception of the history of revolutions, in which the Bolivian process is inscribed:

> Thus, revolutions appear not as infinite upward lines but as waves (Marx) that flow and ebb, with exceptional moments of universality in

collective action, and long periods of abatement, of corporativism, of demobilized everyday life.[24]

This allows García Linera not only to justify top-down processes, but also to anticipate a possible future postcapitalist stage, and, at the same time, paradoxically, to declare his faith in the autonomous capacity of the subaltern sectors in a future passage from post-neoliberalism to postcapitalism.[25]

With these rhetorical acrobatics, García Linera seeks to resolve two more problems: despite having been critical of the failed "cultural revolution," he justifies rapprochement with conservative sectors and parts of the dominant classes.[26] On the other hand, as to the question of leadership, he maintains that "The historical leader does not replace collective action as the supreme creator of social life, but it is its identifying and unifying symbol."[27] And if strong leadership provokes political regression, this is not the fault of the leader but rather of the classes that have not internalized their "experience of struggle," that is, that remain subaltern.[28] Indirect self-criticism—that is, of a kind that evades responsibility—goes hand in hand with a counterattack against the left. García Linera accuses what he calls the "café left" (*izquiera de cafetín*) and green Trotskyites (*troskos verdes*) of complicity with imperialism and the right. Rafael Correa likewise declared in 2009 that the greatest danger was "infantile environmentalism and leftism," and Emir Sader, in his editorials, is eager to discredit what he calls the "extreme left" (*ultraizquierda*) at every opportunity.[29] Meanwhile, other spokespeople of the progressive movements declare—frankly—that a left opposition is acceptable so long as it does not allow itself to be assimilated or instrumentalized by the strategies of the right, and so long as "at critical defensive moments—at points of cleavage—they join forces with the national and popular governments against the common enemy."[30]

Without this coarseness proper to the propaganda and polemics of what Gramsci called *piccola politica* (petty or small politics), López Segrera reproduces, from a position sympathetic to the progressive governments, the basic arguments elaborated by García Linera, insisting on the point of the absence of a counter-hegemonic culture and being more explicit and categorical in his criticisms, connecting the limits of progressivism with the rise of the right.[31]

Similarly, but from a critical leftist position internal to progressivism, where many of the Venezuelan governments' sympathizers can be situated, Pablo Solana and Gerardo Szalkowicz reluctantly accept the idea of the end of a cycle and try to offer a balanced assessment.[32] On the one hand, they emphasize that these were post-neoliberal governments that had a number of successes: they relegitimized the "electoral route" to state power, taking advantage of the economic conjuncture; they achieved social gains; they revitalized the state through social intervention as well as through nationalizations, as in Venezuela and Bolivia; and they promoted Latin American unity against imperialism. At the same time, because the authors claim to want to reignite the left and to "overcome endogenous limitations and weaknesses," they specify a series of unfinished tasks that, they maintain, can be realized within the framework of the existing progressive governments and political forces: those of overcoming a dependent and extractivist production model, going beyond liberal democracy through participatory structures, "ruling by obeying" (*mandar obedeciendo*), building popular power and not conceiving of the people as a mere administrative support, promoting a true "cultural revolution" against the conception of the people as citizen-clients, and avoiding "triumphant complacency" by fostering debate and self-criticism.[33] Finally, it is worth noting that these authors maintain that the obvious differences between the center-left governments and the radical nationalists did not stop them from identifying with one another and coming together, and that this was more than a simple strategic alliance or an instance of regional diplomacy—that it in fact became the official political discourse of "militants and the official media," blurring the distinctions.[34]

Although a sector of left intellectuals defends progressivism, even in its twilight, holding fast to the persistence of the governments of Venezuela and Bolivia—and to a lesser extent those of Ecuador under Lenín Moreno—many others who supported them in the beginning have, over the years, developed critical positions that distanced them irreconcilably from the core of unconditional defenders and even from ranks of critical sympathizers.[35]

A RAINBOW OF CRITICISM FROM THE LEFT

All the critical or self-critical elements that emerged in the intraprogressivist field of the debate either correspond with or directly respond to questions or positions that emerged over the course of the sometimes fierce debate that raged in both political and academic or intellectual spheres. Those who were unequivocally critical of the progressive governments tend to assume, as a methodological premise, that we are dealing with a unified historico-political phenomenon—without denying the obvious differences and nuances among the different contexts—that reflects a certain synchrony and consonance, arising from an anti-neoliberal momentum that has stagnated, reproducing elements of neoliberalism (consumerism, exploitation, extractivism, and environmental destruction, among others), along with authoritarian, clientelist, and corrupt practices. Notwithstanding their internal heterogeneity, for analytical and expositive purposes it is worth distinguishing some general categories of critical perspectives that are representative of the range of existing left currents in Latin America, excluding of course the national-popular, which tends to identify with the progressive governments.

The rainbow of criticism from the left takes on red, red-black, green, or even multicolored tones (like the Andean *whipala*, a patchwork flag representing some indigenous peoples of the Andes); that is, anticapitalist, autonomist-libertarian, environmentalist, or postcolonial. We can roughly characterize each by identifying the focal point of its critique, the element that it singles out as most conservative or regressive. For the red (anticapitalist) camp, this element consists of the class alliances and the intracapitalist and neo-developmentalist framework of the socioeconomic changes. The greens (environmentalists) and the indigenous peasant movements position themselves against extractivism and the so-called megaprojects and, therefore, also, somewhat like the anticapitalists, against the effects of neo-developmentalism and capitalist modernization. The red-black criticism of the autonomist anticapitalists and other libertarian currents—including those with anarchist roots—mainly opposes the dynamic of authoritarianism, statism, centrism, clientelism, and *caudillismo* (big-man leadership). The multicolor (postcolonialist) position underscores the aggressions toward Mother Earth and communal ways of life, as well as the persistence of racial hierarchy and the absence of a real plurinational landscape in the cases of Bolivia and Ecuador. These critical positions tend to intersect and overlap, though they have their own specific expressions that can end up being incompatible on certain points or in their purest or most essential forms in highlighting one or another central contradiction.[36] We will illustrate this with a few examples of arguments advanced by influential intellectuals who represent these various positions to the left of progressivism.

A good synthesis of these elements can be found in an early text that tried to offer a critical approach to those progressive governments that were considered the most radical: *Promesas en su laberinto: Cambios y continuidades en los gobiernos progresistas de América Latina.*[37] The questions that guide the analyses of the different cases (Venezuela, Ecuador, and Bolivia) correspond to three fundamental levels of inquiry that have cut across the debate. In the first place, they ask whether these governments constitute alternatives to either capitalism or developmentalism, leading to a postextractivist model and a sovereign place in the world market. Second, they ask if the redistributive social policies break with the neoliberal pattern, if property relations and the productive model are altered. Finally, they ask if democracy was deepened beyond its liberal representative version, through popular participation and respect for criticism, dissidence, and protest.[38]

In the introduction to that early text, Edgardo Lander, a Venezuelan intellectual who has been a vocal critic of Chavismo, proposes that no anti-capitalism is possible without questioning the idea of progress and without deepening democracy.[39] On the Venezuelan case, he points out that a rentier logic reinforced a vertical and centralized state, which he considers incompatible with both the project of a communal state and the possibility of true self-government.[40]

In the same vein, Víctor Álvarez[41] analyzes the Venezuelan rentier state, summing it up thus: "we import because we do not produce, we do not produce because we import,"[42] giving data on the tendency toward deindustrialization that accelerated under Chávez.[43] According to the ex-minister of the Bolivarian government, the regime ended up establishing an entrepreneurial state that bureaucratized property without distributing it, merely distributing profits, implementing paternalistic and clientelist modalities of power.[44] For Álvarez, even as unemployment and poverty went down, the Venezuelan economy became more capitalist and workers even more exploited.[45]

In the chapter on Bolivia, Carlos Arze Vargas and Javier Gómez[46] explain the limits of the process of structural transformation in terms of the absence of industrialization and an internal demand that, despite its growth, did not reverse the raw-material export model based on the exploitation of the forces of production as a source of wealth.[47] They also point out the failure to put into practice the structures of direct democracy that appeared in the constitution of 2009. They conclude that the government of Evo Morales has four fundamental limitations: a lack of ideological credibility as a result of the opposition between *buen vivir* and developmentalism; a lack of plurality, since neither public debate nor opposition from social and political organizations is tolerated; and administrative and institutional failures as a result of the centralization of leadership.[48]

In the chapter on Ecuador, Pablo Ospina,[49] while acknowledging changes in the redistribution of wealth and the expansion of social rights (in particular in healthcare and education), points out that during Correa's presidency the model of accumulation was unchanged, private property was untouched, and profits grew exponentially; he argues that, therefore, promises notwithstanding, there was no empowerment of the citizenry but merely institutional mechanisms to control and discipline the social and civil organizations for the sake of "decorporatizing" Ecuadorian politics and fortifying the state.[50] According to Ospina, if Correa was popular for a time, the support he enjoyed was passive and did not involve participation. Ospina therefore concludes that the Citizens' Revolution chose efficacy over democracy.[51]

With regard to the progressive governments of Argentina and Brazil, critical analyses can be found that highlight these same questions and, at the same time, acknowledge the specificity of each experience.[52] In these cases, the line between supporters and critics is shifted toward the right, since, because these governments are clearly more moderate in their projects of socioeconomic transformation and in their anti-imperialism, the criticisms are sharper and the defenses weaker from a leftist perspective.

In a kind of mirror image of the panorama of sympathetic positions, from a socialist perspective, and within critiques of progressivism in general, Venezuela tends to stand out as a special case. For example, Claudio Katz, an Argentinian Marxist economist, questions the neo-developmentalism of the progressive governments, defining it thus:

> Increased state intervention, heterodox economic policies, resuming processes of industrialization, reducing the technological gap and following the example of Southeast Asia. As opposed to traditional developmentalism, it promotes alliances with agrobusiness, attenuates the deterioration of terms of exchange, moves away from a center-periphery paradigm, and prioritizes the management of the exchange rate.[53]

He recognizes in these governments "social gains, democratic conquests, and successes in resisting imperial aggression," but he denounces their extractivism and lack of diversification of production. He does not accept that the post-neoliberal governments can be defined by a failure to break with neoliberalism or by their conflicts with various popular movements, despite the social spending that mitigated frictions. By contrast, Katz insists on not confusing the center-left governments with regimes like the Venezuelan one, which stood out for its anti-imperialist and Latin Americanist stances, because of the socialist character of the transformations it set in motion and the popular support that it generated.[54]

Similarly, though in a more orthodox register, James Petras and Henry Veltmeyer point out that the gains achieved were the result of the class struggle "from below," but that the center-left governments made social pacts with the capitalist class and became their accomplices when the correlation of forces shifted, favoring mining interests and agrobusiness. According to these authors, only in Bolivarian Venezuela, and even there without breaking with capitalism, was there a truly progressive advance, which still cannot be called socialist, because there was no break with the logic and dynamics of capitalism.[55]

The questioning of neo-developmentalism takes on green shades when it focuses on extractivism and its ecoterritorial impact. This position, held by communitarian movements in defense of their territories, NGOs, and environmentalist collectives, finds its most incisive expression in the texts of intellectuals such as Eduardo Gudynas, Maristella Svampa, and Alberto Acosta.[56]

Gudynas argues that these governments are not neoliberal, but rather that they are situated within capitalism, since

> They maintained, and even bolstered, their economic role as suppliers of raw materials, they accepted the structures and dynamics of globalization, and in almost all of these countries the financial sector has grown steadily. They were so intent on maintaining revenues that they perpetuated, through other means, the commodification of social life and of nature.[57]

The environmentalist perspective upholds a critique that is not based solely on the general principle of environmental protection, but that recognizes how intensification of capitalist processes of destruction—in particular at the territorial level with what has been called extractivism—goes hand in hand with the perpetuation of dependency and "rentierism": that is, with the persistence of a raw-materials export model that inhibits the endogenous processes of industrialization and technological advancement.

This line of critique revolves around two alternative core concepts: *buen vivir* and the commons. The notion of *buen vivir* or *vivir bien* (living well) (*sumak kawsay* or *suma qamaña*, in Quechua and Aymara, respectively), which is rooted in indigenous Andean traditions, refers to an anti-developmentalist or degrowth paradigm whose central tenet is that of a harmonious relationship with nature (*pachamama*, or Mother Earth). Its dissemination in tandem with the emergence of indigenous movements was influential in the governments of Bolivia and Ecuador and colored some of the language of their constitutions of 2009 and 2008, respectively. In Ecuador it was adopted as a key concept in development plans since 2009, but, according to the government's critics, it remained a mere rhetorical gesture, neutralized within a developmentalist and state-centric logic.[58]

The notion of the commons has a different trajectory, since it was introduced into the lexicon of certain Latin American groups, associations, and movements from the intellectual and theoretical sphere and has a certain resonance with European anti-globalization movements.[59]

The ecoterritorial question is one of the most critical points of the conflict, since it has ignited a series of movements of resistance against extractivism across Latin America and has an important place among the arguments of the critical sectors not only because it constructs a concrete target of critique but also because it intersects with the anticapitalist and autonomist arguments.

The Argentinian sociologist Maristella Svampa, who has been prolific in her contribution to the elaboration of the critique of extractivism and what she called the "commodities consensus," points out that the crisis of the progressive governments was not produced wholly by external factors but also by intense ideological polarization, the concentration of political power, and rising corruption. This concentration of power refers not only to the leaders themselves but also to forms of discipline within the establishment and within various social, intellectual, academic, and journalistic organizations and movements.[60]

Authors directly connected to the autonomist current have articulated a vigorous critique of the Latin American progressive governments, including those of Ecuador, Bolivia, and Venezuela, along these lines.[61] This position is summarized in a brief but incisive book by Decio Machado and Raúl Zibechi.[62] These authors categorically deny that emancipation can be achieved by electoral or state means and hold that the progressive governments stabilized and repositioned the state, bringing a close to a period of struggle.[63] The progressivist recomposition of the state is therefore presented as a step backward with respect to the series of struggles of the preceding years.[64] They propose four basic common elements of this regression: "the fortification/repositioning of the state, the implementation of compensatory social policies as the core of new models of governability, the extractivist model of production and the export of commodities as the basis of the economy, and the execution of large infrastructure projects."[65] They affirm that participation from below was not stimulated, and, unlike other contributors to the debate, believe that even in the case of the Venezuelan Communes there was not so much as an embryo of a new type of state or a true counterpower, but that these were part of a mechanism that, in the last instance, underpins the government and the central apparatus.[66]

With regard to the Bolivian government, they maintain that MAS is

> A statist political force that is imposing a development/modernization project based on extractivism and, in order to carry it out, must do away with democracy and plurality through cooptation, repression, or the concentration of power, and in effect is doing so through a combination of all of these mechanisms.[67]

Machado and Zibechi highlight the co-optation that is cloaked in a discourse of social justice, the fight against poverty and inequality, popular leadership within the administrative apparatus of the state, the use of repression, and the "appeasement produced by social policies."[68] They also question the redistributive impact of these social policies, demonstrating a persistence of "structural inequality" along with the supposed reduction of poverty, and they further point out that cash vouchers created debt for large sectors.[69] Finally, they examine the emergence of a new bourgeoisie, of new elites, and the recomposition of the dominant classes, in particular in Brazil and Bolivia, where they focus on the unions and mining cooperatives.[70]

Clearly, the critique articulated by authors with autonomist roots deploys various arguments that, as we have seen, are also brandished by anticapitalists, environmentalists, and Indianists, and which are compatible with the hypothesis that characterizes the progressive Latin American governments of the beginning of the twenty-first century as agents of passive revolutions. Following this Gramscian hypothesis, which we will develop at length below, certain Ecuadorian, Argentinian, and Brazilian authors have maintained that the progressive governments can be understood through the lens of the concept of passive revolution—that is, a certain combination of transformation and conservation carried out from the state to preempt the escalation of the class struggle, refashioning the capitalist system through socioeconomic reforms that benefit the subaltern classes but that are designed ultimately for their demobilization and control.

Maristella Svampa, for example, characterizes Kirchnerismo in the following terms:

> Change and, at the same time, conservation; progressivism, a model elaborated in a national-popular key and with Latin Americanist

pretensions, and, at the same time, a model of dispossession, based on the comparative advantages of the Commodities Consensus. After ten years of Kirchnerismo, it has not been easy to escape this trap of "restoration-revolution," since it was the progressive middle classes, with a discourse of change, in their not-always-acknowledged alliance with large power blocs, that were charged with the task of reconstituting the dominant order from above, neutralizing and coopting demands from below.[71]

In Ecuador, in an extensive study of Correa's government, Francisco Muñoz Jaramillo maintains that the period was characterized by passive revolutions with Caesarist elements to pursue a "project of capitalist modernization" and "the foundation of a new bourgeois state."[72]

In Brazil, the conception of the governments of the Workers' Party (PT) as a passive revolution likewise provoked a brief but pertinent debate that involved a number of high-profile intellectuals. In a 2005 article, Ruy Braga and Álvaro Bianchi propose the idea of a social-liberal "Brazilian-style passive revolution," to differentiate the process from neoliberalism in light of the policies of redistribution of revenue and to account for the transformation, which they called the "financialization," of the union bureaucracy.[73] Carlos Nelson Coutinho, a distinguished Brazilian intellectual and pioneer of Gramscian studies in the country, contested this reading, preferring the phrase "hegemony of petty politics," since he now saw substantial modifications tied to demands from below, and he understood consent to be strictly passive. He maintained, therefore, that it was a plain and simple counterreform, continuous with neoliberalism.[74] In 2010, in response to Coutinho, Braga defined Lulismo as passive revolution, characterizing the process as one of conservative modernization tied to the financial sphere as well as to transformations in the world of work, considering Bolsa Familia and other public policies, including wage policies, to constitute mere concessions without an attendant structural change. With regard to hegemony, Braga points out the demobilization of social organizations and movements as well as the passive consent of the subaltern classes as opposed to the active role of the leadership of the PT, which came to manage the state and the pension funds.[75]

For his part, the renowned sociologist Francisco de Oliveira denied that the process was either one of passive revolution or of populism, but recognized elements of transformism, co-optation, and demobilization, characterizing the process with the tongue-in-cheek phrase "hegemony in reverse."

> It is the dominant class that consents to be politically led by the dominated, on the condition that the "moral leadership" not question the capitalist form of exploitation.[76]

Edmundo Fernandes Dias, another distinguished Brazilian Gramscian, also characterizes the period of the PT governments as one of passive revolution, maintaining moreover that the "process of Lulification"—the incorporation within the state apparatus of representatives of the subaltern classes that "decapitated their leadership"—spread throughout Latin America.[77]

Before unpacking the claim that the progressive governments constituted passive revolutions and moving on to a more-focused analysis of the texts that advance these arguments, we must note that, amid the variety of positions, a basic theoretical tension stands out: one between hegemonism and autonomism—two opposing logical and political principles that have been and remain key terms that mark certain actors and moments of the historical process that we are trying to decipher.

It is important to distinguish between the general and abstract principles of autonomy and hegemony—which both belong to the Marxist tradition, in particular its Gramscian branch—from their respective *isms*, the theoretical and practical political tendencies to separate them, essentialize them, and make them into unilateral strategic tools, that is, focused on a single site, the state or the communitarian, or a privileged subject that embodies the political project and becomes the only dynamic factor capable of engendering transformation: the autonomy of the subject of the community, class, or people; the autonomy of the political, that is, of the political structures of mediation—the state, the party, or the leader.

Not by accident, on a theoretical (or political-strategical) level, after the rise of autonomist thought fostered by the period of struggle, as we have discussed above, a consideration of the state and the reclaiming of a statist concept of hegemony has occupied an important place not only in the debate but also in its attendant theorizations. At the same time, in addition to the persistence of the concrete question of autonomy, autonomism itself as a political and intellectual tendency, despite having lost some of its persuasive force as a social alternative, remains a robust and radically critical position in relation to hegemonism and the corresponding statism of the progressive governments' supporters.

A contiguous and parallel question that runs across, and at the same time allows us to organize, the debate that we are outlining, concerns opposing conceptions of the role of intellectuals, in which the organicity to which Gramsci refers translates into two forms that, instead of linking up, are counterposed: that of the critical intellectual and that of the intellectual as an organ of power. In the context of the debate on progressivism, this tension amounted to an irreducible opposition between critics and supporters, in both cases falling back on a militant conception of the intellectual, privileging one feature or another, one justification or another: whether the intellectual be a radical, systematic, and uncompromising critic of all power or instance of domination, or be committed, disciplined, and integrated into the party or government considered to be antisystemic.

Having proposed these broad key concepts for approaching the debate, we conclude this part of the chapter by repeating that our intention in presenting the representative selection of authors, positions, and arguments that we have included here is to offer a preliminary map of the general lines of the conflict between, on the one hand, the official discourse and its variants, and, on the other hand, a broad range of critical positions within a debate that is still raging in the political and intellectual spheres. Even as this dispute loses steam as the defeat of progressivism deepens and the right gains ground in the region, the analysis of the experiences of the progressive Latin American governments of the beginning of the twenty-first century will continue to develop and occupy an ever more important place both in the field of the social sciences and, in the long term, the historiography of the region. As we pointed out in the beginning of this chapter, our subject is a historic debate that marks a watershed in the political and intellectual history of the region.[78]

An Era of Passive Revolutions

This theory, which emerged in the early period of the debate on the achievements and limitations of those progressive Latin American governments, proposes to characterize the period in question as a series of variants of *passive revolution*, that is, following Gramsci, a series of political projects that became significant but limited processes of transformation, with a conservative undercurrent, directed from above and by means of demobilizing and subalternizing political practices, carried out largely through Caesarism and *transformism* as the means of building upward and downward channels of popular organization, participation, and agency.[79]

Considering that, as we saw in previous sections, one of the major analytical problems seems to be that of synthesizing the contradictions and ambiguities that mark these political experiences, the Gramscian concepts open up an original and fruitful line of interpretation that allows us to go beyond the notion of *progressive governments* that has been used in this book and that is in broad circulation in this intense and ongoing debate.

REVOLUTION AS NEO-DEVELOPMENTALISM AND STATISM

The question of the transformative or revolutionary reach of the progressive governments has been at the center of much of the debate, between those who laud their post-neoliberal accomplishments and those who see them as confined to a neo-developmentalism paradigm. Various elements of this aspect of the debate give credence to the theory of passive revolution:

1. The transformations that were put in motion by the progressive governments can be called *revolutions*—assuming a broad and strictly descriptive sense of the term—insofar as they promoted significant alterations of the capitalist model in an anti-neoliberal, post-neoliberal, and neo-developmentalist direction, with the different cases falling somewhere on a spectrum that runs from deep and substantial reforms to a "moderate reformist conservativism," to use a phrase of Gramsci's. Brazil could be said to represent the conservative end of the spectrum, and Venezuela the point of most substantial reformism with real structural changes. In evaluating the extent of the transformations, it is not the same to weigh the public spending that stimulated consumption and the internal market as to recognize the limited activation of the productive sector or the strengthening of a raw-materials export model. All in all, from an impartial perspective, we must recognize a shift—even if a modest one—with respect to neoliberalism insofar as nationalist and social priorities are reflected in a series of sovereignist and redistributive measures. At the same time, as explained in chapter 2, with regard to industrial production, forms of insertion in the world market, and the persistence and even bolstering of the raw-materials export model—with the concomitant environmental costs—there were no substantial changes, and some critics have argued, providing relevant data, that there was in fact a regression. The question as to whether this neo-developmentalism is consistent with or antithetical to the post-neoliberal, anticapitalist, and socialist projects, and whether this last threshold is attainable in the short term, is beyond

the scope of this book. Even if they arise on the spectrum between structural reforms and a "moderate reformist conservativism," the processes under consideration undoubtedly represent a significant break with neoliberalism as it was implemented in Latin America since the 1980s. They can therefore be characterized using Gramsci's conception of *revolution* in a limited sense, that is, along with its conservative counterpart, as a neo-developmentalist revolution, a progressive variant of capitalist modernization.[80]

2 At the same time, initially activated by the antagonistic popular mobilizations but then against these very sectors and on the grounds of their limitations, the process was directed *from above*. Although some demands formulated from below by the subaltern classes were incorporated, the progressive political forces, from the position of the state, forged alliances and even incorporated into their ranks sectors of the dominant classes, and fostered the emergence of new groups both through the accumulation of capital and through the empowerment of new layers of bureaucracy. In this sense the conservative limits of the Latin American passive revolutions lie in the class composition and recomposition of the forces that direct them. We cannot say categorically that the progressive governments are direct expressions of the Latin American dominant classes or bourgeoisie, just as we cannot claim the opposite—that is, that they come strictly from the subaltern classes and the workers. However, amid the interclass mediations and contradictions that, with different nuances, appear in all these cases, we can clearly see a certain organic anchoring in the subaltern classes and some progressive gains, along with conservative limits to the horizon of transformation and ideological tone of the project; in these, we see an obvious and antithetical class element. In other words, without saying that these governments are directly or completely run by the dominant classes, we can say that they are governments whose relative autonomy did not translate into a frontal and systematic opposition to the interests of the local dominant classes, but rather sought to forge an inter- or trans-class hegemony that would break their unity to promote the detachment of a progressive or nationalist sector from the oligarchic bloc toward a reformist conservative project that takes the form of a passive revolution. In accomplishing this and in incorporating other sectors of the middle classes and promoting new dynamics of

accumulation, the social and political composition of the progressive field was considerably altered in a conservative direction.

3 On the other hand, with regard to the political process, reforms were implemented strictly from above, through the apparatus of the state, and, in particular, through presidential power, making use of the existing liberal-democratic institutional and legal structures as the fundamental and almost exclusive instruments of political action. It is universally recognized that the transformations that occurred were carried out from above, and that the center and engine of the reformist and conservative practices compose the state apparatus. Whether we like it or not, it is indisputable that, with various degrees of intensity, the progressive Latin American governments, against the principles of neoliberalism, restored the state—and the public policies that issue from it—as the central instrument of social and economic intervention. Beyond the debate on the vices or virtues of a neo-developmentalist project, the statism or *statolatry* currently in vogue in Latin America corresponds to the model of passive revolution in that it effectively combines a capacity for innovation from above with vertical control. This does not imply an ideological condemnation of the principle of the role of the state, as from an autonomist position, but simply a recognition of the disproportionate role that the state has taken in the context of the Latin American progressive governments. One of the most prominent and well-documented critiques points to the implementation of social assistance programs, which respond in part to demands from below and which were an important feature of all these governments. These programs, on the one hand, redistributed wealth—which must be lauded—while, on the other hand, not only did they not guarantee the poor sustainable and independent means to ensure their own well-being, but they also functioned as powerful tools of clientelism, serving to solidify political loyalties.

DEMOBILIZATION, TRANSFORMISM, AND CAESARISM

In addition to evaluating the transformative reach and class character of these processes, we are equally concerned with identifying the sociopolitical limitations of the Latin American passive revolutions of the beginning of the century.

To this end, we can point out three features that reveal the predominance of action from above, by old and new elites, from the state or political society, and the corresponding or parallel construction of the passivity of the subaltern classes.

1. The political forces located at this governmental level took advantage of and promoted a more or less pronounced *demobilization* of the popular movements and exercised tight social control, or, if you will, hegemony over the subaltern classes. This partially but significantly undermined their fragile and incipient autonomy as well as their antagonist power. It in fact produced, or at least did nothing to counteract, a resubalternization in relation to the stability of a new political equilibrium. Hence the feature of passivity—the shift from an antagonistic politicization to a subaltern depoliticization—became characteristic, salient, decisive, and common to the configuration of the several versions of passive revolution in Latin America at the beginning of the century.[81]
2. Parallel processes of *transformism* took place by which elements, or even whole sectors, of the popular movements were coopted and absorbed by force, by alliances, and by projects that combined progressive and conservative features. They moved into the terrain of institutionality and the state apparatuses, generally in order to implement the public policies directed toward redistribution through assistentialist programs and corresponding processes of demobilization or, occasionally, controlled mobilization.
3. The mode of *passive revolution* stems from the Latin American *caudillist* tradition, and emerged as a kind of *progressive Caesarism*, in that the *catastrophic equilibrium* between neoliberalism and antineoliberalism was resolved through a progressive synthesis of reform and capitalist modernization in a neo-developmentalist direction governed by a charismatic figure, a tipping of the scales in the dynamic center of the process. The progressive governments, in effect, revolve around the figure of a popular *caudillo* who not only guarantees a balance between transformation and conservation, but also ensures the fundamentally passive and delegative nature of the process, while retaining the ability to draw sporadically on targeted and contained forms of mobilization.

It is a fact that the progressive Latin American governments emerged *after* the waves of popular mobilizations that marked the decade between the mid-1990s and the mid-2000s, with different rhythms, forms, and intensities in the various national contexts. This background is relevant as it posits a fundamental interpretative problem that we would like to point out—one that has to do with the adjective in the term *passive revolution*: the so-called progressive governments in Latin America took advantage of, precipitated, or promoted a relative demobilization, depoliticization, or, in the best of cases, a controlled and subordinate mobilization or politicization of the popular sectors and social movements and organizations. In the first years, in particular in Venezuela, Ecuador, and Bolivia, when the right sought to destabilize the anti-neoliberal governments through social and institutional conflict, the levels of mobilization remained relatively high. But since this attack was blocked and the conservative or neoliberal opposition groups turned their main focus back to electoral means, the quantitative decrease in social conflict has been obvious and documented by analysts, while since 2013 there has been a resurgence of protests as a result of the reactivation of the right as well as of the popular organizations and movements.[82] At the same time, the process of demobilization and passivization, at the qualitative level, is reflected in a clear passage from an antagonistic mode of politicization to a subaltern one. It is this qualitative shift that allows us to recognize, even in view of subaltern forms of action, resistance, and protest, a general tendency toward demobilization and passivization.

Among the critical assessments that are circulating with increasing frequency in the countries where progressive governments were or are still in power, the following causes have been cited: the context of the crisis of political institutions and parties; the rise of charismatic governments and leaders who vented the tensions and demands that had catalyzed the social organizations and movements in the preceding years; the co-optation and the voluntary participation of leaders and activists from popular movements in state institutions in order to translate their demands into public policy; pressure and clientelist management and, occasionally, even repression, by government actors.

The moment of the progressive governments, still in their ascent to hegemony, at their most comfortable point, was also the moment of demobilization and politicization, of the missed opportunity to forge a participative democracy, using the forms of organization, mobilization, and politicization that had been developed to strengthen and empower the popular classes.

On the contrary, the political forces located within the governments did not counteract but instead exploited and even promoted the tendency toward a corporative-clientelist regression experienced by many of the organizations and movements that had been at the helm in earlier stages of the process. In this broad overview, we must not lose sight of the political landscape of the process in these countries, in which three general forms of mobilization were employed: those promoted by the governments and by the party and union authorities that supported them; those tied to the opposition from the right; and those of the dissidents on the left.

The first two tended to decline with the introduction of accords and practices of governability, a *pax progresista* (except during election and the attendant routine exercises of mobilization), only to return at the moment of hegemonic crisis and counterattack from the right. The last mode, a surge of antagonistic and relatively autonomous mobilizations of the subaltern classes, might seem to disprove the claim of passivity, but it was really only a reaction against the passive revolutions under way, the embryo of an antithesis that did not quite take shape and remained limited in its ability to gather momentum and to cohere around an alternative project. Regardless of our assessment of the outcomes of the process, we must recognize that it was, by and large, a mass phenomenon, prolonged, or, unlike in the 2000s, with significant effects in terms of the general political equilibrium. The governments did not succeed in reversing the general tendency, but rather confirmed the hypothesis of their resubalternization, that is, of the reconfiguration of subalternity as the subjective framework of domination, as a general condition of possibility of the passive revolution.

By contrast, we must give an account of the limitations of the popular movements that enabled the processes of passive revolution to take place, which we can sum up, paraphrasing Gramsci, as sporadic, rudimentary, and inorganic subversivism without a unified popular project. These are the elements from which arise both the possibility of passive revolution and the necessary conditions for its continuation. Finally, in the context of the tendency toward passivization, there was a turn to controlled mobilization—a familiar formula for Latin American populism, generally applied in a defensive mode against the forces of oligarchic restoration, like that which is now under way—which can sometimes overflow its intended limits.

The absence of reforms that would amount to a true democratization of the state, of the political and party systems, and of direct or participative democracy confirms the general hypothesis as to the passive nature of the political processes set in motion by Latin American progressivism. At first, there appeared to be a certain political will, and innovative ideas were even generated that found some expression in the three new constitutions (in Venezuela, Ecuador, and Bolivia), as a reflection of the programs and demands of the popular movements that had questioned the electoralism and particracy of the Latin American transitions to democracy. But these became more and more diluted in the governmental practices and projects, though they continued to be reproduced on the discursive level and were still upheld by some sectors within the governing coalitions—groups that were not strong enough or influential enough to determine the general course. Democratization conceived as the socialization of power and as a driving force of self-determination remained an unfulfilled promise of Latin American progressivism, confined to the dead letters of the constitutions. Only in Venezuela did direct democracy at some point occupy a central place both at the symbolic level and at the level of public financing, through the creation of the communal councils. But this important step in the direction of participative democracy has been tempered and corrupted by clientelism and by a top-down logic of the government and of the United Socialist Party of Venezuela, the political arm of Chavismo that was created at the same time as a centralizing counterbalance to the decentralization of power that the Communes represented.

Now, we must consider that the ebb of the spontaneous processes of participation tied to specific conjunctures cannot be mechanically resolved by engineering institutional apparatuses for participation. At the same time, though all forms of institutionalization necessarily bring some degree of passivization, this does not mean that the existence of institutional frameworks that include participative channels is irrelevant, so long as these are not devoid of content, or so long as they do not become mere bureaucratic links that operate as mechanisms of social control.

At the same time, without falling into the Manichaeism of an institutionalization/autonomy dichotomy, we see here an underlying trend of political distrust, of a crisis of Western political institutions, that leads us to posit passivity as a general societal tendency. Finally, we must recognize that it was largely the popular movements themselves that sought and, to varying extents, found paths to the institutions of the state in a process of construction of power that was partially successful, but that implied an institutionalization of political action despite the relative demobilization and loss of agency of the social organizations and movements.

Transformism played a fundamental role here. The rise of the progressive governments led to a co-optation from the state apparatus that drained popular sectors of leaders and activists to the point of disrupting the social movement conceived as a whole. This process is central in explaining passivization, subalternization, social control, controlled mobilization, or heteronomy.

Likewise, it is particularly telling that there is a resemblance between the political form that emerged and the caudillist model—that is, in the terms that we are proposing, a progressive Caesarism that fulfills a fundamental function in that it not only stabilizes and neutralizes conflict but also affirms and sanctions verticality, delegation, and passivity as central and decisive features.

Focusing, then, on the question of processes of political subjectification, we must acknowledge a regression to subalternity, a loss of both antagonistic capacity and autonomy on the part of the actors and social movements that spearheaded the social struggles in Latin America in the initial moment of the anti-neoliberal period. On the side of the state, tendencies became apparent toward institutionalization, delegation, demobilization, and depoliticization (and even toward authoritarianism, bureaucratization, clientelism, co-optation, and selective repression) that characterized the political scenes dominated by the progressive governments. "Perversions" of the projects of transformation emerged that, notwithstanding declarations of intent, either dismissed, denied, or limited the development of the political subjectivity of the subaltern classes, focusing instead on initiatives from above that, far from promoting emancipatory and democratic processes, reproduced subalternity as a necessary condition of domination. Regardless of our assessment of the outcome and socioeconomic accomplishments of the public policies implemented by the progressive governments, the old forms of statism and partisanship reappeared that, far from operating as mechanisms of real democratization and the socialization of politics, became obstacles and instruments of passive revolution. In exploiting, controlling, limiting, and, ultimately, obstructing the development of forms of participation, the occupation of spaces from which to exercise self-determination, and the constitution of popular power or counterpowers from below, not only did the governing forces deny a substantial element of any fully emancipatory project, but they also diminished the possibilities of continuing the process of reform, not to mention of deepening it and steering it in a revolutionary direction. This happened because the fundamental political condition for a history of the subaltern classes—initiative from below, and the capacities for organization, mobilization, and struggle—had disappeared.

THE END OF THE PROGRESSIVE PERIOD AND THE REGRESSIVE TURN

As a result of the economic crisis, of political attrition after more than a decade of government, and of the internal contradictions of any passive revolution, between 2013 and 2015, the so-called progressive governments of Latin America entered into a critical phase that some authors are calling the "end of the era," opening up a debate on the nature of the conjuncture with important strategic implications for the immediate future. We will briefly advance the argument that, strictly speaking, the period ended not only because of the right's return to power in Argentina and Brazil but also because the loss of hegemony had become obvious, leading to a series of consequences, including this turn to the right in these major countries of the region, but also situations of turbulence in others.

Since passive revolution is a process that finds a hegemonic solution to a situation of a balance of forces, or "catastrophic stalemate" (*empate catastrófico*)—a phrase that was used in progressivist discourse in Latin America in the 2000s—we can analyze and problematize the notion of the end of an era by revealing a central and critical feature: the relative loss of hegemony, that is, a diminished capacity for the construction and maintenance of broad interclass consensus along with a strong popular base that characterized the phase of consolidation of these governments.

In effect, between 2013 and 2015, the phase of hegemonic consolidation came to a close. This hegemony had been expressed repeatedly in election results and plebiscites but was forged fundamentally through the efficient exercise of a series of state and party mediations, displacing the right from strategic institutional networks and ideological apparatuses of the state and establishing a series of core ideas, watchwords, and political values with a national-popular tenor like sovereignty, nationalism, progress, development, social justice, redistribution, plebeian dignity, and so on. In some countries this displacement was accompanied by a direct confrontation with attempts at restoration through coups or other extra-institutional means—as in the cases of Bolivia, Ecuador, and Venezuela, but also in Argentina with its 2008 agricultural taxation crisis—whose ultimate failure weakened the right in these countries and, therefore, paved the way for a more vigorous exercise of hegemony on the part of the progressive forces, including reformulating the constitutional frameworks and setting the scene for what was called a "change of epoch."[83]

This phase has ended. At least since 2013, as outlined in chapter 1, there has been a turn, with some formal and temporal variations, from a progressive agenda to an increasingly regressive one.[84] This turn was particularly noticeable in the fiscal responses to the economic crisis that hit the region, which privileged capital over both labor and the environment, as well as in the attitude toward the social organizations and movements to the left of the governments, which tended to toughen both discursively and in practice.

Gramsci maintained that one can—and must—distinguish between a progressive and a regressive Caesarism. He added that this antinomy constitutes a lens through which we can analyze different forms and stages of passive revolutions, since it allows us to see different combinations of progressive and regressive features and to identify which of the two predominates in each of the successive moments of the historical process.[85] Since the emergence of the social and political blocs and alliances that have driven the progressive Latin American governments, divergent tendencies have coexisted within them. If in the initial stage the progressivist tendency, with which they have been labeled, predominated, we can identify a subsequent conservative turn that took them backward in relation to the progressive character of their hegemonic stage. This turn appeared organically within the blocs and alliances that sustained these governments and was expressed in the shifts in public policy that were justified, from the perspective of the defense of their positions of power, by the need to compensate for the loss of broad hegemony by veering toward the center.

This move to the center, we might add, seemed to contrast with the logic of the left–right and people–oligarchy polarization that characterized the establishment of these governments, propelled by the emergence of robust antineoliberal movements and the subsequent clashes with the right that opened the doors for the consolidation of hegemony. At the same time, if we follow Maristella Svampa's theory of a return to populist strategies, a real, organic, political movement toward the center does not preclude the use of a confrontational rhetoric, which is typical of populism, though it would have to become more moderate over time as it gains coherence between form and content.[86]

In any case, we are witnessing a fundamental historical and structural shift in the political composition of these governments, and therefore marking a significant moment in the political history of the present in Latin America. The regressive turn within progressivism was more pronounced in some countries (Argentina, Brazil, Ecuador) than in others (Venezuela, Bolivia, Uruguay), since in the latter the social and political blocs linked to the progressive governments remained relatively compact, there were no major cleavages of the left, and the right was weaker (except in Venezuela, where this is debatable). Although the regressive turn within progressivism was fundamentally a question of molecular shifts at the level of social and political alliances, class influence, sectors of classes and social and political groups and their counterparts in terms of the redirection of public policy, we will mention here, by way of example (because it would be impossible to give a comprehensive panorama of the Latin American landscape), only some of the most salient instances of this in the sphere of party politics and leadership turnover.

In Argentina the conservative turn was obvious, and it was sealed with Daniel Scioli's presidential candidacy in 2015 in the Front for Victory (FpV), with Scioli's not being a part, to use an Argentinian expression, of the Kirchnerist *riñon* (kidney), unlike the vice-presidential candidate, Carlos Zannini. This indicated a shift to the center-right of the Peronist microcosm of the political system (as Juan Carlos has called it) that was already under way in the preceding few years in which a gradual weakening of Kirchnerismo occurred.[87] In a sense, this is also the case with the 2019 Argentinian elections, with the return of Kirchnerism in diluted form, as Cristina Fernández de Kirchner receded to the vice-presidency and Alberto Fernández assumed the presidential seat.

In Brazil, for some time several authors had been describing a genetic mutation, beyond the corruption scandals, within the PT. The sociologist Francisco "Chico" de Oliveira has identified this as the rise of the *platypus*—a hybrid figure, half syndicalist and half financial speculator, managing immense pension funds that navigate the financial markets.[88] In this context Lula's possible return would not have substantially modified the political direction taken by Dilma Rousseff, just as there was no major alteration when she took office, yet the turn to the center was evident more in their conjuncture than with a reduction in social spending relative to the persistent direct and indirect bolstering of processes of capital accumulation. This same tendency appeared in Ecuador with the shift of the leftist sectors within the PAIS Alliance (AP) and the election of Jorge Glas, a vice president who clearly identifies with the private sector, to accompany Correa in the 2013 elections.[89] This directionality matured with Lenín Moreno's rise to the presidency, as discussed in chapter 1. In Uruguay the regression on the ideological level from "Pepe" Mujica's leadership to Tabaré Vázquez's was obvious, as a reflection of the internal and external equilibrium of the Broad Front that moved to the right, even with the continuity that comes with a stable political force and a well-defined project. As we saw in chapter 1, this trajectory helped lay the groundwork for the assumption of the genuine right-wing to power in the figure of Luis Lacalle Pou in 2020.

With regard to the Andean cases (Bolivia and Ecuador), Maristella Svampa points out a breach of promises that represented "the loss of the emancipatory dimension of the regimes' politics and a trend toward traditional modes of domination, grounded in charismatic leadership and identification with the state."[90] In the case of Bolivia, beyond the emergence of an "Aymara bourgeoisie" and the bureaucratization and institutionalization of broad sectors of the leadership of the social movements that ignited the anti-neoliberal struggles, the shift toward the center in terms of the political composition of the ruling bloc, while Evo Morales was still in power, was less apparent. At the same time, the question of Morales's reelection opened up a delicate debate, despite the fact that no solid electoral alternative had emerged, since the right, with the exception of some local results, had not yet fully raised its head, and since the Movimiento Sin Miedo had not managed to configure an alternative on the left. This dynamic would change, of course, with the coup of 2019 and the seizure of power by Jeanine Áñez. Such internal regressive tendencies within progressivism were even less apparent in Venezuela, because the political and economic crises polarized the opposing camps, rallying the subaltern classes beyond the leaders of the Bolivarian Revolution despite the fact that the circumstances of a particularly fragile economy did not allow for a deepening of this process, generated internal tensions, and strengthened its most authoritarian tendencies.

Such national differences were reflected in the greater or lesser influence of the reactivation of a social and political opposition from the left. Indeed, in the majority of these countries, despite the relative recovery of the right, there has been a rise in protests by popular actors, organizations, and movements, though they have not ultimately taken root and solidified an antagonistic and autonomous position against their own subalternization and the passive revolutions. Due to a lack of persistence over time, a lack of organizational cohesion, and a lack of political coordination, unfortunately there has been no real emergence within the Latin American political landscape of a new politics of the left. In fact, despite the slow recovery of autonomy and the capacity for struggle, no significant processes of accumulation of political force were evident over the course of the past several years of the waning hegemony of progressivism, with the possible exception of the Workers' Left Front (FIT) in Argentina, whose prospects and potential for growth are uncertain—see, for example, its decline in the 2019 presidential contest as described in chapter 1. The eruption of protests in Ecuador traversed various sectors and demands, weakening Correa and compelling him to back the candidacy of Lenín Moreno, whose victory inaugurated a new phase of post-Correa progressivism. But despite rising discontent in the popular sectors—in particular among the organized indigenous and labor groups—this did not lead to the consolidation of a political alternative but, on the contrary, Moreno and the anti-Correa turn fractured the sphere of popular organizations. Although it remains too early to tell, the October 2019 rebellions may represent a change in this regard, insofar as they represent a new coherence on the part of popular forces, led by the rearticulation of the CONAIE.

This situation is due in part to the effect of the ebb, following the rising tide of anti-neoliberal struggles, of the popular sectors toward a clientelism and corporativism rooted in a subaltern political culture. But, by contrast and to a significant extent, it is the result of the initiatives, or lack thereof, among the progressive governments that were more interested in building up electoral support, guaranteeing governability, and eliminating social conflict than in fostering, or even respecting, the antagonistic and autonomous organizational dynamics or the construction of channels and forms of participation and self-determination in the service of a genuine transformation of the conditions of life, beyond the mere power of consumption, of the subaltern classes.

This weakening, or absence of empowerment, suggests that the passivizing measures that operated as a counterpart to the structural transformations and redistributive policies (without considering here the controversial continuation of extractivist and raw-export practices) resulted in a lost decade in terms of accumulation of political force from below, from the autonomous capacity of the popular sectors, against the ascent that marked the 1990s and that broke with neoliberal hegemony, leading to the current historical conjuncture.

This failure is what impedes, for the moment, an engagement with a double deviation to the right: that of the relative strengthening of the political forces of the right itself, and that of the conservative and regressive turn that has altered the balance and the political orientation of the power blocs that sustain Latin America's progressive governments.

In conclusion, in times of turmoil, some of the passive revolutions, in a phase of decline, remain under way, surrounded by a growing opposition from both the right and the left, internally marked by a conservative and regressive turn, slipping dangerously down a slope on which they are losing their hegemonic luster, and even announcing the end of a historical process, of an era, that seems to be inexorably approaching.

CONCLUSION

In this book we have offered an overarching assessment of the politics, economics, and strategies of the Latin American left in the twenty-first century. The objective has been to capture the dynamism of the extra-parliamentary explosions of the late 1990s, the promise and contradictions of the period of progressive hegemony between 2003 and 2011, and the unraveling of that hegemony and the rise of new rights since 2013.

On the terrain of the political, we have charted the complexities of class struggle and the dynamic relationships between popular movements and progressive parties and governments from the 1990s to the present. We have demonstrated how the popular rebellions of the late 1990s emerged in response and opposition to the neoliberal hegemony of the Washington Consensus over the 1980s and 1990s. It was on the basis of this extra-parliamentary resistance that electoral victories of center-left and national-popular governments were eventually consolidated in a number of Latin American countries over the course of the first decade of the twenty-first century. In an uneven political process, radical impulses from below were channeled and crystalized by an eclectic range of progressive parties, often led by charismatic figures, toward a strategic perspective of electoralism and state power.

Following a "golden age" of progressive hegemony between roughly 2003 and 2011, a variety of state-capitalist programs of governance and development were consolidated across distinct countries under the rule of mainly center-left, but also some left, administrations. The overarching ideological characters of these governments were far from the revolutionary or anti-capitalist orientations of much of the Latin American left in the 1970s. Assessing the region as a whole, during the 2006–2013 period, regime types split along three axes: neoliberal/conservative; social-liberal and/or populist left; and national-popular with anti-imperialist accents. The latter type is best characterized by the governments of Venezuela, Ecuador, and Bolivia. Across the second and third regime types, there was a similar return of the social elements of the state, the reinforcement of various social programs, and the development of new infrastructures for neo-developmental economic plans. And yet none of these programs implied a serious confrontation with the interests of the ruling classes, while, politically, they involved the co-optation and institutional integration of popular movements, with some social movement and union leaderships directly incorporated into the state apparatuses.

With time, the golden age faded and new authoritarian characteristics emerged in some of the progressive experiences in power, new layers of bureaucratic sclerosis were consolidated, and tensions began to emerge among popular movements and progressive governments beginning around 2012–2013; this marks the putative "end of the cycle" of progressivism. At the same time, sensing the weakness of progressive administrations, a series of new right movements and electoral initiatives became emboldened and made advances in several countries since 2013. It would appear that the experience of governing capitalist state apparatuses, even in cases where that apparatus had been partially reformed through new constitutions, had deleterious effects over time on the actions, policies, and ideological worldviews of progressivism in office. New elites within the state began to emerge, together with mergers with fractions of the extant ruling classes, simultaneous to, and imbricated in, accelerating processes of corruption and bureaucratization. In Venezuela, for example, such trends were already evident under Hugo Chávez, even though they only exploded under Nicolás Maduro. Brazil, perhaps, represents the clearest and most regularized manifestation of merging interests between Workers' Party elites, trade union officials, and the world of finance. As conservative tendencies within progressive governments became more amplified, tensions and even open confrontations with popular movements increased. Without understanding the contradictions and limitations of progressive experiments such as the PT in Brazil, one cannot hope to explain subsequent right-wing resurgences, such as the subsequent rise of Jair Bolsonaro to that country's presidency.

In the current conjuncture, four political trends are evident. One involves the destabilization of social-liberalism and the ascension in its place of more-orthodox neoliberal forces, with Uruguay under Pou and Chile under Piñera standing out as two prominent examples. A second phenomenon sees national-popular governments remaining in office, but in degraded or even regressive forms. This trend is most evident in Venezuela, Ecuador, and Nicaragua. A third is the anti-democratic removal of progressivism from office through coups d'état of distinct varieties—the standouts here are Brazil 2016 and Bolivia 2019, though it is also worth remembering Honduras 2009 and Paraguay 2012. A final trend is the return or rise to office of center-leftism in extremely challenging economic and political circumstances, with Argentina's Alberto Fernández representing the former and Mexico's Andrés Manuel López Obrador representing the latter.

Throughout Latin America, authoritarian features of the state seem to be gaining strength. The return of various right-wing forces to government is evidence of the right's continuing political influence and power in the region, as well as its enduring capacity to adapt to new scenarios and to capitalize on the weaknesses of the left, even to the extent of reinventing itself on the streets. At the same time, popular disaffection with progressivism as it has been practiced in early twenty-first century regimes is finding expression in renewed popular movements and repertoires of collective action: peasant mobilizations, urban struggles, movements of students and the youth, novel forms of worker militancy and unionism, new feminist formations, and indigenous politics, among many others. To a certain extent, this is a return to the plural forms of plebeian politics that we witnessed in the 1990s. The incipient return of independent working-class mobilization augurs well for the possibility of left-wing recomposition in the streets and the renewal of class struggle from below. Such myriad examples of renewed self-activity among the popular classes is evidence once again that any hopes for an emancipatory future ought to be oriented to those movements from below, and to the left. It is here where we will find social forces capable of overcoming the limits and contradictions of the progressive cycle, without aligning with the resurgent forces of domestic and imperial reaction.

On the terrain of the economic, we have demonstrated how Latin American state forms are today, as they were historically, doubly determined. On the one side, the timing and pattern of Latin America's subordinate incorporation into the international division of labor and the rhythms of the core historical cycles of accumulation unfolding on the global scale have helped to determine the region's state forms. At the same time, on the other side, such state forms are shaped and conditioned by the central conflicts generated among the principal domestic antagonistic social classes, along with the shifting balance of forces between them—economic, sociological, ideological, and political—as each attempts to defend and advance its interests against the other.

We have shown how the period of progressive hegemony between 2003 and 2011 was intimately linked to the Chinese-driven international boom in commodities, together with the concomitant upturn in agro-industrial mono-cropping, mining, and natural gas and oil extraction across much of the region. The rents generated from such resource extraction provided the means with which progressive governments could establish regimes in which modest redistributive gains were achieved for the lower social classes, even while class structures and social-property relations underlying these societies were largely untouched.

The compensatory redistribution of progressive governments, we have argued, were, from the beginning, structurally vulnerable to an eventual slowdown in commodity prices, and by 2012 this was the main mechanism through which the global economic crisis of 2008 made its delayed landing on the shores of South America. Economic crises in the wake of the downturn undermined the material bases of redistribution, which helped to stoke political tensions between progressive governments and popular movements, while also opening up political opportunities for right-wing rearticulation.

The international economic features of our analysis have also been combined with attentiveness to the influence of imperialism, and particularly the geopolitical strategies of the United States and China vis-à-vis Latin America in recent decades. We have demonstrated how the United States remains the key imperial power influencing political outcomes in the region, even if it has suffered relative decline across various economic and geopolitical dimensions of its foreign power projection. China, meanwhile, still does not represent an imperial rival in military terms to the United States in Latin America. However, it clearly has a prominent and growing imperial influence in terms of patterns of foreign direct investment (FDI), as a determinant commercial destination point for important Latin American commodity exports, and also as an alternative line of credit with distinct loan conditionalities from those often attached to loans from the World Bank, International Monetary Fund, or Inter-American Development Bank.

Against such imperial machinations, we have also paid close attention to the efforts made by progressive movements and governments in the region to establish alternative regional geopolitical formations to counter the influence of the United States, in particular. On the radical wing of such institutional experiments were the Bolivarian Alliance for the Peoples of Our America (ALBA), the Bank of the South, and the Sucre currency. More-moderate expressions of regional bodies designed to contest US hegemony—at least in a limited way—included the Southern Common Market (MERCOSUR), the Union of South American Nations (UNASUR), and the Community of Latin American and Caribbean States (CELAC). The central conclusions we have drawn are that such counter-regional initiatives, radical and more modest alike, clearly weakened US dominance and power in Latin America to a certain extent. However, the most radical initiatives decomposed as the economic crisis hit and the legitimacy of a number of progressive governments faltered, most crucially in the case of the Bolivarian process in Venezuela. While the moderate expressions of counter-regionalism persist, they never represented the same potential as ALBA, the Bank of the South, and the Sucre, given that they were never grounded in expressly anti-imperialist politics. At the same time, new right-wing regional integration projects like PROSUR are gaining ground. In the current moment, both China and the United States are consolidating existing pathways of influence in Latin America, while forging a number of new domains of power in the region, as counter-regional efforts to establish relative autonomy for Latin American countries through regional cooperation are in retreat.

Finally, on the terrain of intellectual production in Latin America, we have surveyed the general coordinates of the debates on the left regarding the character and composition of the progressive turn in the twenty-first century, paying particular attention to national-popular, populist, anti-capitalist, libertarian-autonomist, ecological, and postcolonial currents of thought. We have identified central theoretical and political tensions running through these debates, between those emphasizing hegemony versus autonomy, and between those, on the one hand, emphasizing initiatives from above, through the state, and rooted in multiclass alliances and programs of limited reform, and those, on the other hand, defending initiatives from below, oriented toward anti-systemic radicalism.

While opposition to neoliberalism in Latin America had been, in a certain sense, a point of articulation and consensus on the intellectual left, the contradictory experience of progressive governments occupying offices of state became a point of internal divergence and disarticulation, a process that intensified over time. In socioeconomic terms, debates unfolded through the prisms of post-neoliberalism, neo-developmentalism, and anti-capitalism. In the intersecting realms of economy and ecology, disputes emerged around extractivism and dependency. On the state and democracy, controversies arose over populism, clientelism, transformism, and passive revolution. Finally, the question of cultural diversity was taken up through the lenses of plurinationalism and postcolonialism.

For intellectuals closest to the progressive governments in office, the primary contradiction facing Latin American countries was the axis of imperialism versus anti-imperialism, and what made these governments worthy of support were their ostensible anti-imperial positions within global geopolitics. Secondarily, what made these governments *popular* governments was their commitment to social justice, an orientation embedded in their post-neoliberal economic policies. Renewed state intervention by progressive governments on both fronts—first, through the assertion of popular sovereignty in the international arena, and second, through state policies of redistribution—was for such leftist intellectuals the bases on which they anchored their support for and ideological commitment to progressive governments.

Leftist critics of progressive governments, meanwhile, recognized that these administrations had emerged from, and been made possible by, the extra-parliamentary surge in anti-neoliberal resistance in the late 1990s and early 2000s. However, for leftist critics, the new left and center-left governments tended to dampen those early anti-neoliberal impulses, rather than push them forward. More than that, they reproduced crucial elements of neoliberalism in their political-economic policies and development plans—consumerism, exploitation, extractivism, and environmental destruction. Politically, over time, many also became prone to authoritarian, clientelistic, and corrupt practices.

Such left intellectual oppositions emerged from various quarters, including anti-capitalism, libertarian-autonomism, environmentalism, and postcolonialism. Anti-capitalist critics pointed to the limits of multiclass alliances and neo-developmental political-economic programs. Militant environmentalists and peasant movements positioned themselves against capitalist extractivism and megaprojects of development. Libertarian-autonomists focused mainly on combinations of authoritarianism, statism, centralism, clientelism, and *caudillismo* (big-man leadership). Postcolonial critics, finally, homed in on aggressions against Mother Earth and communitarian ways of life, as well as continuities in racist hierarchies, plus the failure to achieve genuinely plurinational transformation in countries such as Bolivia and Ecuador. Again, overriding tensions running through these conflicts turned on hegemony versus autonomy, class versus "the people" as the predominant revolutionary subject, and self-emancipation from below versus emancipation mediated through the state, party, and leadership.

Following insights developed in the work of Antonio Gramsci, we have argued that progressive governments in twenty-first-century Latin America can best be understood through the concept of passive revolution. These political projects have involved significant but strictly limited transformations, with conservative undertones, pushed forward from above and through political practices aimed at the demobilization of subaltern classes. Passive revolution, in this sense, has found expression in modalities of Caesarism and transformism, both of which have hollowed out popular infrastructures of organization, participation, and self-activity.

The decline of left hegemony has not meant a smooth alteration to right hegemony, but rather entry into a period of chaotic, unpredictable, and volatile political impasse.[1] In certain instances, left governments have remained in office, but are no longer characterized by their transformative potential.[2] In Venezuela, for example, Nicolás Maduro was reelected to the presidency in May 2018, yet the Bolivarian process has since ossified into an increasingly bureaucratic and militarized distortion of its early phases.[3] Meanwhile, in Ecuador, Lenín Moreno, Rafael Correa's former vice president, and since 2017 the country's president, has introduced a series of orthodox neoliberal restructuring measures, reneging on promises in his electoral platform to continue the popular social expenditures carried out during the Correa administrations.[4] In Nicaragua, Daniel Ortega's Sandinistas remain in power, but it is increasingly evident that they have "dressed in a leftist discourse their attempt to establish a populist multiclass political alliance around this project of capitalist development under the firm hegemony of capital and Sandinista state elites."[5] As the economic crisis internationally began to undermine the Nicaraguan political economy, Ortega announced pension cuts and other regressive measures, sparking off a student and worker uprising in April and May 2018, which has been met with brutal state and paramilitary repression, further undermining the legitimacy of his regime.[6]

In October 2018, the modestly left candidate Andrés Manuel López Obrador (or "AMLO," as he is known) won the Mexican presidential elections.[7] However, his coalition, Morena, has moved significantly to the center over the last few years, and this capitulation to realpolitik sped up during the electoral contest and his first months in office. AMLO's presidency, therefore, so far closely resembles the centrist orientation of Luiz Inácio "Lula" da Silva (Lula) during his first term in office in Brazil.[8]

Elsewhere, the center-left has imploded electorally, and the right has ascended in its place. In Chile, for example, in the second round of the December 2017 elections, the ultra-conservative Sebastián Piñera won 55 percent of the popular vote, soundly defeating Alejandro Guillier, the candidate of the center-left New Majority coalition. Piñera's 55 percent was the best electoral result for a party of the Chilean right in almost a century of republican history.[9] In Argentina, similarly, the Peronist candidate, Daniel Scioli, was defeated in the November 2015 presidential election by the center-right businessman and former Buenos Aires mayor Mauricio Macri, putting a temporary end to the Kirchnerist experiment. Macri, against a political backdrop of rising trade union and social movement opposition along with a growing economic crisis, attempted to return the country to the orthodox neoliberalism of the 1990s, negotiating a major loan agreement between Argentina and the IMF in May 2018.[10] Large-scale demonstrations against Macri's austerity measures contributed to his declining popularity and profile, paving the way for Alberto Fernández's electoral victory in 2019.

In Brazil, Dilma Rousseff was removed from office through a parliamentary coup in 2016, and her former vice president, Michel Temer, sat in as interim president until the October elections in 2018. As noted, the elections witnessed the victory of the region's most extreme right-wing government to date, under the leadership of Bolsonaro. However, the limits of the new right have been expressed both in the infinitesimally low popularity of Temer's interim regime and in the disaster of Bolsonaro's first year and a half in office, characterized as they were by policy paralysis and a deep dive in that president's popularity.[11] Meanwhile, in Colombia, Iván Duque, a representative of paramilitarism, backed by former President Álvaro Uribe, won the presidency in June 2018, jeopardizing the future of the peace agreement.[12]

We have entered a period of right-wing advance and left-wing retreat or ossification, but the right has no solution to the economic and political crises it has inherited. As a result, we are likely to witness a period of intensifying coercive and authoritarian forms of rule on the part of right-wing governments, accompanied by novel iterations of social resistance from the extra-parliamentary left. Significant signs of left renewal in the streets could be seen in the 2019 rebellions across Chile, Colombia, Ecuador, and Puerto Rico. In an effort to inform the struggles of the latter, it is imperative that we study intensively the limits as well as the contradictions of the progressive experiments of early twenty-first-century Latin America. This book represents a modest contribution to that effort.

COVID-19 POSTSCRIPT

Already by mid-June 2020, Latin America, accounting for only 8 percent of the global population, was already suffering half the world's new coronavirus deaths.[1] By August 3, the Pan-American Health Organization (PAHO) reported 2,707,977 cumulative COVID-19 cases in Brazil alone, as well as 93,563 deaths in the country attributable to the virus. This placed President Bolsonaro's stomping ground second only to President Trump's United States in cases and deaths in the entire world. Mexico, Peru, and Chile were the other Latin American cases with high and rising confirmed counts as of late summer 2020. In contrast, along with low rates across most of the Caribbean island states, the countries of Paraguay, Uruguay, and Cuba were at the time of writing relative success stories, with respective cumulative cases at 5,485 (Paraguay), 2,646 (Cuba), and 1,278 (Uruguay), and deaths at 52 (Paraguay), 35 (Uruguay), and 26 (Cuba).[2]

To be clear, in terms of the sheer number of cases and fatalities, all existing official numbers provided by states in the region should be treated with caution, as should the figures of the World Health Organization and its regional affiliates like the Pan-American Health Organization, even if some of the discernible trends they indicate are indisputable. In the medium term, the most reliable data will be, rather, the distinction between average death rates over the last several years and death rates during the pandemic period. Such general mortality analysis is particularly revealing both because such figures do not depend on the highly variable (and thus incomparable) testing capacities and programs of different countries and they are more difficult for governments to conceal or manipulate. General mortality figures also capture deaths both from COVID-19 and those excess indirect deaths caused by people with other underlying health conditions who were not able to access necessary medical attention due to saturated capacity in the health system as a result of the pandemic. The full extent of this information will only be known fully some distance into the future, and perhaps never fully in the most under-resourced states of Latin America and the Caribbean.

Nonetheless, some initial studies have already focused on this kind of general mortality comparison of select cities and intra-country regions, and the results are alarming. According to a May 2020 investigation carried out by the *New York Times*, for example, Manaus, the biggest city of the Brazilian Amazon, with a population of 2 million, registered a total municipal mortality figure of 2,800 for April alone, which is roughly three times the historical average of deaths for that month.[3] By the end of July, the six cities with the highest COVID-19 exposure in Brazil were all situated on the Amazon River, with the pandemic spreading from Manaus, "with its high-rises and factories, to tiny, seemingly isolated villages deep in the interior," where "the fragile health care system has buckled under the onslaught."[4] According to PAHO's data, as of August 3, 2020, Ecuador had 86,232 cumulative cases and 3,064 cumulative deaths.[5] However, *Financial Times* COVID-19 data analysis is revealing of the limits of such real-time estimates. According to the *Financial Times*, between the end of February 2020, when the virus arrived in Ecuador, and July 1, 2020, the last day of data analyzed, there had been 23,600 excess deaths in Ecuador compared to the country's historical averages over the same time span—that is, a general mortality increase of 117 percent.[6] The long and the short of it is that the ultimate numbers of deaths we will surely read about in coming years that resulted directly or indirectly from COVID-19 in Latin America is very likely to be significantly higher than the available daily statistics that appear in newspaper headlines. Also, while absolute numbers of deaths are important—and thus Bolsonaro is deserving of his notoriety for elevating Brazil to second place in the world on this measure—it is also critical to examine coronavirus deaths as a proportion of population. On the measure of deaths per 100,000, for example, Peru (64.55) and Chile (53.17) had worse results as of August 8, 2020, than Brazil (47.54). Meanwhile, Mexico, Bolivia, Colombia, Guatemala, and Argentina joined Peru, Chile, and Brazil among the top twenty countries in the world.[7]

It is clear that even before the onset of COVID-19 the social and economic situation in much of Latin America and the Caribbean had deteriorated gravely since at least 2013, and many of the modest but important improvements in poverty rates and income inequality achieved during the era of progressive governments and capitalist dynamism driven by a global commodity boom (2003–2012) had already been significantly reversed. Between

2016 and 2019, for example, the major regional economies suffered negative or anemic rates of GDP growth—Argentina (−2.1%, 2.7%, −2.5%, −3.0%); Brazil (−3.3%, 1.3%, 1.3%, 1.0%); Chile (1.7%, 1.3%, 4.0%, 0.8%); and Mexico (2.9%, 2.1%, 2.0%, 0.0%). For the same period, similar dynamics were visible in aggregate growth rates for Latin America and the Caribbean as a whole (−1.7%, 1.2%, 1.0%, 0.1%).[8] Venezuela's GDP contracted by an extraordinary 26.8 percent in the first quarter of 2019 alone.[9]

Setbacks in poverty and extreme poverty levels, according to the metrics of the United Nations Economic Commission for Latin America and the Caribbean (ECLAC), have been particularly evident since 2015, partially reversing progress made in these areas between 2002 and 2014.[10] The end of the commodity boom and an associated slowdown in economic growth, together with a shift to the right politically in a number of countries, fueled austerity measures that reduced antipoverty policies and more inclusionary social and labor legislation. In the new setting, unemployment also rose in parallel with a return to informalization processes in the world of work that had only partially improved before 2015.[11] Between 2002 and 2014, regional average poverty declined from 45.4 percent to 27.8 percent, as 66 million people rose above the poverty line. Over the same period, extreme poverty fell from 12.2 percent to 7.8 percent. However, by 2018, the last year for which ECLAC's regional statistics are available, regional poverty had risen to 30.1 percent, alongside a rise to 10.7 percent in extreme poverty. In absolute terms, this translated into 185 million people living in poverty in 2018, with 66 million of them people in extreme poverty. There were 21 million more people living in poverty in 2018 than in 2014, and 20 million of them were considered extremely poor.[12] These aggregate trends conceal as much as they reveal, however. In fact, the increase in the overall regional rate between 2015 and 2018 was in the main a product of trends in Venezuela and Brazil, where both poverty and extreme poverty rates rose significantly, whereas in the other countries poverty continued to decline, but at a slower pace than between 2008 and 2014.[13] Based on the available data, ECLAC had already predicted considerable worsening of aggregate conditions of poverty and extreme poverty over the course of 2019; of course, all of this was before COVID-19 and the interrelated economic collapse of early 2020.

The pandemic has exacerbated these conditions sharply. Latin America has long been the most unequal region in the world, and it remained so even after the progressive experiments of left and center-left governance in the early part of this century. That inequality feeds directly into deeply stratified underlying health conditions and health access among the population. The effects of COVID-19 are being filtered through a situation of low or negative economic growth, growing labor informality, and heightening problems of inequality and poverty. In a joint report published at the end of July 2020, ECLAC and PAHO predicted a 9.1 percent decline in overall GDP across Latin America and the Caribbean in 2020, with an expected 5.4 percent bump in the official unemployment rate. If these projections prove correct, this will be the most severe economic contraction in the region since recordkeeping began in 1901. This would also mean an estimated rise in the region's poverty rate by 7.1 percentage points in 2020 to 37.3 percent, with an increase in extreme poverty by 4.5 percentage points, to 15.5 percent. In absolute terms, then, by the close of 2020 there were expected to be 45 million more people living in poverty in the region (leading to a total of 231 million), with 28 million more being extremely poor (leaving a total of 96 million in extreme poverty).[14]

Poor Latin Americans and Caribbeans are more vulnerable to COVID-19 due to the higher prevalence in this layer of the population to existing conditions like lung or heart disease, diabetes, and a general lack of access to sufficient medical attention. Likewise, class injustice is interlaced with and intensified by the complex and specific oppressions of gender and sexuality, ethnicity and race, disability, homelessness, incarceration, and migration—all of which will mean disproportionate suffering by specific sectors of the population. Women, for example, constitute 60 percent of the workforce in accommodation and food service industries in the region, as well as 72.8 percent of laborers in the healthcare sector. They are also more likely than men to be employed in the informal economy. In addition, they face heightened demands of unpaid social reproductive labor during the pandemic in the form of primary caregiving and household maintenance. Finally, in periods of quarantine and economic downturn associated with the pandemic, sexual and gender violence, including the incidence of femicide, has increased. Income inequality is also expected to increase throughout Latin America and the Caribbean, considerably reversing gains made in the first decade and a half of the twenty-first century. Other components of inequality—access to healthcare, nutrition, basic infrastructure, and social service protections—are also expected to deteriorate further.[15]

Informal workers—amounting to 53 percent of the region's economically active population (or EAP)—are particularly vulnerable to job and income loss in the context of the pandemic and related recession, given that they lack any legal social protections. Again, informal workers are mostly women.

Formal workers, too, are in a vulnerable situation, with only eleven countries in all of Latin America and the Caribbean—Argentina, Aruba, Bahamas, Barbados, Brazil, Chile, Colombia, Ecuador, Honduras, Uruguay, and Venezuela—offering some kind of unemployment insurance, and these are in the main meager and short-term in character. Labor conditions of class combine, moreover, with housing vulnerabilities in Latin America's cities, given the extraordinary acceleration of unplanned urbanization in recent decades along with inadequate dwellings for the poor. People in poor and working-class urban communities tend to be unable to work from home and thus, to survive, they need to venture outside for work. Their housing tends to be overcrowded and often lacks adequate access to water and sanitation services. All this makes them disproportionately vulnerable to COVID-19.[16]

At a general regional level—and thus necessarily concealing a heterogeneous reality—health systems throughout Latin America and the Caribbean tend to lack both skilled medical professionals and medical supplies. At 20 per 10,000 population the average availability of physicians in Latin America and the Caribbean is sharply below the 35 per 10,000 average figure for rich countries in the Organization for Economic Cooperation and Development (OECD). Likewise, hospital bed figures are merely 2 per 1,000 population on average across Latin America and the Caribbean, compared to 4.8 in OECD countries.[17] There has long been an underinvestment in health by central governments, reaching an average aggregate regional level of only 3.7 percent of GDP, including fiscal and social security health contributions.[18] Only two countries—Argentina and Uruguay—have healthcare financing figures approximating the average level in the OECD. Meanwhile, Cuba spends much more proportionally on its healthcare system than the OECD countries, which helps to explain its exceptionality during the COVID-19 crisis—more on this below.

Most countries of the region have fragile and unintegrated health systems, which have not been able—nor will they likely ever be able—to cope properly with COVID-19 as the crisis expands and endures. In most countries, public healthcare is only directed toward low-income sectors of the population, and thus is underfunded and inadequate. Formal-sector workers are often able to access the health system through social security services attached to their employment. Across the region, households must cover on average one-third of healthcare costs with direct payments from their own pockets.[19] The rich and powerful rely on private healthcare, whether in their home countries or abroad. Again, with variation, health systems in the region tend to be unequal in terms of access and quality. The region's medical supplies and inputs depend heavily on global health supply chains that are breaking down logistically and politically at the moment, and most states in the region cannot compete with the bulk-buying power of imperial states in the world system, which are able to monopolize purchases of tests and personal protective equipment, among other supplies and equipment. Hospital beds and ventilators per capita are in most countries far less available than what is necessary there even in normal times. To make matters still worse, several health systems in the region were already coping—or, more precisely, were failing to cope—with an outbreak of more than 3 million cases of Dengue virus alone in 2019—over 2.2 million cases in Brazil.[20]

In the midst of constant shifts in the evolution of the pandemic, together with renewals and reconfigurations of a wider set of co-constitutive socioeconomic and ecological crises, it would be foolhardy to make any speculative predictions about political directions in the region with any sense of confidence. The most we can conclude this book with are several initial observations of emerging trends. One standout figure is that of Jair Bolsonaro, whose cavalier disregard for human life is directly related to an explosion of infections and deaths in Brazil. On a world stage, his criminal negligence has few serious rivals—perhaps limited to Donald Trump in the United States, and Boris Johnson in the United Kingdom. Bolsonaro's government is, of course, the most important expression of the far-right in office in Latin America. Brazil, moreover, has the region's biggest population, is its biggest economy, and is its most power country in geopolitical terms. Brazil is, in several senses, a sort of exemplary condensation of the kind of socioeconomic and political crises in the region that predated the pandemic and that have since been interacting with it as it has evolved.

In Brazil—as in the wider international alt-right ideological milieu of post-truth irrationalism—we had already witnessed a formal attack by the Bolsonaro regime on the legitimacy of scientific evidence and the pursuit of scientific truths per se. This was perhaps starkest in Bolsonaro's well-known climate-change denialism. Accompanying this, before COVID-19, were legislative attacks on funding for healthcare infrastructure and scientific institutions alike. All this has highlighted a kind of hyper-irrationalism, at the center of all far-right positions historically, at the heart of the most culturally authoritarian section of the Bolsonaro government—which is only about one-third of the actual composition of the government, but an extremely important one, including the president himself. This hard core of the Bolsonaro regime has seized on the COVID-19 conjuncture and declared the virus a petty cold, a mere sniffle—"nothing to see here, continue as usual."

In early July 2020, Bolsonaro himself contracted COVID-19. This occurred after months of his denying the seriousness of the virus, cavorting unmasked at mass rallies with his evangelical supporters, and battling against the quarantine and social-distancing measures adopted by opposition state governors and municipal mayors. "Some authorities even forbade people from going to the beach," Bolsonaro carped on the day he announced he had tested positive. Next, he declared that the "majority of Brazilians contract this virus and don't notice a thing."[21] In April 2020, Bolsonaro fired his first health minister, Enrique Mandetta, who became well known for his scientifically rigorous press conferences and open disagreements with the executive on most matters concerning the virus. Mandetta had soon eclipsed Bolsonaro in approval ratings. Mandetta's successor, Nelson Teich, was drawn from the private healthcare sector and was seemingly more in-step with Bolsonaro's agenda, but he, too, would soon receive the president's boot. As of late summer 2020, Brazil still lacked a permanent health minister in the midst of a colossal escalation of deaths and cases.[22]

In 2015–2016, with an economic contraction of 7.4 percent, Brazil experienced its worst recession in over a century, followed by three years of stagnation. Per capita income of the poorest 20 percent of the population fell by 11.5 percent between 2015 and 2019, while the richest 20 percent captured 6 percent more in real terms. At the outset of the pandemic in Brazil there were already 12 million unemployed, with only 500,000 enjoying access to unemployment insurance. Fifteen million people live in *favelas* (shantytowns), some 25 million lack access to potable water, and 40 million do not have access to adequate sanitation.[23] These were extant failures of fourteen years of PT rule, where instead of investments in a genuine network of social protection, improvements in urban infrastructure, and quality housing schemes, emphasis was placed on access to credit, mass consumption, and targeted antipoverty programs like Bolsa Familia. Bolsonaro's flouting of social distancing and confrontation with governors and municipalities, however, has tremendously amplified the effects of coronavirus. Politically, the logic of his regime is rooted in the constant reproduction of crisis and continuous radicalization, both of which are essential for the ongoing mobilization of his hardcore supporters. By August 2020, politically this translated into the division of Brazilian society into thirds: a third *bolsonarista*, a third *lulista* (devoted to former president Luis Inácio "Lula" da Silva), and a third unstably aligned to either of those poles.[24]

Early in the pandemic's spread through Latin America, Ecuador was a site of particular viral intensity. Its president, Lenín Moreno, was comparable in the first moments of the outbreak in that country to Bolsonaro in terms of his efforts to minimize mortality figures and in his basic indifference to the mounting death toll.[25] Moreno had already entered into an agreement with the International Monetary Fund (IMF), which involved austerity measures designed to hollow out public infrastructure and the social functions of the state, including healthcare. Austerity measures lay at the heart of the popular rebellion in October 2019. In the context of the pandemic, the rightward trajectory of the Moreno government is being further concretized, as the president moves to renegotiate debt with creditors and renew agreements with the IMF. It is difficult to imagine the momentum of the rebellions of October 2019 being completely eclipsed in the coronavirus interregnum.

The results of Daniel Ortega's COVID-19 denialism in Nicaragua have been enigmatic. Ortega's regime stands out for having introduced no quarantines, no masks, no tests, and no social distancing. On the contrary, Ortega has rallied demonstrations of government supports and promoted high-density festive events in the country, all the while implementing zero restrictions to Nicaragua's border crossings. Flagrantly disregarding the advice of epidemiologists, Ortega advised Nicaraguan citizens that reading the Bible was the best way to deal with the pandemic. And yet, cases there remain low. Claudio Katz hypothesizes that this may have something to do with the country's economic underdevelopment, signaled, for example, by its weak integration into the global economy and by weak internal transportation networks.[26] This hypothesis corresponds with analysts who have linked the spread of the virus with the central logistical and commercial corridors of the globalized neoliberal economy.[27]

The virus was relatively late in arriving to Bolivia, but was quickly overwhelming the country's healthcare system by August 2020. The country's unelected president—as a result of the coup ousting Evo Morales in 2019—Jeanine Áñez has utilized the cover of the pandemic to twice postpone scheduled general elections. No doubt influencing her actions are the polling data that indicate a lead for Luis Arce, presidential candidate for the Movement Toward Socialism (MAS) party. At the time of writing, the first round of voting is now scheduled for October 2020.[28]

In Chile, political tendencies and countertendencies can be observed, the precise momentum of which remain difficult to discern with any precision. On the one hand, Sebastián Piñera's regime has seemingly benefited in the short term, as the virus has provided cover for a suppression of the popular movements of recent months. His approval ratings have risen from a low of 9 percent to 25 percent, and the use of security forces in the streets to enforce mandatory physical distancing has been met with wide-scale approval—the same security forces that were so roundly discredited only weeks earlier. Distinct from Bolsonaro, the Chilean government did implement a series of public health measures, but these proved inadequate to stem the rising tide of cases and deaths, as did similar early lockdowns in Peru. The informalization of the world of work in preceding decades, and the erosion of public health infrastructure in both Chile and Brazil, minimized the effectiveness of any coronavirus emergency measures. Thus, Piñera's relative rise in popularity occurred in spite of the fact that the number of coronavirus deaths in his country, measured as a proportion of population, is second only to those in Peru in Latin America.

On the other hand, regarding political tendencies and countertendencies, the depth of the crisis of legitimacy facing the Piñera government will not be lessened overnight. It is important to recall that at the close of 2019, not only was the president's approval rating at 9 percent, but also only 14 percent of Chileans identified with any party whatsoever; polling data suggested that confidence levels in the government, Congress, and political parties stood at 5, 3, and 2 percent, respectively.[29] What is more, the momentum of street politics and, in particular, the militant feminist wave is unlikely to simply disappear. Rather, it is set to play a decisive role in the battles over the "new normal" to come, once street politics is once again a reasonably safe pursuit. Karina Nohales, a militant involved in both the Committee for Workers and Unionists and the International Committee of the country's most important umbrella feminist collective, the Coordinadora Feminista 8M, explained recently that, despite being locked down, activists have managed to launch a Feminist Organization of workers. It is envisioned as a space in which women and militant workers come together from the perspective of their labor, whether it be formal, informal, paid, or unpaid. Nohales describes the initiative as seeking to unite, in this way, wide layers of Chilean non-unionized workers with existing trade-union militants in a space where all can participate and contribute, realizing in this way the potential power of

Chilean workers that until now has remained fragmented. The uniting strategic horizon is the Feminist General Strike.[30] Piñera's government has also been vulnerable to the ongoing threat of social movement renewal in the streets, as evidenced dramatically by his administration's reluctant submission to the popular demand that a constitutional amendment be introduced such that 10 percent of savings of pensioners be made available to them immediately—amounting to as much as $US 20 billion.[31]

In Argentina, where Alberto Fernández sits at the head of a center-left administration, the government is thus far enjoying a boost in popularity, despite a catastrophic economic crisis in which debt negotiations are ongoing and a major sovereign debt default is a possibility in the near future. Fernández took early, concerted action to enforce physical distancing measures, which won popular approval and also favorable treatment in much of the media. It helps to have neighboring President Bolsonaro as the standard against which one is measured. The right-wing opposition has been discredited, and basically has subordinated itself to Fernández's handling of the crisis. Mauricio Macri, leader of the preceding center-right government, introduced a 23 percent cut to the health budget, further undermining the country's capacity to deal with the present crisis. Public health provision and the role of healthcare workers are being revalorized in the public consciousness in the midst of the crisis, laying the basis for future potential inroads against neoliberalism.

As Claudio Katz has explained, the pandemic managed to push the looming issue of debt repayment temporarily to the back burner, as public funding was immediately needed to service the viral crisis. Momentum has been behind a more confrontational stance with international creditors. At the same time, as elsewhere, Argentine social movements are crippled by their inability to assemble in the streets. There is a danger that the use of much-hated security forces to enforce mandatory physical distancing and isolation measures will be normalized post-pandemic, together with the extension of surveillance mechanisms. Illegitimate repressive measures taken by the security forces during the opening months of 2020 have not been met with any reprisal from the Fernández government. Alongside emergency cash-transfer measures that target informal workers and that seem to run against the logic of neoliberalism, Fernández is at the same time making austerity moves, such as delinking unionized workers' future salary increases from inflation increases. As is the case elsewhere, we also have to include in this measure of the conjuncture the increasing pressures from capital in

Argentina on the government to fully reopen the economy, whatever the cost to lives.[32] In Argentina, as in Colombia under the right-wing government of Iván Duque, early strict measures to combat the virus had some initial successes, but these were subsequently partially undermined as cases and deaths mounted after a few months. This likely has to do with the growth of the informal economy in recent decades in both cases, as well as the lack of an adequate social safety net, making it an impossibility for many workers to continue to quarantine. In addition, inadequate healthcare infrastructure plays a role in both countries.[33]

In Mexico, the initial response of center-leftist President Andrés Manuel López Obrador (AMLO) was catastrophic. He refused to break from traveling on his normal trips around the country and was ensconced in a variation of the sort of denialism afflicting the governments of Brazil, Nicaragua, and Ecuador. A low point was a press conference in late March 2020, during which AMLO exhibited a pair of amulets that he claimed would protect him and the country from the virus.[34] AMLO belatedly shifted gears, placing an epidemiologist, Hugo López Gatell, in charge of public management of the crisis and introducing the promotion of social distancing along with various partial and temporary restrictive measures on non-essential activities. These measures have, however, failed to stem the alarming tide of cases and deaths in Mexico.

Making matters significantly worse, Mexico was already in recession when the virus arrived. The country's economy contracted 17.3 percent in the second quarter of 2020 relative to the previous three months, making it one of the worst hit—in economic terms—of countries in the Global South. This was its fifth quarter of consecutive contraction. Relative to the same period in 2019, the decline in the second quarter of 2020 was 18.9 percent, representing the biggest plunge on record in national statistics. The IMF projected an overall contraction of 10.5 percent in Mexico for 2020.[35]

Cuba, meanwhile, has stood out for having some of the lowest levels of cases and deaths in the Americas. As is well known, one of the major enduring successes of Cuba's revolution is the island's healthcare system, which has an unusually high number of doctors per capita, together with a history of well-coordinated preventative care arrangements. Early regulation on incoming flights from abroad, strict controls of mandatory physical isolation, extensive medical surveys, and widespread check-ups on households by medical students, among other measures, have translated into weeks of declining new cases and a low death rate.[36]

Continuing its history of international medical solidarity, Cuba has dispatched more than 2,000 doctors and healthcare workers to some twenty countries, adding to the existing 37,000 or so Cuban medical personnel stationed in sixty-seven countries around the globe. It is possible to maintain simultaneously that the Cuban efforts are both a measure of solidarity and a measure to generate foreign exchange for the Cuban state. Cuba's health brigades have charged for their services since the collapse of the Soviet Union, and they have become the country's principal source of foreign exchange—generating $6.2 billion in 2018.[37] Cuba remains only a partial exception to the wider negative trend in the Americas, despite these impressive details, mainly because the internal economic contradictions in the country are severe, and the socioeconomic fallout of declining remittances from the Cuban diaspora, plus a prolonged slump in tourism, will likely have a serious impact on overarching conditions, even if the health system remains highly functional. The US sanctions of the regime stay in place, and could even escalate in the lead-up to the American November 2020 elections.

Let us pause by relating the pandemic more explicitly to some of the central themes taken up in the book thus far. It is evident that the pandemic arrived in a situation in which the world's people witnessed three dynamics occurring simultaneously: newly formed right-wing governments in many countries; weakened and rightward-moving left governments where they remain; and, the main source of hope, new extra-parliamentary social movements—reaching semi-insurrectionary levels in places like Chile—especially in countries where the right is in power. This new protest wave, including the popular explosions in Ecuador, Colombia, and Puerto Rico in 2019 (as part of an international uplift in radical protest that year), but also elsewhere in the region on a less visible scale, was rarely connected or well-integrated into any traditional left formations, especially given the relative delegitimating of center-left and left parties from their recent time in office in a number of cases. At the center of the protest wave in many locales has been a resurgent popular feminism, with an intensity and depth perhaps without historical precedence in the region, as well as ecological struggles against intensifying extractivism.

These, then, were three of the prominent pre-pandemic political dynamics. It should be stressed that the new right governments in office were very far away from enjoying some sort of new hegemony, in the sense of replacing the old center-left hegemony achieved at the height of the commodity boom. They were generally having difficulties governing, with extremely low rates of approval. In part, this is because they were unable to generate a kind of renewal of capitalist dynamism, a way out of the economic crisis—dependent as this has been in the region on the restoration of life in the world market. So as the viral pandemic arrived, it interacted with a number of these extant political-economic scenarios.

We need also to relate the unfolding pandemic in the region to the crisis of capitalism on a global scale—insofar as the recent, robust rate of growth in Latin America between 2003 and 2011 was massively dependent on external dynamics. Overwhelming such forces were China's rapid industrialization, high commodity prices, and so on. The latest projections of the IMF suggest negative 4.9 percent global growth in 2020—a remarkable contraction from the positive 2.9 percent growth rate of the global economy in 2019.[38] The World Bank predicts that global trade will fall more in 2020 than it did during the global crisis of 2008, given COVID-19's particular disruption of global value chains. The Bank expects a 13.4 percent contraction of global trade in 2020.[39] According to the United Nations Conference on Global Trade and Development (UNCTAD), the value of merchandise trade already fell 5 percent in the first quarter of 2020, and the institution expects a 20 percent annual decline in the entirety of 2020.[40]

These economic phenomena on a world scale will find particular transmission routes into Latin America: a fall in export prices for both primary commodities and manufactured goods (as we demonstrated in chapter 2, the region's economy has become increasingly dependent on export earnings since the transition to neoliberalism in the 1980s, a subordinate incorporation into the international division of labor intensified rather than reversed under "pink tide" rule); declining terms of trade for the region; collapse of remittances from migrant labor; capital flight (both the withdrawal of foreign capital into safer assets as well as the capital flight of domestic Latin American capitalists as they, too, shift their fortunes even more than usual into foreign banks and off-shore tax havens); a breakdown of global value chains for those countries most heavily involved in manufacturing (Brazil and Mexico, especially); and a collapse in tourism (the Caribbean small-island states are likely be particularly brutalized by this factor, though its effects will be widely felt throughout Latin America and the Caribbean itself).

Altogether, this poses a crisis of unprecedented scale and complexity, even harkening a truly global depression—as the Eurozone, China, and the United States are all in turmoil. A global recession was already in motion prior to COVID-19, rooted among other things in problems of massive corporate, household, and government debt, all facilitated by quantitative easing (or cheap money), alongside low rates of profitability, little investment, and escalating inequality as cheap money flowed into speculative financial investment schemes. The viral pandemic has made this underlying economic trajectory monstrously worse.[41]

At the heart of all of this is the monumental question of debt. On the one hand, there is the issue of debt weighing down centers of global accumulation such as the United States and China (a product of their response to the 2008 crisis), which, quite apart from all the unknowns that persist with regard to COVID-19, calls into question the viability of any massive countercyclical intervention reanimating these economies and in turn providing an engine source for the world market, as China briefly managed to do following the 2008 meltdown. On the other hand, as Adam Hanieh has demonstrated so effectively, there is the problem of the extraordinary indebtedness of countries in much of the Global South—and not just the poorest ones—which is inhibiting their ability to meet the public spending challenges necessary for any effective response to COVID-19. Even before the latest world conjuncture, two years ago, in 2018, a total of forty-six countries devoted more government spending to servicing public debts than they did on their healthcare systems as a proportion of GDP.[42]

In Latin America, the 1980s and 1990s witnessed a surge in the influence of the World Bank, the IMF, and the Inter-American Development Bank. As key institutional vectors of imperialism they made access to lines of credit conditional on neoliberal structural adjustment programs. During the height of the "pink tide" era and the associated commodity boom, these institutions receded dramatically from the regional picture. As the global crisis of 2008 made its entry into South America by 2012–2013, however, these institutions followed in its wake. Before the pandemic, as we have seen, both Argentina and Ecuador had already entered into agreements with the IMF, and both were struggling to repay their debts. Ecuador and Venezuela were also massively indebted to China—today, China is the world's biggest public creditor to the Global South through its Belt and Road Initiative, and, along with all the other imperial debt collectors, it is now calling for repayment from the impoverished states of sub-Saharan Africa and Latin America to which it loaned hundreds of billions of dollars.[43] All this means that, already in crisis, Latin American states are now in situations of extreme vulnerability, though the specific channels through which the global crisis is making its way into Latin America varies according to each country's specificities.

To make matters worse, alongside the economic crisis, there are the ongoing ecological contradictions of extractive capitalism—a major focus of our book. As Rob Wallace, Alex Liebman, Luis Fernando Chaves, and Rodrick Wallace have pointed out, structural transformations in extractive sectors such as agro-industry worldwide—along with associated patterns of planetary hyper-deforestation—are deeply associated with the origins of COVID-19 and of potential future viral threats of a similar variety.[44] It is no coincidence that within the dynamics of world capitalism, some of Latin America's most potent social struggles and conflicts between the reproduction of life and ecosystems, on one side, and the interests of capital, on the other, in recent years have been rooted in those sectors that express the particular regional manifestations of the rise of extractive capital globally—agro-industrial mono-cropping, oil and natural gas extraction, and mining mineral extraction. Such battlegrounds are in today's altered world assuming novel dimensions, given what we know about the political-economic and ecological origins of COVID-19, and specifically its connection to agro-industrial food production, rural displacement, deforestation, and subsequent flow through global value chains, logistics processes, and so on.

In addition to the ecological crisis, there is, of course, the crisis of social reproduction, with that element understood in the broadest sense of the best new Marxist feminist analyses, as all activities extending through the realms of paid and unpaid gendered labor involved in the generational reproduction of the working class.[45] This can involve everything from the unpaid toil of raising children and feeding and clothing family members, to the waged work of a teacher providing education, or to a healthcare worker providing care to the sick.

In Latin America and the Caribbean, as we have seen, women are particularly affected by the aggravated pressure on health systems, because they constitute the vast majority of the employees in the sector, region wide. In addition to assuming the front-line crisis work in the health system as the pandemic spreads, women are disproportionately burdened with the excess social reproductive labor involved in quarantine, such as caring for and home-schooling children. Paid domestic workers in Latin America tend to be disproportionately migrants, indigenous, or Afro-descendant women. They typically lack access to social security and increasing levels of unemployment as employer families readjust their home budgets in the face of the crisis. As mentioned, in Latin America and throughout Caribbean, as elsewhere in the world, instances of domestic violence against women and children are intensifying in contexts of quarantine and collapse of household finances. The social-reproductive elements of the Latin American crises were visible long before the pandemic, and they were raised to the foreground of political life in recent years through what is arguably the biggest wave of popular feminism in Latin American history. The last five years have seen massive movements in Argentina and Chile, along with important feminist currents in Mexico, Brazil, and elsewhere. The popular feminist movement in Chile, for example, was the most important articulating factor of the largest wave of rebellions that country experienced since the fights against Pinochet at the end of the 1980s. Latin American popular feminism today possesses an extraordinary vibrancy.

Of course, the insights of the ecological and feminist struggles, important as they were in recent years, are still more important in the present scenario facing the region, and indeed the rest of humanity. The fact that these movements were among the stronger popular forces of recent years is one of the positive factors that will play into the contending balance of forces between life and capital as we emerge from the first phases of the pandemic and disputes over the character of the "new normal" that will emerge to replace it. In world history there have been few moments when the competition between the value of production for profit versus the reproduction of life has been so starkly posed.

ACKNOWLEDGMENTS

We thank Bruno Bosteels and Geo Maher for their early interest in this project. Their Radical Américas series at Duke University Press is one of the more exciting recent publishing initiatives in Latin American Studies, and we are very pleased that our book has found shelter under its umbrella. At Duke, we thank Courtney Berger for shepherding the manuscript through to completion, and Sandra Korn for her timely assistance. We also benefited from the incisive commentary on the manuscript by two blind reviewers. Finally, our sincere appreciation to David Broder and Anne Freeland for their excellent translations of early versions of chapters 1 and 3.

NOTES

INTRODUCTION
1. See, for example, Aloizio Mercadante and Marcelo Zero, eds., *Gobiernos del PT: Un legado para el futuro* (Buenos Aires: CLACSO-Fundação Perseu Abramo-Partido dos Trabalhadores, 2018); Fander Falconi, "¿Qué significa ser progresista hoy?," *Nodal*, August 25, 2018, http://www.nodal.am/2018/03/significa-progresista-hoy-fander-falconi-especial-nodal/. Incidentally, Falconi never uses the word "left" in his article, but instead points to the necessity of participatory democracy as being the basis of a radical republicanism; Alfredo Serrano Mansilla, "El nuevo progresismo latinoamericano," *La Jornada* (Mexico), April 28, 2018.

CHAPTER 1. Conflict, Blood, and Hope
1. See, for example, Gustavo Carlos Guevara, ed., *Sobre las revoluciones latinoamericanas del siglo XX* (Buenos Aires: Newen Mapu, 2017); Fernando Mires, *La rebelión permanente: Las revoluciones sociales en América Latina* (Mexico City: Siglo XXI editores, 2001); and Alan Knight, *Revolución, democracia y populismo en América Latina* (Santiago: Centro de Estudios Bicentenario y Pontificia Universidad Católica de Chile, 2005).
2. Michael Löwy, *El marxismo en América Latina: Antología desde 1909 hasta nuestros días* (Santiago: LOM, 2007).
3. For collective reflection on this theme, see, among others, GESP, ed., *Movimientos sociales y poder popular en Chile: Retrospectivas y proyecciones políticas de la izquierda latinoamericana* (Santiago: Tiempo robado editoras, 2015); Miguel Mazzeo, *El sueño de una cosa (introducción al poder popular)* (Buenos Aires: Editorial El Colectivo, 2007); and, for a work centered on the Chilean experience, Franck Gaudichaud, *Chile 1970–1973: Mil días que estremecieron al mundo: Poder popular, cordones industriales y socialismo durante el gobierno de Salvador Allende* (Santiago: LOM, 2016).
4. James Petras and Henry Veltmeyer, eds., *The Class Struggle in Latin America: Making History Today*, Critical Development Studies (London: Routledge, 2017).
5. Examples of excessive optimism include multiple statements by Noam Chomsky and some of the writings of Tariq Ali, notably *Pirates of the Caribbean: Axis of Hope* (London: Verso, 2006).

6. François Houtart, "Amérique latine: Fin d'un cycle ou épuizement du post-néolibéralisme?," CETRI, 2016, https://www.cetri.be/Amerique-latine-fin-d-un-cycle-ou.

7. Many different schools and currents have tried to define today's movements, sometimes on the basis of the "new social movements" theory (following in the wake of Alain Touraine) or on the basis of works on "resource mobilization" and "the rationality of collective action," in particular following Mancur Olson and Sidney Tarrow.

8. See Jeffery R. Webber, "Late-Fascism in Brazil? Theoretical Reflections," *Rethinking Marxism* 32, no. 2 (2020): 151–167; "A Great Little Man: The Shadow of Jair Bolsonaro," *Historical Materialism* 28, no. 1 (2020): 3–49.

9. The departments of Beni, Pando, Santa Cruz, and Tarija, which form a geographic "half-moon" around the Andes. On the coup, see Jeffery R. Webber and Forrest Hylton, "The Eighteenth Brumaire of Macho Camacho: Jeffrey R. Weber (with Forrest Hylton) on the Coup in Bolivia," interview by Ashley Smith, *Verso Blog*, November 15, 2019, https://www.versobooks.com/blogs/4493-the-eighteenth-brumaire-of-macho-camacho-jeffery-r-webber-with-forrest-hylton-on-the-coup-in-bolivia. Listen also to the extensive interview with Webber conducted by Daniel Denvir, "Coup in Bolivia with Jeff Webber," *The Dig* (podcast), November 28, 2019, https://www.thedigradio.com/podcast/coup-in-bolivia-with-jeff-webber/.

10. Valério Arcary, "Quatro critérios para definir se uma mobilização social é progressiva ou reacionária," *Esquerda on line*, December 6, 2016, http://esquerdaonline.com.br/2016/12/06/quatro-criterios-para-definir-se-uma-mobilizacao-social-e-progressiva-ou-reacionaria/.

11. Hernán Ouviña, "La política prefigurativa de los movimientos populares en América Latina: Hacia una nueva matriz de intelección para las Ciencias Sociales," *Acta Sociológica* 62 (September–December 2013): 77–104. For a theoretical approach, see Massimo Modonesi, *Subalternidad, antagonismo, autonomía* (Buenos Aires: Editorial Prometeo-clacso, 2010).

12. This chapter builds on individual and collective reflections over the last decade. See in particular Franck Gaudichaud, ed., *Le volcan latino-américain: Gauches, mouvements sociaux et néolibéralisme en Amérique latine* (Paris: Textuel, 2008); and Franck Gaudichaud, ed., *Amériques Latines: Emancipations en construction* (Paris: Éditions Syllepse, 2013).

13. While we do not share a considerable part of the analytical perspectives and conclusions proposed by Katu Arkonada and Paula Klachko, we largely identify with the periodization that they suggest at the end of their work: Katu Arkonada and Paula Klachko, *Desde abajo, desde arriba: De la resistencia a los gobiernos populares: Escenarios y horizontes del cambio de época en América Latina* (Havana: Editorial Caminos, 2016).

14. For a historical synthesis, see Mónica Bruckmann and Theotonio Dos Santos, "Balance histórico de los movimientos sociales en América Latina," CETRI, May 2018, https://www.cetri.be/Los-movimientos-sociales-en.

15. Still a strong presence in the Latin American collective memory are memories of the crushing of the Chilean revolution (1973); of "Che" Guevara, murdered together with his guerrillero comrades in Bolivia; coups d'état against democratic governments (for instance, those of Jacobo Árbenz in Guatemala in 1954, General Torres in Bolivia

in 1971, and João Goulart in Brazil in 1964); and the counterrevolutionary war in Nicaragua in the 1980s.

16. Many of these debts could be considered "odious" from a legal standpoint, for they were contracted by dictatorships and thus, by definition, by unelected regimes. We discuss the role of debt in the onset of neoliberalism in chapter 2.

17. Atilio Borón, *Tras el buho de Minerva: Mercado contra democracia en el capitalismo de fin de siglo* (Buenos Aires: FCE/CLACSO, 2000).

18. Claudio Katz, "Au-delà du néolibéralisme," in "L'Amérique latine rebelle: Contre l'ordre impérial," special issue, *Contretemps*, no. 10 (2004): 27.

19. Steve Ellner, "Memories of February 27: Uncovering the Deadly Truth," *Commonweal* 117, no. 22 (1990): 740–741.

20. Bernard Duterme, "Amérique latine: 20 ans d'échec du néolibéralisme," *Revue Démocratie*, May 2016, http://www.revue-democratie.be/index.php/international/709-amerique-latine-20-ans-dechec-du-neoliberalisme.

21. Maristella Svampa and Sebastián Pereyra, *Entre la ruta y el barrio: La experiencia de las organizaciones piqueteras* (Buenos Aires: Editorial Biblos, 2003).

22. There are many and varied examples of such struggles: see José Seoane, Emilio Taddei, and Clara Algranati, *Desafíos para los movimientos sociales y los proyectos emancipatorios de Nuestra América* (Buenos Aires: Ediciones Herramienta y El Colectivo, 2013).

23. Julie Massal, *Les mouvements indiens en Equateur: Mobilizations protestataires et démocratie* (Paris: Karthala, 2005).

24. Bruno Konder Comparato, *L'action politique des sans-terre au Brésil* (Paris: L'Harmattan, 2004); Ana María Rocchietti, "El Movimiento de los Trabajadores sin Tierra (MST) del Brasil: Sus orígenes y el carácter de su lucha," *Revista Herramienta*, 2001, https://herramienta.com.ar/articulo.php?id=42.

25. Maristella Svampa, "Movimientos sociales y nuevo escenario regional: Las inflexiones del paradigma neoliberal en América Latina," *Sociohistórica*, nos. 19–20 (2006): 141–155; http://www.memoria.fahce.unlp.edu.ar/art_revistas/pr.3612/pr.3612.pdf.

26. Jorge Castañeda, *Utopia Unarmed: The Latin American Left after the Cold War* (New York: Knopf, 1993).

27. Gloria Muñoz Ramírez, *EZLN: 20 et 10, le feu et la parole* (Paris: Nautilus, 2004); Jérôme Baschet, *La Rébellion zapatiste: Insurrection indienne et résistance planétaire* (Paris: Flammarion, 2005).

28. Geoffrey Pleyers, *Alter-globalization: Becoming Actors in the Global Age* (Cambridge, UK: Polity, 2010).

29. The CLOC (Coordination of Latin American Peasants' Organizations), founded in 1994, is the direct product of this peasant and indigenous "new internationalism."

30. Jules Falquet, "Une analyse du mouvement féministe latino-américain et caribéen dans la mondialization," in Gaudichaud, *Le volcan latino-américain*, 137–156.

31. Ruth Berins Collier and Samuel Handlin, eds., *Reorganizing Popular Politics: Participation and the New Interest Regime in Latin America* (University Park: Pennsylvania State University Press, 2009).

32. Franck Gaudichaud and Thomas Posado, "Introduction: Syndicats et gouvernements latino-américains: une réinstitutionnalization?," *Cahiers des Amériques latines*, no. 86 (2017): 17–29, http://journals.openedition.org/cal/8347.

33. Thomas Posado, "Itinéraire d'un syndicaliste devenu candidat à la présidentielle: Utilization et contention d'un militant ouvrier dans le Venezuela de Chávez," *Amérique Latine Histoire et Mémoire: Les Cahiers* 23 (2013), http://journals.openedition.org/alhim/4828.

34. Marc St. Upéry, "¿Hay patria para todos? Ambivalencia de lo público y 'emergencia plebeya' en los nuevos gobiernos progresistas," in "Lo público: Estado y sociedad civil en América Latina," dossier, *Iconos* 32 (2008), https://doi.org/10.17141/iconos.32.2008.284.

35. Cf. John Holloway, *Change the World without Taking Power: The Meaning of Revolution Today* (London: Pluto, 2002), and *Contra y más allá del Capital: Reflexiones a partir del debate sobre el libro "Cambiar el mundo sin tomar el poder"* (Puebla, Mexico: Universidad Autónoma de Puebla; Buenos Aires: Ediciones Herramienta, 2006). For a far-reaching presentation and discussion of this debate, see Franck Gaudichaud, "América Latina actual: Geopolítica imperial, progresismos gubernamentales y estrategias de poder popular constituyente," interview by Bryan Seguel, in Grupo de Estudios Sociales y Políticos, ed., *Movimientos sociales y poder popular en Chile: Retrospectivas y proyecciones políticas de la izquierda latinoamericana* (Santiago: Tiempo robado editoras, 2015), 237–278.

36. Sidney Tarrow, *Power in Movement: Collective Action, Social Movements and Politics* (Cambridge: Cambridge University Press, 1994).

37. Christophe Ventura, "Brève histoire contemporaine des mouvements sociaux en Amérique," *Mémoires des Luttes*, August 2, 2012, http://www.medelu.org/breve-histoire-contemporaine-des.

38. Claudio Katz, "Las nuevas rebeliones latinoamericanas," *Rebelión*, October 2007, http://www.rebelion.org/noticia.php? id=58138.

39. Nicolas Pinet, "Introduction: Éléments pour une grammaire de la révolte," *Figures de la révolte: Rébellions latino-américaines (XVIe–XXe siècles)*, Collection Coyoacán (Paris: Syllepse, 2016), 7–29.

40. Franklin Ramírez Gallegos, "Ascenso, des-fragmentación y desperdicio: Luchas sociales, izquierda y populismo en el Ecuador (2007–2017)," CETRI, August 25, 2017, https://www.cetri.be/Ascenso-des-fragmentacion-y.

41. See Pino Solanas's film *Memoria del saqueo* (Argentina, 2003).

42. See Maristella Svampa, "Las fronteras del gobierno de Kirchner," *Revista Crisis*, no. 0 (December 2006), http://maristellasvampa.net/archivos/period15.pdf; and Ana Soledad Montero, *¡Y al final un día volvimos! Los usos de la memoria en el discurso kirchnerista (2003–2007)* (Buenos Aires: Prometeo, 2011).

43. Jeffery R. Webber, *Red October: Left-Indigenous Struggles in Modern Bolivia* (Chicago: Haymarket, 2012); Forrest Hylton and Sinclair Thomson, *Revolutionary Horizons: Past and Present in Bolivian Politics* (London: Verso, 2008).

44. Hervé Do Alto and Pablo Stefanoni, *Nous serons des millions: Evo Morales et la gauche au pouvoir en Bolivie* (Paris: Raisons d'agir, 2008).

45. More accurately, a renegotiation of the contracts with the multinationals.

46. According to García Linera, multitudes refer to a "bloc of collective action that brings the autonomous organized structures of the subaltern classes together around discursive and symbolic hegemonic constructs, which have the particularity that their origins vary among different segments of [these same] classes." See Álvaro García Linera, *La potencia plebeya. Acción colectiva e identidades indígenas, obreras y populares en Bolivia* (Buenos Aires: CLACSO-Prometeo Libros, 2008).

47. Hervé Do Alto, "La 'revolution' d'Evo Morales ou les voies sinueuses de la refondation de la Bolivie," in Gaudichaud, *Le volcan latino-américain*, 205–224.

48. See Laurent Delcourt, "Le Brésil de Lula: une dynamique de contradictions," in *Le Brésil de Lula: Un bilan contrasté*, Alternatives Sud (Paris: Syllepse, 2010), 7–34; and Frédéric Louault, "Lula, père des pauvres?," *La Vie des idées*, October 29, 2010.

49. Emir Sader, "The Weakest Link? Neoliberalism in Latin America," *New Left Review* 52 (July/August 2008), https://newleftreview.org/issues/ii52/articles/emir-sader-the-weakest-link-neoliberalism-in-latin-america.

50. It also includes the Sandinistas, the Farabundo Martí National Liberation Front (FMLN), the Brazilian PT, the Uruguayan Broad Front, Venezuela's Cause R, and Mexico's Revolutionary Democratic Party (PRD).

51. Frei Betto, *A mosca azul: Reflexao sobre o poder* (Brazil: Rocco, 2006).

52. Pablo González Casanova, "Democracia, liberación y socialismo: Tres alternativas en una," *Observatorio Social de América Latina*, no. 8 (September 2002): 175–180, http://biblioteca.clacso.edu.ar/clacso/osal/20110215062252/11casanova.pdf. For a feminist perspective on this neoliberal violence, see Jules Falquet, *Pax Neoliberalia: Perspectivas feministas sobre (la reorganización de) la violencia* (Buenos Aires: Madreselva, 2017).

53. Maristella Svampa proposes that we distinguish between a "middle-class populism"—the Kirchners' presidencies in Argentina or the presidency of Correa in Ecuador—and a "plebeian populism"—Morales in Bolivia or Chávez in Venezuela. See Maristella Svampa, *Del cambio de época al fin de ciclo: Gobiernos progresistas, extractivismo, y movimientos sociales en América Latina* (Buenos Aires: Edhasa, 2017).

54. Immanuel Wallerstein, "How Has Latin America Moved Left?," *Commentary*, no. 187 (June 15, 2006), https://www.iwallerstein.com/commentaries. See also the analysis by the same author nine years later, regarding the difficulties the forces of the left now faced in the region: "The Latin American Left Moves Rightward," *Commentary*, no. 404 (July 1, 2015), https://www.iwallerstein.com/commentaries.

55. Unusually detailed information on US involvement in Venezuela under Chávez and Bolivia under Morales was made publicly available thanks in part to the heroism of Chelsea Manning. See WikiLeaks, *The WikiLeaks Files: The World According to US Empire* (London: Verso, 2016).

56. See Jeffery R. Webber, *From Rebellion to Reform in Bolivia: Class Struggle, Indigenous Liberation and the Politics of Evo Morales* (Chicago: Haymarket, 2011).

57. Eric Toussaint, "Les leçons de l'Équateur pour l'annulation de la dette illégitime," CADTM, May 29, 2013, http://www.cadtm.org/Les-lecons-de-1-Equateur-pour-1.

58. For a liberal-conservative interpretation of the two lefts, see Jorge Castaneda, "Latin America's Left Turn," *Foreign Affairs*, May–June 2006; for a "Bolivarian" analysis,

see Arkonada and Klachko, *Desde abajo, desde arriba*. See also Jeffery Webber and Barry Carr, eds., *The New Latin American Left: Cracks in the Empire* (Lanham, MD: Rowman and Littlefield, 2013); M. Harnecker, *La izquierda después de Seattle* (Madrid: Siglo XXI, 2001); and Marc Saint-Upéry, *Le rêve de Bolivar: Le défi des gauches sud-américaines* (Paris: La Découverte, 2007).

59. Franklin Ramírez Gallegos, "Mucho más que dos izquierdas," *Nueva Sociedad*, no. 205 (September–October 2006), http://nuso.org/articulo/mucho-mas-que-dos-izquierdas/.

60. Mabel Thwaites Rey, ed., *El Estado en América Latina: Continuidades y rupturas* (Santiago: Editorial Arcis—CLACSO, 2012).

61. Comision Economica para America Latina y El Caribe, *Panorama Social de América Latina* (Santiago: Comision Economica para America Latina y El Caribe, 2015).

62. Constanza Moreira, "El largo ciclo del progresismo latino-americano y su freno: Los cambios políticos en América Latina de la última década (2003–2015)," *Revista Brasileira de Ciências Sociais* 01.3, no. 93 (2017), https://dx.doi.org/10.17666/329311/2017.

63. Luciana Mourão and Anderson Macedo de Jesus, "'Bolsa Família' Program: An analysis of Brazilian Income Transfer Program," *Field Actions Science Reports*, Special Issue 4 (2012), http://journals.openedition.org/factsreports/1560; and Pierre Salama, "Brésil: Bilan économique: Succès et limites," *Problèmes d'Amérique Latine*, no. 78 (Autumn 2010), http://pierre.salama.pagesperso-orange.fr.

64. Bernard Duterme, "Recherche percepteurs désespérément," *Le Monde Diplomatique* (Paris), April 2018.

65. Pierre Salama, "¿Cambios en la distribución del ingreso en las economías de América Latina?," *Foro Internacional* 209, vol. 52, no. 3 (2012): 628–657, http://pagesperso-orange.fr/pierre.salama/art/cambios.pdf; Pierre Salama, *Les Économies émergentes latino-américaines, entre cigales et fourmis* (Paris: Armand Colin, 2012).

66. For a positive perspective, despite everything, see Dario Azzellini, "Class Struggle in the Bolivarian Process Workers' Control and Workers' Councils," *Latin American Perspectives*, August 22, 2016.

67. See Franck Gaudichaud, "Amérique latine: Fin d'un âge d'or? Progressismes, post-néolibéralisme et émancipation radicale: Entretien avec Edgardo Lander et Miriam Lang," *ContreTemps*, April 2018, https://www.contretemps.eu/amerique-latine-progressismes-neoliberalisme-emancipation.

68. Cristóbal Kay and Leandro Vergara-Camus Volver, eds., *La cuestión agraria y los gobiernos De izquierda en América Latina Campesinos, agronegocio y neodesarrollismo* (Buenos Aires: CLACSO, 2018).

69. Jeffery R. Webber, "Evo Morales, *Transformismo*, and the Consolidation of Agrarian Capitalism in Bolivia," *Journal of Agrarian Change* 17, no. 2 (2017): 330–347.

70. Virginie Poyetton, "Bolivie: Une réforme agraire mi-figue mi-soja," *Le Courrier* (Geneva), October 11, 2014. See also Bruno Fornillo, "¿Existe una reforma agraria en la Bolivia del Movimiento al Socialismo?," *Íconos: Revista de Ciencias Sociales*, no. 42 (January 2012): 153–166.

71. On Bolivia, see Salvador Schavelzon, *El Nacimiento del Estado Plurinacional: Etnografía de una Asamblea Constituyente* (La Paz: Plural/CLACSO/CEJIS, 2012),

http://biblioteca.clacso.edu.ar/clacso/coediciones/20130214112018/ElnacimientodelEstadoPlurinacional.pdf.

72. Matthieu Le Quang, "Le Bien Vivre, une alternative au développement en Equateur?," *Revue du MAUSS*, October 4, 2016, http://www.journaldumauss.net/?Le-Bien-Vivre-une-alternative-au.

73. See George Ciccariello Maher, *Building the Commune: Radical Democracy in Venezuela* (London: Verso, 2016); and Dario Azzellini, *Communes and Workers' Control in Venezuela: Building 21st Century Socialism from Below* (Chicago: Haymarket, 2018).

74. Cited by Mathieu Uhel, "La démocratie participative entre subordination et autonomization politique: Les Conseils communaux à Maracaibo (Venezuela)," *Cahiers des Amériques latines* 69 (December 26, 2013), http://journals.openedition.org/cal/970.

75. Margarita López Maya, *El ocaso del chavismo: Venezuela 2005–2015* (Caracas: Editorial Alfa, 2015); and Margarita López Maya, "Socialismo y comunas en Venezuela," *Nueva Sociedad* 274 (March–April 2018), http://nuso.org/articulo/socialismo-y-comunas-en-venezuela.

76. Roxana Liendo, "Bolivie: Vivir bien, Evisme et Mouvements sociaux," *Etat des résistances dans le Sud—Amérique Latine* 24, no. 4 (2017): 31–39.

77. Jeffery Webber, *The Last Day of Oppression, and the First Day of the Same: The Politics and Economics of the New Latin American Left* (Chicago: Haymarket, 2017).

78. Liendo, "Bolivie."

79. Jeffery R. Webber, "State, Bureaucracy, and Rentier Capital," *Dissent*, February 7, 2020.

80. See Franck Gaudichaud and Thomas Posado, eds., "Syndicalismes et gouvernements progressistes," dossier, *Cahiers des Amériques Latines* 86 (2017), https://journals.openedition.org/cal/8339.

81. The different CGTs decided to reunite in August 2016, with a collegiate leadership now led by the historic confederation.

82. Thomas Posado, "Renouvellement et institutionnalization des centrales syndicales au Venezuela sous Chávez (2001–2011)," *revue IdeAs*, June 15, 2015, https://journals.openedition.org/ideas/832.

83. Julien Dufrier, "Le syndicalisme au Nicaragua depuis le retour du *Frente Sandinista de Liberación Nacional* (2007–2016)," *Cahiers des Amériques latines*, no. 86 (2017), http://journals.openedition.org/cal/8364.

84. Eduardo Gudynas, "Si eres tan progresista, ¿por qué destruyes la naturaleza? Neoextractivismo, izquierda y alternativas," *Ecuador Debate* 79 (2010): 61–82.

85. Svampa, *Del cambio de época al fin de ciclo*.

86. See www.olca.cl and http://ocrn.info.

87. See, in particular, Fernando Pairican Padilla, *Malón: La rebelión del movimiento mapuche 1990–2013* (Santiago: Pehuén Editores, 2014); and Thomas Klubock, *La Frontera: Forests and Ecological Conflict in Chile's Frontier Territory* (Durham, NC: Duke University Press, 2014).

88. Alvaro García Linera, *El Oenegismo, enfermedad infantil del derechismo (O como la reconducción del proceso de cambio es la restauración neoliberal)* (La Paz: Vicepresidencia del Estado, Presidencia de la Asamblea Legislativa Plurinacional, 2011). For a dissection

of García Linera's evolution as a thinker during his time as vice president, see Jeffery R. Webber, "Burdens of a State Manager," *Viewpoint*, February 25, 2015, https://www.viewpointmag.com/2015/02/25/burdens-of-a-state-manager/.

89. Decío Machado, "El progresismo latinoamericano en su laberinto," in Eduardo Gudynas et al., *Rescatar la esperanza: Más allá del neoliberalismo y el progresismo* (Barcelona: Entrepueblos, 2016), 106.

90. Robert Michels, *Political Parties: A Sociological Study of the Oligarchical Tendencies of Modern Democracy* (New York: Hearst's International Library, 1915).

91. Eric Toussaint, *Banque du sud et nouvelle crise internationale* (Paris: Syllepse, 2008); Eric Toussaint, "Venezuela, Equateur et Bolivie: la roue de l'histoire en marche," CADTM, November 2009, http://cadtm.org/Venezuela-Equateur-et-Bolivie-la.

92. Manuel Sutherland advances the figure of $700 billion. See "Economista Manuel Sutherland: El control cambiario propició pérdida de $700 mil millones," Aporrea-UR, February 5, 2018, https://www.aporrea.org/contraloria/n320642.html.

93. Patrick Guillaudat, "Vers un thermidor au Venezuela?," *ContreTemps*, January 16, 2018, https://www.contretemps.eu/thermidor-venezuela-maduro/.

94. See Webber, "State, Bureaucracy and Rentier Capital." On sanctions, see Mark Weisbrot and Jeffrey Sachs, *Economic Sanctions as Collective Punishment: The Case of Venezuela* (Washington, DC: Center for Economic and Policy Research, April 2019).

95. Huáscar Salazar Lohman, *"Se han adueñado del proceso de lucha": Horizontes comunitario-populares en tensión y la reconstitución de la dominación en la Bolivia del MAS* (Cochabamba: Sociedad Comunitaria de Estudios Estratégicos, 2015).

96. Webber and Hylton, "Eighteenth Brumaire." Also see Denvir, "Coup in Bolivia"; and Nicole Fabricant and Bret Gustafson, "The Fall of Evo Morales," *Catalyst* 4, no. 1 (Spring 2020): 105–131.

97. Bernard Duterme, *Toujours sandiniste, le Nicaragua?* (Brussels: Couleur Livres, 2018). See also Dan La Botz, *What Went Wrong? The Nicaraguan Revolution: A Marxist Analysis* (Chicago: Haymarket, 2018).

98. There are more than 80,000 "political" posts in Brazil, of which 47,000 are directly appointed by the president's office.

99. André Singer, *Os sentidos do lulismo: Reforma gradual e pacto conservador* (São Paulo: Cia das Letras, 2012); André Singer and Isabel Loureiro, eds., *As contradições do Lulismo: A que ponto chegamos?* (São Paulo: Boitempo, 2016).

100. See Maria Chavez Jardim, *Entre a solidariedade e o risco: sindicatos e fundos de pensão em tempos de governo Lula*, Coleção Trabalho e Contemporaneidade (São Paulo: Annablume/Fapesp, 2009); and a work pulling together different perspectives on this question, by Raúl Zibechi, *Brasil Potencia: Entre la integración regional y un nuevo imperialismo* (Lima: PDTG ed., 2013), 61–87.

101. See Armando Boito and Andréa Galvão, eds., *Política e classes sociais no Brasil dos anos 2000* (São Paulo: Alameda, 2012); and Armando Boito, Andréia Galvão, and Paula Marcelino, "La nouvelle phase du syndicalisme brésilien (2003–2013)," *Cahiers des Amériques latines* 80 (2015), http://journals.openedition.org/cal/4184.

102. Francisco Cunha Lima Cintra and Rémy Herrera, "De Lula à Dilma, quel développement pour le Brésil? O menor dos males?," *Marché et organizations* 2014/1, no. 20

(2014): 183–205, https://www.cairn.info/revue-marche-et-organisations-2014-1-page-183.htm.

103. Ernesto Herrera, "Uruguay: El cerrojo progresista," *Rebelion*, March 19, 2018. http://www.rebelion.org/noticia.php?id=239173. See also Diego Castro, "Cierre del ciclo progresista en Uruguay y América Latina: Balance para relanzar horizontes emancipatorios" (Ponencia, LASA, Lima, 2017), https://www.academia.edu/32929779/_2017_Cierre_del_ciclo_progresista_en_Uruguay_y_Ame_rica_Latina._Balance_para_relanzar_horizontes_emancipatorios._Ponencia_LASA_Lima.

104. Rosario Queirolo, "¿Qué significa el 'giro a la deracha' uruguayo?," *Nueva Sociedad* 287 (May–June 2020): 98–107.

105. Franck Gaudichaud, *Las fisuras del neoliberalismo chileno: Trabajo, crisis de la "democracia tutelada" y conflictos de clase* (Buenos Aires: CLACSO, 2015), http://biblioteca.clacso.edu.ar/clacso/becas/20151203023022/fisuras.pdf.

106. Bello, "Days and Nights of Rage in Chile," *Economist*, October 26, 2019.

107. Jeffery R. Webber, "¡Fuera Piñera! Revolt in Chile," *Spectre*, April 15, 2020, https://spectrejournal.com/fuera-pinera/.

108. Michael Stott and Benedict Mander, "Chile President Sebastián Piñera: 'We Are Ready to Do Everything to Not Fall into Populism,'" *Financial Times*, October 17, 2019.

109. See Decio Machado and Raúl Zibechi, *Cambiar el mundo desde arriba: Los límites del progresismo* (Bogotá: Ediciones desde abajo, 2016); or see a plural approach to this same phenomenon in Gerardo Szalkowicz and Pablo Solana, eds., *América Latina: Huellas y retos del ciclo progresista* (Caracas: Editorial El perro y la rana, 2018).

110. For a critique of the vision of revolution promoted by García Linera, an essential influence on the region's progressive currents, see Salvador Schavelzon, "Teoría de la revolución en Álvaro García Linera: Centralización estatal y elogio de la derrota," *Rebelion*, April 23, 2018. http://rebelion.org/noticia.php?id=240668.

111. Michael Löwy, "Brésil: Le coup d'Etat," *Mediapart*, May 14, 2016, https://blogs.mediapart.fr/michael-lowy/blog/140516/bresil-le-coup-detat.

112. Andrew Fishman et al., "Breach of Ethics: Exclusive: Leaked Chats between Brazilian Judge and Prosecutor Who Imprisoned Lula Reveal Prohibited Collaboration and Doubts over Evidence," *The Intercept*, June 9, 2019, https://theintercept.com/2019/06/09/brazil-lula-operation-car-wash-sergio-moro/; Glenn Greenwald and Victor Pougy, "Hidden Plot: Exclusive: Brazil's Top Prosecutors Who Indicted Lula Schemed in Secret Messages to Prevent His Party from Winning 2018 Election," *The Intercept*, June 9, 2019, https://theintercept.com/2019/06/09/brazil-car-wash-prosecutors-workers-party-lula/; Glenn Greenwald, Leandro Demori, and Betsy Reed, "How and Why *The Intercept* Is Reporting on a Vast Trove of Materials about Brazil's Operation Car Wash and Justice Minister Sergio Moro," *The Intercept*, June 9, 2019, https://theintercept.com/2019/06/09/brazil-archive-operation-car-wash/.

113. Perry Anderson, *Brazil Apart, 1964–2019* (London: Verso, 2019).

114. See the lecture he gave in Madrid: Claudio Katz, "¿Qué pasa en Venezuela?," Plaza de los Comunes, July 13, 2017, https://www.youtube.com/watch?v=49znMBBsUdo.

115. Susan Spronk and Jeffery R. Webber, "February Traumas: The Third Insurrectionary Moment of the Venezuelan Right," *New Politics*, February 25, 2014.

116. For a first balance-sheet of the Venezuelan crisis, based on a plurality of views, see Daniel Chávez, Hernán Ouviña, and Mabel Thwaites Rey, eds., *Venezuela: Lecturas urgentes desde el Sur* (Buenos Aires: CLACSO/TNI, 2017), https://www.tni.org/files/publication-downloads/venezuela-sur.pdf.

117. Manuel Sutherland, "La ruine du Venezuela n'est due ni au 'socialisme' ni à la 'revolution,'" *Barril.info*, May 11, 2018, https://barril.info/fr/actualites/venezuela-crise-socialisme-revolution-petrole-importations?lang=fr.

118. "Llamado internacional urgente a detener la escalada de violencia en Venezuela: Mirar a Venezuela, más allá de la polarización," *Llamado Internacional Venezuela* (blog), May 30, 2017, http://llamadointernacionalvenezuela.blogspot.com/2017/05/urgent-international-call-to-stop.html.

119. REDH, "Who Will Accuse the Accusers? Statement in Defense of Venezuela," Venezuelanalysis.com, June 1, 2017. https://venezuelanalysis.com/analysis/13177.

120. Gaudichaud, "Amérique latine." See also Edgardo Lander, *La implosión de la Venezuela rentista* (Amsterdam: TNI, 2016), https://www.tni.org/es/publicacion/la-implosion-de-la-venezuela-rentista.

121. Franklin Ramírez, "El 4 de febrero y la descorreización de Ecuador," *Nueva Sociedad*, January 2018, http://nuso.org/articulo/el-4-de-febrero-y-la-descorreizacion-de-ecuador-ramirez.

122. John Cajas Guijarro, "¿Hacia dónde va el Ecuador de Lenín Moreno? Entre una crisis persistente y un nuevo neoliberalismo," *Nueva Sociedad*, June 2008, http://nuso.org/articulo/hacia-donde-va-ecuador-lenin-moreno-/.

123. Jeffery R. Webber, "Rebellion, Reformism, and Reaction in Latin America," interview by Ashley Smith, *Verso Blog*, November 6, 2019, https://www.versobooks.com/blogs/4477-rebellion-reformism-and-reaction-in-latin-america-an-interview-with-jeffery-r-webber.

124. Pablo Ospina Peralta, "Ecuador contra Lenín Moreno," *Nueva Sociedad*, October 2019, https://nuso.org/articulo/ecuador-lenin-moreno/.

125. Lamia Oualalou, *Jésus t'aime! La déferlante évangélique* (Paris: Cerf, 2018).

126. Forrest Hylton, "Colombia's Disappeared," *London Review of Books* (blog), July 16, 2020, https://www.lrb.co.uk/blog/2020/july/colombia-s-disappeared.

127. Emiliano Terán Mantovani, "América Latina en el cambio de época: ¿Normalizar el estado de excepción?," ALAI, March 22, 2018, https://www.alainet.org/es/articulo/191765.

128. Jeffery R. Webber, "Revolution against 'Progress': Neo-extractivism, the Compensatory State, and the TIPNIS Conflict in Bolivia," in *Crisis and Contradiction: Marxist Perspectives on Latin America in the Global Political Economy*, ed. Susan Spronk and Jeffery R. Webber (Chicago: Haymarket, 2015), 302–333.

129. Laetitia Perrier-Bruslé, "Le conflit du Tipnis et la Bolivie d'Evo Morales face à ses contradictions: Analyse d'un conflit socio-environnemental," *EchoGéo*, January 26, 2012, http://journals.openedition.org/echogeo/12972.

130. Matthieu Le Quang, "La trajectoire politique de l'initiative Yasuní-ITT en Équateur: Entre capitalisme vert et écosocialisme," *Cahiers d'histoire: Revue d'histoire critique* 130 (January 2016), http://journals.openedition.org/chrhc/4998.

131. On the struggles of 2013–2015, see Alejandra Santillana Ortíz and Jeffrey R. Webber, "Cracks in Correísmo?," *Jacobin*, August 14, 2015, https://www.jacobinmag.com/2015/08/correa-ecuador-pink-tide-protests-general-strike/.

132. Verónica Gago, *La potencia feminista: O el deseo de cambiarlo todo* (Madrid: Traficantes de Sueños, 2019).

133. Bruno Bringel and Geoffrey Pleyers, "Les mobilizations de 2013 au Brésil: Vers une reconfiguration de la contestation," *Brésil(s)* 7 (2015), http://journals.openedition.org/bresils/1417.

134. Webber, "Rebellion, Reformism, and Reaction."

135. Another significant case: in El Maizal commune in Lara state, the commune's leader Ángel Prado defeated the PSUV candidate, but the CNE ultimately overruled his election and attributed the votes he had secured to the PSUF candidate.

136. Michael Stott, "More than 5m Set to Flee Venezuela by the End of This Year," *Financial Times*, June 19, 2019; Michael Stott and Gideon Long, "Venezuela: Refugee Crisis Tests Colombia's Stability," *Financial Times*, February 19, 2020.

137. Rafael Bernabe, "The Puerto Rican Summer," *New Politics* 17, no. 4 (2020), https://newpol.org/issue_post/the-puerto-rican-summer/; Forrest Hylton, "Algo está pasando en Colombia," *Nueva Sociedad*, January 2020, https://nuso.org/articulo/algo-esta-pasando-en-colombia/.

138. Ernesto Laclau, *On Populist Reason* (London: Verso, 2007).

139. Claudio Katz, "Estrategias socialistas en América Latina," *Revista Viento Sur*, no. 94 (January 2007).

140. Decío Machado, "Revitalizar el pensamiento crítico en América Latina," *Brecha*, February 15, 2018, https://brecha.com.uy/revitalizar-pensamiento-critico-america-latina/.

141. Emilio Taddei, "Relegitimación de la gobernabilidad neoliberal, resistencias populares y desafíos emancipatorios en la Argentina y en Nuestra América," in *Fórum Social Mundial 2016, Montreal–Canadá, 12 de agosto de 2016*, http://docplayer.es/41978630-Forum-social-mundial-2016-foro-social-mundial-2016-world-social-forum-2016-montreal-canada-12-de-agosto-de-2016.html.

142. Alberto Acosta and Ulrich Brand, *Salidas del laberinto capitalista: Decrecimiento y Postextractivismo* (Quito: Fundación Rosa Luxemburg, 2017).

143. Michael Löwy, *Écosocialisme: L'alternative radicale à la catastrophe écologique capitaliste* (Paris: Mille et une nuits, 2011); Jorge Riechmann, *El socialismo puede llegar sólo en bicicleta* (Madrid: Los libros de la catarata, 2012); Jérôme Baschet, *Adieux au capitalisme: Autonomie, société du bien vivre et multiplicité des mondes* (Paris: La Découverte, 2014).

CHAPTER 2. **World Market, Patterns of Accumulation, and Imperial Domination**

1. Claudio Katz, *Neoliberalismo, neodesarrollismo, socialismo* (Buenos Aires: Batalla de Ideas, 2016), 74.

2. Jeffery R. Webber, *The Last Day of Oppression, and the First Day of the Same: The Politics and Economics of the New Latin American Left* (Chicago: Haymarket, 2017);

Kenneth M. Roberts, *Changing Course in Latin America: Party Systems in the Neoliberal Era* (New York: Cambridge University Press, 2015); Steven Levitsky and Kenneth M. Roberts, eds., *The Resurgence of the Latin American Left* (Baltimore: Johns Hopkins University Press, 2011); Claudio Katz, *Las disyuntivas de la izquierda en America Latina* (Buenos Aires: Ediciones Luxemburg, 2008).

3. George Ciccariello-Maher, *We Created Chávez: A People's History of the Venezuelan Revolution* (Durham, NC: Duke University Press Books, 2013); Salvador Schavelzon, *El nacimiento del Estado Plurinacional de Bolivia: Etnografía de una Asamblea Constituyente*, (Buenos Aires: CLACSO, 2013); Salvador Schavelzon, *Plurinacionalidad y vivir bien/buen vivir: Dos conceptos leídos desde Bolivia y Ecuador post-constituyentes* (Buenos Aires: CLACSO, 2016).

4. Salvador Schavelzon, "El fin del relato progresista en América Latina," *La Razón* (La Paz), June 22, 2015.

5. Katz, *Neoliberalismo, neodesarrollismo, socialismo*, 386–387.

6. Carlos Eduardo Martins, "La Integración Regional en América Latina y Sus Desafíos Contemporáneos," *Cuadernos del Pensamiento Crítico Latinoamericano* 12 (May 2014); Daniele Benzi, ALBA-TCP, *Anatomía de la integración que no fue* (Buenos Aires: Imago Mundi, 2017).

7. Katz, *Neoliberalismo, neodesarrollismo, socialismo*, 74.

8. James M. Cypher and Tamar Diana Wilson, "Introduction—China and Latin America: Processes and Paradoxes," *Latin American Perspectives* 42, no. 6 (2015): 6.

9. Giovanni Andrea Cornia, "Inequality Trends and Their Determinants: Latin America over the Period 1990–2010," in *Falling Inequality in Latin America: Policy Changes and Lessons*, ed. Giovanni Andrea Cornia (Oxford: Oxford University Press, 2014), 24–49; Giovanni Andrea Cornia, "Recent Distributive Changes in Latin America: An Overview," in Cornia, *Falling Inequality in Latin America*, 4–23; Kenneth M. Roberts, "The Politics of Inequality and Redistribution in Latin America's Post-adjustment Era," in Cornia, *Falling Inequality in Latin America*, 50–71.

10. Pablo Ospina Peralta, "El reformismo progresista," *Nueva Sociedad*, May 2016, http://nuso.org/articulo/el-reformismo-progresista/.

11. Duncan Green, *Silent Revolution: The Rise and Crisis of Market Economics in Latin America*, 2nd ed. (New York: Monthly Review Press, 2003), 72–118.

12. Alfredo Saad-Filho, "The Political Economy of Neoliberalism in Latin America," in *Neoliberalism: A Critical Reader*, ed. Alfredo Saad-Filho and Deborah Johnston (London: Pluto, 2005), 222–229.

13. ECLAC, *Economic Survey of Latin America and the Caribbean 2017: Dynamics of the Current Economic Cycle and Policy Challenges for Boosting Investment and Growth* (Santiago: United Nations Economic Commission for Latin America and the Caribbean, 2017), 93.

14. Saad-Filho, "Political Economy of Neoliberalism," 227.

15. Araceli Damián and Julio Boltvinik, "A Table to Eat On: The Meaning and Measurement of Poverty in Latin America," in *Latin America after Neoliberalism: Turning the Tide in the 21st Century?*, ed. Eric Hershberg and Fred Rosen (New York: New Press, 2006), 145.

16. Luis Reygadas, Eric Hershberg, and Fred Rosen, "Latin America: Persistent Inequality and Recent Transformations," in Hershberg and Rosen, *Latin America after Neoliberalism*, 122.

17. Steven Levitsky and Kenneth M. Roberts, "Introduction—Latin America's 'Left Turn': A Framework for Analysis," in Levitsky and Roberts, *Resurgence of the Latin American Left*, 3, 9–10; Jeffery R. Webber and Barry Carr, "Introduction: The Latin American Left in Theory and Practice," in *The New Latin American Left: Cracks in the Empire*, ed. Jeffery R. Webber and Barry Carr (Lanham, MD: Rowman and Littlefield, 2013), 1–29.

18. ECLAC, *Economic Survey*, 93.

19. José Seoane, Emilio Taddei, and Clara Algranati, *Extractivismo, despojo y crisis climática: Desafíos para los movimientos sociales y los proyectos emancipatorios de Nuestra América* (Buenos Aires: Ediciones Herramienta, 2013); Anthony Bebbington and Jeffrey Bury, eds., *Subterranean Struggles: New Dynamics of Mining, Oil, and Gas in Latin America*, repr. ed. (Austin: University of Texas Press, 2014).

20. ECLAC, *Economic Survey*, 113.

21. José Seoane, "El retorno de la crisis y la ofensiva extractivista," in *Extractivismo, despojo y crisis climática: Desafíos para los movimientos sociales y los proyectos emancipatorios de Nuestra América*, ed. José Seoane, Emilio Taddei, and Clara Algranati (Buenos Aires: Herramienta, 2013), 23.

22. William I. Robinson, *Latin America and Global Capitalism: A Critical Globalization Perspective* (Baltimore: Johns Hopkins University Press, 2008).

23. Claudio Katz, "Dualities of Latin America," *Latin American Perspectives* 42, no. 4 (2015): 12, https://doi.org/10.1177/0094582X15574714.

24. Maristella Svampa, "'Consenso de los commodities' y lenguajes de valoración en América Latina," *Nueva Sociedad* 244 (2013): 30–46.

25. Eduardo Gudynas, "Los ambientalismos frente a los extractivismos," *Nueva Sociedad* 268 (2017): 111.

26. Maristella Svampa, "Cuatro claves para leer América Latina," *Nueva Sociedad* 268 (2017): 56.

27. Gudynas, "Los ambientalismos frente a los extractivismos," 112.

28. Svampa, "'Consenso de los commodities,'" 32. It should be noted that although Svampa's notion of re-primarizaton of Latin American economies exaggerates the extent of industrial decline—industry remains important, if reduced—she nonetheless captures important features of the current political-economic conjuncture and their attendant political and ideological expressions. For a thoughtful critique of Svampa, see Juan Grigera, "La insoportable levedad de la industrialización," *Batalla de Ideas* 4 (2013): 46–57.

29. Gudynas, "Los ambientalismos frente a los extractivismos," 113.

30. Svampa, "'Consenso de los commodities,'" 34.

31. Eduardo Gudynas, "Estado compensador y nuevos extractivismos: Las ambivalencias del progresismo sudamericano," *Nueva Sociedad* 237 (2012): 128–146. See also Eduardo Gudynas, *Extractivismos: Ecología, economía y política de un modo de entender el desarrollo la Naturaleza* (Cochabamba: CEDIB, 2015).

32. Julio C. Gambina and Germán Pinazo, "La crisis y las trayectorias de América Latina: Neoliberalismo, neo-desarrollismo y proyectos alternativos," in *América Latina*

en medio de la crisis mundial: Trayectorias nacionales y tendencias regionales, ed. Jairo Estrada Álvarez (Buenos Aires: CLACSO, 2014), 95.

33. Gambina and Pinazo, "La crisis y las trayectorias," 102–103.
34. Cypher and Wilson, "Introduction," 6–7.
35. Katz, *Neoliberalismo, neodesarrollismo, socialismo*, 34.
36. Leandro Vergara-Camus and Cristóbal Kay, "The Agrarian Political Economy of Left-Wing Governments in Latin America: Agribusiness, Peasants, and the Limits of Neo-developmentalism," *Journal of Agrarian Change* 17, no. 2 (2017): 415–437, https://doi.org/10.1111/joac.12216.
37. Katz, *Neoliberalismo, neodesarrollismo, socialismo*, 34.
38. Grigera, "La insoportable levedad de la industrialización."
39. Katz, *Neoliberalismo, neodesarrollismo, socialismo*, 35.
40. Katz, *Neoliberalismo, neodesarrollismo, socialismo*, 387.
41. Katz, *Neoliberalismo, neodesarrollismo, socialismo*, 36.
42. Katz, *Neoliberalismo, neodesarrollismo, socialismo*, 37.
43. Javier Santiso, *The Decade of the Multilatinas* (Cambridge: Cambridge University Press, 2014).
44. Katz, *Neoliberalismo, neodesarrollismo, socialismo*, 39.
45. Katz, *Neoliberalismo, neodesarrollismo, socialismo*, 40.
46. Katz, *Neoliberalismo, neodesarrollismo, socialismo*, 42–43.
47. Alejandro Portes and Kelly Hoffman, "Latin American Class Structures: Their Composition and Change during the Neoliberal Era," *Latin American Research Review* 38, no. 1 (2003): 41–82, https://doi.org/10.1353/lar.2003.0011; Amy Hite and Jocelyn S. Viterna, "Gendering Class in Latin America: How Women Effect and Experience Change in the Class Structure," *Latin American Research Review* 40, no. 2 (2005): 50–82, https://doi.org/10.1353/lar.2005.0023.
48. Katz, *Neoliberalismo, neodesarrollismo, socialismo*, 44.
49. Katz, *Neoliberalismo, neodesarrollismo, socialismo*, 44.
50. David McNally, *Global Slump: The Economics and Politics of Crisis and Resistance* (Oakland, CA: PM, 2010); Anwar Shaikh, "The First Great Depression of the 21st Century," in *Socialist Register 2011: The Crisis This Time*, ed. Leo Panitch, Greg Albo, and Vivek Chibber (New York: Monthly Review Press, 2010), 44–63.
51. Webber, *The Last Day of Oppression*, 23–24.
52. CEPAL, *Anuario estadístico de América Latina y el Caribe, 2012* (Santiago: Comisión Económica para América Latina y el Caribe, 2012), 77.
53. Esteban Actis, "América Latina y su contexto externo: del 'doble' al 'frágil boom,'" *Nueva Sociedad*, December 2017, http://nuso.org/articulo/america-latina-y-su-contexto-externo/; Martín Abeles and Sebastián Valdecantos, "América del Sur, recesión y después . . . ," *Nueva Sociedad* 265 (2016): 14–21; Claudio Katz, "Los atolladeros de la economía latinoamericana," *Herramienta*, 2011, https://herramienta.com.ar/articulo.php?id=1600; Claudio Katz, "The Singularities of Latin America," in *Socialist Register 2012: The Crisis and the Left*, edited by Leo Panitch, Greg Albo, and Vivek Chibber (New York: Monthly Review Press, 2011), 200–216; Claudio Katz, "The Three Dimensions of the Crisis," in *Crisis and Contradiction: Marxist Perspectives on Latin America in the Global*

Political Economy, ed. Susan Spronk and Jeffery R. Webber, Historical Materialism Book Series (Leiden: Brill Academic, 2014), 273–301.

54. Webber, *The Last Day of Oppression*, 20–21.

55. Cypher and Wilson, "Introduction," 6.

56. ECLAC, *Economic Survey*, 117.

57. Luis Morano et al., *Between a Rock and a Hard Place: The Monetary Policy Dilemma in Latin America and the Caribbean* (Washington, DC: World Bank, October 1, 2017), 13, http://documents.worldbank.org/curated/en/809541512048064994/Between-a-rock-and-a-hard-place-the-monetary-policy-dilemma-in-Latin America-and-the-Caribbean.

58. Morano et al., *Between a Rock*, 11.

59. Morano et al., *Between a Rock*, 5.

60. CEPAL, *Explorando nuevos espacios de cooperación entre América Latina y el Caribe y China* (Santiago: Comisión Económica para América Latina y el Caribe, 2018), 18; CEPAL, *Balance preliminar de las economías de América Latina y el Caribe* (Santiago: CEPAL, 2019), 101.

61. ECLAC, *Preliminary Overview of the Economies of Latin America and the Caribbean 2019* (Santiago: Economic Commission for Latin America and the Caribbean, 2019), 11.

62. ECLAC, *Preliminary Overview*, 12.

63. ECLAC, *Preliminary Overview*, 14.

64. ECLAC, *Preliminary Overview*, 14.

65. ECLAC, *Economic Survey*, 89.

66. ECLAC, *Economic Survey*, 87.

67. ECLAC, *Economic Survey*, 135.

68. ECLAC, *Economic Survey*, 136.

69. ECLAC, *Economic Survey*, 136.

70. Claudio Katz, *Bajo el imperio del capital* (Buenos Aires: Ediciones Luxemburg, 2011), 41, 161.

71. Ellen Meiksins Wood, *Empire of Capital* (London: Verso, 2005).

72. Wood, *Empire of Capital*, 12.

73. Colin Mooers, *Imperial Subjects: Citizenship in an Age of Crisis and Empire* (New York: Bloomsbury Academic, 2014), 5.

74. Katz, *Bajo el imperio del capital*, 45.

75. Paul A. Baran and Paul M. Sweezy, *Monopoly Capital*, New Impression ed. (Harmondsworth, UK: Pelican/Penguin Books, 1973); John Bellamy Foster and Robert Waterman McChesney, *The Endless Crisis: How Monopoly-Finance Capital Produces Stagnation and Upheaval from the USA to China* (New York: Monthly Review Press, 2012).

76. Katz, *Bajo el imperio del capital*, 143.

77. Katz, *Bajo el imperio del capital*, 45.

78. Katz, *Bajo el imperio del capital*, 43, 51.

79. Katz, *Bajo el imperio del capital*, 54.

80. Katz, *Bajo el imperio del capital*, 50.

81. Claudio Katz, "La nueva estrategia imperial de Estados Unidos," in *Estados Unidos y la nueva correlación de fuerzas internacional*, ed. Marco A. Gandásegui (Buenos Aires: CLACSO, 2017), 120.

82. Katz, "La nueva estrategia imperial," 121.
83. Katz, *Bajo el imperio del capital*, 104–110.
84. Katz, *Bajo el imperio del capital*, 64.
85. Katz, *Bajo el imperio del capital*, 65.
86. Leo Panitch and Sam Gindin, *The Making of Global Capitalism: The Political Economy of American Empire* (London: Verso, 2012); Perry Anderson, *American Foreign Policy and Its Thinkers* (London: Verso, 2017).
87. Tony Norfield, *The City: London and the Global Power of Finance* (London: Verso, 2017), 105.
88. Norfield, *The City*, 105.
89. Norfield, *The City*, 110–111.
90. Norfield, *The City*, 108.
91. Peter Dicken, *Global Shift: Mapping the Changing Contours of the World Economy, Seventh Edition*, 7th ed. (New York: Guilford, 2015); William I. Robinson, *A Theory of Global Capitalism: Production, Class, and State in a Transnational World* (Baltimore: Johns Hopkins University Press, 2004).
92. Todd Gordon and Jeffery R. Webber, *Blood of Extraction: Canadian Imperialism in Latin America* (Winnipeg: Fernwood, 2016), 2–30.
93. ECLC, *Foreign Direct Investment in Latin America and the Caribbean 2017* (Santiago: Economic Commission for Latin America and the Caribbean, 2017), 13, 40, https://www.cepal.org/en/publications/type/foreign-direct-investment-Latin America-and-caribbean.
94. ECLC, *Foreign Direct Investment*, 13.
95. ECLC, *Foreign Direct Investment*, 40.
96. ECLC, *Foreign Direct Investment*, 42.
97. Robinson, *Latin America and Global Capitalism*; William I. Robinson, "Promoting Polyarchy in Latin America: The Oxymoron of 'Market Democracy,'" in Hershberg and Rosen, *Latin America after Neoliberalism*, 96–119.
98. Brian Loveman, ed., *Addicted to Failure: US Security Policy in Latin America and the Andean Region* (Lanham, MD: Rowman and Littlefield, 2006).
99. Katz, "La nueva estrategia imperial," 124.
100. Katz, "La nueva estrategia imperial," 124.
101. Jairo Estrada Álvarez, "Alianza del Pacífico: ¿Hacia una redefinición del campo de fuerzas en nuestra América?," in *América Latina en medio de la crisis mundial: Trayectorias nacionales y tendencias regionales*, edited by Jairo Estrada Álvarez (Buenos Aires: CLACSO, 2014), 110.
102. Darío Salinas Figueredo, "Cambios en la ecuación de poder, constantes estratégicas estadounidenses y procesos políticos en América Latina," in Gandásegui, *Estados Unidos y la nueva correlación*, 297.
103. Estrada Álvarez, "Alianza del Pacífico," 112.
104. Estrada Álvarez, "Alianza del Pacífico," 113.
105. Katz, "La nueva estrategia imperial," 129.
106. Katz, *Neoliberalismo, neodesarrollismo, socialismo*, 51–51; Estrada Álvarez, "Alianza del Pacífico," 118.

107. Leandro Morgenfeld, "Estados Unidos y sus vecinos del sur en las cumbres de las Américas: De la subordinación al desafío," in Gandásegui, *Estados Unidos y la nueva correlación*, 349.

108. Luis Suárez Salazar, "La política hacia América Latina y el Caribe de la segunda presidencia de Barack Obama: Una mirada desde la prospectiva crítica," in Gandásegui, *Estados Unidos y la nueva correlación*, 312–338.

109. Dana Frank, *The Long Honduran Night: Resistance, Terror, and the United States in the Aftermath of the Coup* (Chicago: Haymarket Books, 2018).

110. Suárez Salazar, "La política hacia América Latina," 323–324. See also Todd Gordon and Jeffery R. Webber, "Post-coup Honduras: Latin America's Corridor of Reaction," *Historical Materialism* 21, no. 3 (2013): 16–56, https://doi.org/10.1163/1569206X-12341316. For the most thorough discussion of the United States and Honduras, see Frank, *Long Honduran Night*.

111. Suárez Salazar, "La política hacia América Latina."

112. Bruce M. Bagley and Jonathan D. Rosen, eds., *Drug Trafficking, Organized Crime, and Violence in the Americas Today* (Gainesville: University Press of Florida, 2017).

113. Adam Isacson et al., *Time to Listen: Trends in US Security Assistance to Latin America and the Caribbean* (Washington, DC: Washington Office on Latin America, 2013), 2.

114. Isacson et al., *Time to Listen*, 1.

115. Katz, "La nueva estrategia imperial," 125.

116. Katz, "La nueva estrategia imperial," 126.

117. Katz, "La nueva estrategia imperial," 126.

118. Atilio Borón, *América Latina en la geopolítica del imperialismo* (Hondarribia, Spain: Editorial Hiru, 2013), 106–109.

119. Borón, *América Latina*, 237–239.

120. Borón, *América Latina*, 220–221.

121. Suárez Salazar, "La política hacia América Latina," 317.

122. Isacson et al., *Time to Listen*, 20.

123. Peter Watt and Roberto Zepeda, *Drug War Mexico: Politics, Neoliberalism and Violence in the New Narcoeconomy* (London: Zed Books, 2012); Dawn Paley, *Drug War Capitalism* (Oakland, CA: AK, 2014).

124. Katz, "La nueva estrategia imperial," 126.

125. Isacson et al., *Time to Listen*, 8.

126. Katz, "La nueva estrategia imperial," 126.

127. Mark Weisbrot and Jeffrey Sachs, *Economic Sanctions as Collective Punishment: The Case of Venezuela* (Washington, DC: Center for Economic and Policy Research), 15, http://cepr.net/publications/reports/economic-sanctions-as-collective-punishment-the-case-of-venezuela.

128. Weisbrot and Sachs, *Economic Sanctions as Collective Punishment*.

129. Katz, "Dualities of Latin America," 20.

130. Katz, *Neoliberalismo, neodesarrollismo, socialismo*, 50.

131. Svampa, "Cuatro claves para leer América Latina," 57.

132. Katz, *Neoliberalismo, neodesarrollismo, socialismo*, 50.

133. Katz, *Neoliberalismo, neodesarrollismo, socialismo*, 388.

134. Svampa, "Cuatro claves para leer América Latina," 58.
135. CEPAL, *Explorando nuevos*, 39.
136. CEPAL, *Explorando nuevos*, 39.
137. Svampa, "Cuatro claves para leer América Latina," 59.
138. CEPAL, *Explorando nuevos*, 51.
139. CEPAL, *Explorando nuevos*, 52.
140. CEPAL, *Explorando nuevos*, 52.
141. Cypher and Wilson, "Introduction," 14.
142. CEPAL, *Explorando nuevos*, 57.
143. CEPAL, *Explorando nuevos*, 56.
144. CEPAL, *Explorando nuevos*, 56.
145. CEPAL, *Explorando nuevos*, 22.
146. CEPAL, *Explorando nuevos*, 22.
147. CEPAL, *Explorando nuevos*, 23.
148. CEPAL, *Explorando nuevos*, 23.
149. CEPAL, *Explorando nuevos*, 23.
150. CEPAL, *Explorando nuevos*, 58.
151. CEPAL, *Explorando nuevos*, 24.
152. Svampa, "Cuatro claves para leer América Latina," 58.
153. Morgenfeld, "Estados Unidos y sus vecinos del sur," 351–353.
154. Morgenfeld, "Estados Unidos y sus vecinos del sur," 353.
155. Svampa, "Cuatro claves para leer América Latina," 58.
156. Estrada Álvarez, "Alianza del Pacífico," 111.
157. Morgenfeld, "Estados Unidos y sus vecinos del sur," 353.
158. Katz, "Dualities of Latin America," 25.
159. Katz, *Neoliberalismo, neodesarrollismo, socialismo*, 58.
160. Katz, *Neoliberalismo, neodesarrollismo, socialismo*, 58.
161. Estrada Álvarez, "Alianza del Pacífico," 112.
162. Salinas Figueredo, "Cambios en la ecuación de poder," 302.
163. Katz, *Neoliberalismo, neodesarrollismo, socialismo*, 72.
164. Raúl Zibechi, *Brasil potencia: Entre la integración regional y un nuevo imperialismo* (Málaga, Spain: Zambra/Baladre, 2012).
165. Katz, "Dualities of Latin America," 24.
166. Raúl Zibechi, "Progressive Fatigue?," NACLA *Report on the Americas* 48, no. 1 (2016): 26, https://doi.org/10.1080/10714839.2016.1170298.
167. Marcelo Dias Carcanholo and Alexis Saludjian, "Integração sul-americana, dependência da China e subimperialismo brasileiro," in *América Latina en medio de la crisis mundial: Trayectorias nacionales y tendencias regionales*, ed. Jairo Estrada Álvarez (Buenos Aires: CLACSO, 2014), 197.
168. Katz, *Neoliberalismo, neodesarrollismo, socialismo*, 55–56.
169. Perry Anderson, "Bolsonaro's Brazil," *London Review of Books*, February 7, 2019, 11–22.
170. Svampa, "Cuatro claves para leer América Latina," 58–59.

CHAPTER 3. **Latin American Progressivism**

1. We have not included Honduras and Paraguay, which, under the governments of Zelaya and Lugo, during a brief period, before the so-called "white coups," were part of this "cycle"; nor have we included Peru, since the government of Ollanta Humala did not have a sufficiently clear or lasting progressive moment. We cannot include Chile because of the neoliberal features of the governments of the Concertación prior to the most recent government of the New Majority headed by Michelle Bachelet, which does not coincide chronologically with the emergence of this conjuncture.

2. The debate, broadly defined, should take into account the right-wing or centrist critiques that proliferated both in the press and in the academic sphere, which oscillated between frankly and openly reactionary positions and others with liberal, liberal-democratic, social-liberal, or social-democratic overtones.

3. The notion of a change of epoch (*cambio de época*), as noted in chapter 1, comes from an expression of Ecuadorian President Rafael Correa, who in 2007 said that the present was "not an era of change, but a change of era." This idea was taken up, that same year, in the title of the Congress of the Latin American Sociology Association (ALAS) in Guadalajara, where Modonesi presented a paper on the subject: Massimo Modonesi, "Crisis hegemónica y movimientos antagonistas en América Latina: Una lectura gramsciana del cambio de época," subsequently published in *A Contracorriente* 5, no. 2 (2008): 115–140. In the same year, Maristella Svampa published a book whose title contributed to the broad dissemination of this notion in academic debates: Maristella Svampa, *Cambio de época: Movimientos sociales y poder político* (Buenos Aires: CLACSO-Siglo XXI, 2008).

4. Elements of this connection between past and present can be found in the broad survey by Maristella Svampa, *Debates latinoamericanos: Indianismo, desarrollo, dependencia, populismo* (Buenos Aires: Edhasa, 2016).

5. We must recognize that, for example, the question of populism as well as the notion of passive revolutions both tend to incorporate the issue of post-neoliberalism, which, in turn, is connected to extractivism, at an intersection that corresponds to what we have been calling neo-developmentalism. Svampa proposes other possible intersections. Svampa, *Debates latinoamericanos*, 454–455.

6. See the self-description of the network's history and objectives at Red en Defensa de la Humanidad (REDH), https://www.ecured.cu/REDH#Objetivos.

7. Meanwhile, critical forums with unquestionable leftist credentials are few. At the national level, in the Venezuelan case, aporrea.org played this role, as did the online magazines lalineadefuego.info in Ecuador and izquierdadiario in Argentina. At the regional level, *Nueva Sociedad* (nuso.org), despite its explicitly social democratic origins, opened its pages to interventions by intellectuals from various leftist traditions under the auspices of its editor, Pablo Stefanoni, who, moreover, has been an important and prolific author on the question of the progressive governments, at first supporting Evo Morales's government in Bolivia and later becoming critical of progressivism in general, from a position that eludes conventional labels and that is certainly not homologous to that of the right or of social democracy.

8. CLACSO maintained a position that was ostensibly sympathetic to Latin American progressivism, particularly during the tenure of the current secretary general, Pablo

Gentili, through declarations, invitations, publication, and events, while respecting both the diversity of positions in its working groups and, for a few years, the critical position that predominated in its publication OSAL: https://www.clacso.org.ar/libreria-latinoamericana/libros_por_programa.php?campo=programa&texto=6.

9. This is with the exception of Hugo Chávez's project of the creation of the Communal Councils, which entailed a formal break, but whose depth and breadth has been, as we will see below, subject to debate.

10. Ernesto Laclau, *La razón populista* (Buenos Aires: Fondo de Cultura Económica, 2005). It should be noted that Laclau publicly supported the Kirchner governments and was enshrined as one of its ideologues.

11. See, for example, a wide-ranging study with a degree of argumentative diversity within it containing a recent and cogent text by Valeria Coronel and Luciana Cadahia, "Populismo republicano más allá de Estado vs Pueblo," *Nueva Sociedad* 273 (January–February 2018): 72–82.

12. But this turn occurred very early in the so-called "process of change" in Bolivia, as is mentioned in Massimo Modonesi, "De la autonomía a la hegemonía," *A Contracorriente* 7, no. 3 (Spring 2010): 563–571.

13. See Álvaro García Linera, "Fin de ciclo o proceso por oleadas revolucionarias," 2017, https://www.vicepresidencia.gob.bo/IMG/pdf/fin_de_ciclo-2.pdf; and Álvaro García Linera, "Del Estado aparente al Estado integral," 2012, http://blogs.ffyh.unc.edu.ar/garcialinera/files/2015/10/Conferencia-UNC.pdf.

14. Atilio Borón, who explicitly associates Castrismo and the Cuban revolution institutionalized in the state with the current period of Latin American progressivism, is particularly insistent on this link. Atilio A. Borón and Paula Klachko, "Sobre el 'post-progresismo' en América Latina: Aportes para un debate," *Rebelión*, September 24, 2016, http://rebelion.org/noticia.php?id=217125.

15. Following this idea, Arkonada and Klachko, who have collaborated with García Linera and Borón, respectively, and who have defended the "struggle from above" citing Lenin, maintain, by means of an argument that recalls the discourse of the popular fronts of the 1930s, that the current governments are carrying out "a bourgeois-democratic revolution based on an interclass alliance that takes up 'unfinished tasks.'" Katu Arkonada and Paula Klachko, *Desde abajo, desde arriba: De la resistencia a los gobiernos populares: Escenarios y horizontes del cambio de época en América Latina* (Havana: Editorial Caminos, 2016).

16. Álvaro García Linera, "Socialismo comunitario, un horizonte de época," 2015, https://www.vicepresidencia.gob.bo/IMG/pdf/socialismo_comunitario-2.pdf.

17. With the exception, as we will see below, of some aspects of Bolivarian socialism. For example, Claudio Katz offers a sharp criticism of neo-developmentalism and, at the same time, highlights some socialist and anticapitalist elements in the policies implemented by the Venezuelan and Bolivian governments. Claudio Katz, *Neoliberalismo, neodesarrollismo, socialismo* (Buenos Aires: Batalla de Ideas, 2017).

18. See some interesting approaches to this question in *Chavismo: Genealogía de una pasión política* (Buenos Aires: CLACSO, Fundación Centro de Estudios Latinoamericanos

Rómulo Gallegos, Centro Internacional Miranda, Escuela Venezolana de Planificación, 2017).

19. See, for example, Atilio Borón, who makes this distinction: "between the Bolivarian governments and those of the Southern Cone; between political projects engaged in—or moving in the direction of—building a socialism of the twenty-first century—as is the case in Venezuela, Bolivia, and Ecuador—and those that, on the contrary, have undertaken to found a 'serious and rational capitalism,' as the successive governments of Argentina, Brazil, and Uruguay have done," in "Una reflexión sobre el progresismo latinoamericano," in *América Latina: Huellas y retos del ciclo progresista*, ed. Gerardo Szalkowicz and Pablo Solana (Caracas: El Perro y la Rana, 2018), 21. In the same vein, Arkonada and Klachko differentiate between two levels of progressivism, one of state capitalism and one of transition to socialism, in *Desde abajo, desde arriba*, 107.

20. The statements can be found here: "Llamado internacional urgente a detener la escalada de violencia en Venezuela," CETRI, May 30, 2017, https://www.cetri.be/Llamado-internacional-urgente-a?lang=fr; and "¿Quién acusará a los acusadores? Respuesta a la solicitada de intelectuales contra el proceso bolivariano de Venezuela," Contrahegemonia Web, June 3, 2017, http://contrahegemoniaweb.com.ar/quien-acusara-a-los-acusadores-respuesta-a-la-solicitada-de-intelectuales-contra-el-proceso-bolivariano-de-venezuela/. A little later, in a laudable attempt to reorient the debate toward a less confrontational mode, different positions on the Venezuelan conjuncture were compiled in Daniel Chávez, Hernán Ouviña, and Mabel Thwaites Rey, *Venezuela: Lecturas urgentes desde el sur* (Buenos Aires: IEALC-UBA, 2017).

21. Francisco López Segrera, *América Latina: Crisis del posneoliberalismo y ascenso de la nueva derecha* (Buenos Aires: CLACSO, 2016), 13.

22. García Linera has been regarded as the principal theorist of progressivism, explicitly taking up the term in a general and inclusive sense, for example when he calls for the "construction of a progressive and sovereign Latin American International." Álvaro García Linera, "¿Fin de ciclo progresista o proceso por oleadas revolucionarias?," *Rebelión*, June 24, 2017.

23. García Linera, "¿Fin de ciclo progresista."

24. García Linera, "¿Fin de ciclo progresista."

25. García Linera, "¿Fin de ciclo progresista."

26. Distorting Gramsci and simplifying Lenin, he writes: "The strategy, then, will be to defeat the enemy culturally (Gramsci); to defeat the enemy politically and militarily (Lenin); and to incorporate the defeated enemy as such within the overall program of the new power. Because otherwise, left with nothing, sooner or later the enemy will seek to destroy the new power, to create an alternative power over the long term." García Linera, "¿Fin de ciclo progresista."

27. García Linera, "¿Fin de ciclo progresista."

28. García Linera, "¿Fin de ciclo progresista."

29. See, for example, Emir Sader, "El fracaso de la ultra izquierda," *Rebelion*, January 27, 2016, but see also the reiteration of the same argument in several articles collected at http://www.rebelion.org/autores.

30. Arkonada and Klachko, *Desde abajo, desde arriba*, 207.

31. "But it is necessary to identify the factors that led to the rise of a new right: a lack of alternative media sources to counterbalance those on the right; the limited development of a political culture of civic values beyond consumerism, of a revolutionary culture; organizational deficits that often meant inadequate engagement with the base; incidents of corruption; the rejection of criticism and a lack of self-criticism; insufficient management of resources and economic programs; inability to develop an alternative productive model to reduce dependency on the commodities market; the superficial and sometimes merely cosmetic nature of many of the changes in the political system; unproductive application of the independent Latin American integration agreements." Arkonada and Klachko, *Desde abajo, desde arriba*, 129.

32. Pablo Solana and Gerardo Szalkowicz, "Apuntes para el reimpulso," *Rebelion*, October 5, 2017, http://www.rebelion.org/noticia.php?id=226457.

33. Solana and Szalkowicz, "Apuntes para el reimpulso."

34. Solana and Szalkowicz, "Apuntes para el reimpulso."

35. Many of them, including the authors of this book, appear on the list of signatories of the aforementioned statement on the Venezuelan crisis.

36. As suggested by Maristella Svampa, who identifies three fundamental types of criticism: democratic, socioeconomic, and ecoterritorial. *Debates latinoamericanos*, 454–455.

37. Edgardo Lander et al., *Promesas en su laberinto: Cambios y continuidades en los gobiernos progresistas de América Latina* (Quito: IEE/CEDLA/CIM, 2013).

38. Lander et al., *Promesas en su laberinto*, xix–xx.

39. Edgardo Lander, "Tensiones/contradicciones en torno al extractivismo en los procesos de cambio: Bolivia, Ecuador y Venezuela," in Lander et al., *Promesas en su laberinto*, 12–13.

40. Lander et al., *Promesas en su laberinto*, 32. The question of the absence of participation and of Chavista authoritarianism is analyzed in detail in Margarita López Maya, *El ocaso del chavismo: Venezuela 2005–2015* (Caracas: Editorial Alfa, 2016).

41. Victor Alvarez, "La transición al socialismo de la Revolución Bolivariana: Transiciones logradas y transiciones pendientes" in Lander et al., *Promesas en su laberinto*, 279–396.

42. Alvarez, "La transición al socialismo," 244.

43. Alvarez, "La transición al socialismo," 246.

44. Alvarez, "La transición al socialismo," 257.

45. Alvarez, "La transición al socialismo," 266–268.

46. Carlos Arze Vargas and Javier Gómez, "Bolivia: ¿El 'proceso de cambio' nos conduce al 'Vivir Bien'?," in Lander et al., *Promesas en su laberinto*, 45–175.

47. Arze Vargas and Gómez, "Bolivia," 99.

48. Arze Vargas and Gómez, "Bolivia," 122–123.

49. Pablo Ospina, "'Estamos haciendo mejor las cosas con el mismo modelo antes que cambiarlo': La revolución ciudadana en Ecuador (2007–2012)," in Lander et al., *Promesas en su laberinto*, 177–277. On the Ecuadorian case, see also the edited volume *Correismo al desnudo* (Quito: Montechristi vive, 2013), which includes a text by Ospina.

50. Ospina, "'Estamos haciendo mejor,'" 193.

51. Ospina, "'Estamos haciendo mejor,'" 206.

52. For an incisive reading of the Argentinian case, informed by class-based and Marxist analysis from an autonomist perspective, see Alberto Bonnet, *La insurrección como restauración: El Kirchnerismo* (Buenos Aires: Prometeo, 2015); see also Adrián Piva, *Economía y política en la Argentina kirchnerista* (Buenos Aires: Batalla de ideas, 2015). On the Brazilian case, for a variety of critical perspectives from the left, see André Singer and Isabel Loubeiro, eds., *As contricioes do Lulismo: A que ponto chegamos?* (São Paulo: Boitempo, 2016); Gilberto Maringoni and Juliano Medeiros, eds., *Cinco mil días: O Brasil na era do Lulismo* (São Paulo: Boitempo, 2017); and Marcelo Badaró Mattos, ed., *Estado y formas de dominación no Brasil contemporáneo* (Rio de Janeiro: Consecuencia, 2017).

53. Claudio Katz, "Desenlaces del ciclo progresista," *Rebelión*, January 25, 2016, http://www.rebelion.org/noticia.php? id=208177.

54. Katz, "Desenlaces del ciclo progresista."

55. James Petras and Henry Veltmeyer, *The Class Struggle in Latin America* (New York: Routledge, 2018). Originally published as James Petras and Henry Veltmeyer, *Espejismos de la izquierda en América Latina* (Mexico: Lumen, 2009), 23–25.

56. Alberto Acosta et al., *Renunciar al bien común: Extractivismo y (pos) desarrollo en América Latina* (Buenos Aires: Mardulce, 2012).

57. Eduardo Gudynas, "La identidad de los progresismos latinoamericanos," *América Latina en Movimiento* 39, no. 510 (December 2015): 5.

58. On this question, among others, see the Indianist position of Pablo Mamani and the publication *Wilka*, which he edits; also see either a critique of *pachamamismo* by Pablo Stefanoni, or Arturo Escobar, "¿Pachamamicos versus Modernicos?," *La Línea de Fuego*, March 6, 2012, https://lalineadefuego.info/2012/03/06/pachamamicos-versus-modernicos-por-arturo-escobar/. In a less polemical vein, see Salvador Schavelzon, *Plurinacionalidad y Vivir Bien/Buen Vivir: Dos conceptos leídos desde Bolivia y Ecuador* (Quito: Abya Yala-CLACSO, 2015); and Massimo Modonesi and Mina L. Navarro, "El buen vivir, lo común y los movimientos antagonistas en América Latina: Elementos para una aproximación marxista," in *Buena Vida, Buen vivir: Imaginarios alternativos para el bien común de la humanidad*, ed. Giancarlo Delgado (Mexico: UNAM-CEIICH, 2014), 205–215.

59. With key texts such as those of Antonio Negri and Michael Hardt, and of Pierre Dardot and Christian Laval.

60. Maristella Svampa, "Cuatro claves para leer América Latina," *Nueva Sociedad* 268 (March–April 2017).

61. There are other autonomist positions that not only are critical, but that absolutely condemn the progressive governments, claiming that neoliberalism and post-neoliberalism and their corresponding forms of statism have been totally equivalent in their assault on "the common." See, for example, Verónica Gago and Diego Sztulwark, "La temporalidad de la lucha social en el fin de ciclo 'progresista' in América Latina," *EuroNomade*, September 6, 2016, http://www.euronomade.info/?p=7862; or Raquel Gutiérrez Aguilar et al., "¿Puede ser fértil la noción de '(re)formismo desde abajo' para pensar los caminos cotidianos—y fundamentales—de transformación social? Reflexiones desde algunas experiencias de lucha más allá, contra y más del Capital y del Estado

en Venezuela," in *Los gobiernos progresistas latinoamericanos: Contradicciones, avances y retrocesos*, ed. Carrillo Nieto et al. (Mexico: UAM-Ítaca, 2017), 205–231.

62. Decio Machado and Raúl Zibechi, *Cambiar el mundo desde arriba: Los límites del progresismo* (Santiago: Editorial Quimantú, 2016).

63. Machado and Zibechi, *Cambiar el mundo desde arriba*, 25.

64. Machado and Zibechi, *Cambiar el mundo desde arriba*, 31–32.

65. Machado and Zibechi, *Cambiar el mundo desde arriba*, 31–32.

66. Machado and Zibechi, *Cambiar el mundo desde arriba*, 19. They add that "they have no economic or financial autonomy, since they manage resources transferred by the state or by state institutions. The nonexistence of their own economy limits their autonomy. It is not the same thing to be organs of administration and participation as to be organs of power. However, it is possible for them to take a different path than that anticipated by the law that created them" (80). But they maintain that the Bolivarian government has "promoted and supported the experiences that arose spontaneously from the popular sectors" (69).

67. Machado and Zibechi, *Cambiar el mundo desde arriba*, 24.

68. Machado and Zibechi, *Cambiar el mundo desde arriba*, 29.

69. Machado and Zibechi, *Cambiar el mundo desde arriba*, 162.

70. Machado and Zibechi, *Cambiar el mundo desde arriba*, 123–124. With respect to the continuities between neoliberalism and progressivism in terms of the circulation of elites, the conception of the state, and public policy, see the extensive study by Beatriz Stolowicz, *El misterio del Posneoliberalismo*, 2 vols. (Bogotá: ILSA-Espacio crítico, 2017).

71. Maristella Svampa, "La década kirchnerista: Populismo, clases medias y revolución pasiva," *LASA Forum* 44, no. 4 (Fall 2013): 14–17. On the other hand, Svampa combines this focus with the concept of populism and distinguishes between plebeian and middle-class populisms—the former that of Venezuela and Bolivia, and the latter that of Ecuador and Argentina. Svampa, *Debates latinoamericanos*, 458.

72. Francisco Muñoz Jaramillo, ed., *Balance crítico del gobierno de Rafael Correa* (Quito: Universidad Central del Ecuador, 2014), 296.

73. Cited in Álvaro Bianchi, "Gramsci interprète du Brésil," *Actuel Marx* 57 (2015): 106.

74. Carlos Nelson Coutinho, "Hegemonia da pequeña política," in *Hegemonia a avessas*, ed. Francisco de Oliveira, Ruy Braga, and Cibele Risek (Rio de Janeiro: Boitempo, 2010), 32.

75. Ruy Braga, "Apresentacao," in Oliveira, Braga, and Risek, *Hegemonia a avessas*, 7–14.

76. Francisco de Oliveira, "Hegemonía a avessas," in Oliveira, Braga, and Risek, *Hegemonia a avessas*, 27; Francisco de Oliveira, "Brasil: Una hegemonía al revés," interview by Massimo Modonesi, OSAL no. 30 (November 2011): 67–75.

77. Edmundo Fernandes Dias, *Revolução passiva e modo de vida: Ensaios sobre as classes subalternas, o capitalismo e a hegemonia* (São Paulo: Editora José Luís e Rosa Sundermann, 2012), 154.

78. We must point out that a more academic body of literature has been emerging recently, often making use of question marks or seeking to take a more balanced stance. However, the question is so fraught that even these efforts, wittingly or unwittingly, end up locating themselves somewhere on the pro–con spectrum, and substantially reproduc-

ing the arguments of the debate that we have presented. See, for example, Gerónimo de Sierra, ed., *Los progresismos en la encrucijada: Argentina, Bolivia, Brasil, Uruguay, Venezuela* (Montevideo: Universidad de la República, 2017); Juan Carlos Gómez Leyton, ed., *Bolivia hoy: ¿Una Democracia Poscolonial o Anticolonial?, Seis estudios y una bibliografía seleccionada 1990–2016* (Santiago: Escaparate, 2017); Gerardo Caetano, "¿Milagro en Uruguay?, Apuntes sobre los gobiernos del Frente Amplio," *Nueva Sociedad* 272 (November–December 2017); Franklin Ramírez and Soledad Stoessel, "Una década de Revolución Ciudadana: posneoliberalismo y conflictividad," in Szalkowicz and Solana, *América Latina*.

79. The text in this section concisely restates—while omitting references to concrete cases and literature that now seem outdated or that appear in this or other chapters of the present book—the arguments developed in two articles published in 2012 and 2015, both included in Massimo Modonesi, *Revoluciones pasivas en América Latina* (Mexico: Itaca, 2017).

80. Carlos Nelson Coutinho, in an attempt to understand neoliberalism, suggested that rather than *passive revolution* we should think in terms of *counterreform*, because the fundamental element of the partial incorporation of demands from below does not occur. Not only do we share this view of neoliberalism, but we would add that this element is present in the current process and completes the picture that allows us to affirm that, where the progressive forces are governing in Latin America, a process of passive revolution is in fact under way. Coutinho, "L'epoca neoliberale: rivoluzione passiva o controriforma?," *Critica Marxista*, no. 2 (2007).

81. See Massimo Modonesi, *Subalternidad, antagonismo, autonomía: Marxismo y subjetivación política* (Buenos Aires: Prometeo-CLACSO-UBA, 2010).

82. This happened when the conservative or neoliberal opposition groups did not adhere pragmatically or did not willingly form alliances with the progressive government waiting for their moment of revenge, or for a time when another political option would be more profitable, which in fact occurred.

83. Álvaro García Linera spoke of a "point of rupture" in describing this strategic shift in the correlation of forces that opened up the possibility of exercising hegemony. See Linera, "Empate catastrófico y punto de bifurcación," *Crítica y emancipación*, no. 1 (June 2008): 23–33.

84. Massimo Modonesi pointed this out in "Conflictividad socio-política e inicio del fin de la hegemonía progresista en América Latina," in *Anuario del conflicto social 2013*, ed. Jaime Pastor and Nicolás Rojas Pedemonte (Barcelona: Universidad Autónoma de Barcelona, 2014), 1081–1095.

85. See Modonesi, *Revoluciones pasivas en América*, chap. 1.

86. Maristella Svampa, "América Latina: De nuevas izquierdas a populismos de alta intensidad," *Memoria*, no. 256 (November 2015): 32–37.

87. Mabel Thwaites, "Argentina fin de ciclo," *Memoria*, no. 254 (May 2015).

88. Oliveira, "Brasil."

89. Francisco Muñoz Jaramillo, ed., *Balance crítico del correísmo* (Quito: Universidad Central del Ecuador, 2014).

90. Maristella Svampa, "Termina la era de las promesas andinas," *Revista Ñ*, August 25, 2015.

CONCLUSION

1. Jeffery R. Webber, *The Last Day of Oppression, and the First Day of the Same: The Politics and Economics of the New Latin American Left* (Chicago: Haymarket, 2017), 273–300.

2. Pablo Ospina Peralta, "El Final Del Progresismo," *Nueva Sociedad*, August 1, 2016, http://nuso.org/articulo/el-fin-del-progresismo/.

3. Manuel Sutherland, "La ruina de Venezuela no se debe al 'socialismo' ni a la 'revolución,'" *Nueva Sociedad* 274 (2018): 142–151.

4. Marc Becker and Thea N. Riofrancos, "A Souring Friendship, a Left Divided," NACLA *Report on the Americas* 50, no. 2 (April 3, 2018): 124–127, https://doi.org/10.1080/10714839.2018.1479452.

5. William I. Robinson, "Capitalist Development in Nicaragua and the Mirage of the Left," *Truthout*, May 18, 2018, https://truthout.org/articles/capitalist-development-in-nicaragua-and-the-mirage-of-the-left/.

6. Lori Hanson and Miguel Gomez, "Deciphering the Nicaraguan Student Uprising," NACLA, June 15, 2018, https://nacla.org/news/2018/06/15/deciphering-nicaraguan-student-uprising.

7. David Agren and Tom Phillips, "'Amlo': The Veteran Leftwinger Who Could Be Mexico's Next President," *Guardian*, May 7, 2018, http://www.theguardian.com/world/2018/may/07/who-is-amlo-mexico-andres-manuel-lopez-obrador-election.

8. Massimo Modonesi, "Cuando puede ganar la que ya no es izquierda," *Desinformémonos*, June 11, 2018, https://desinformemonos.org/cuando-puede-ganar-la-ya-no-izquierda/.

9. Carlos Ominami, "Chile: El Segundo Suicidio de La Centroizquierda," *Nueva Sociedad* 274 (2018): 4–12.

10. Phillip Inman, "Argentina Forced to Seek IMF Aid over Fears for Economy," *Guardian*, May 18, 2018, http://www.theguardian.com/world/2018/may/18/argentina-forced-to-seek-imf-aid; "Argentina Agrees to $50bn Loan from IMF amid National Protests," *Guardian*, June 8, 2018, http://www.theguardian.com/business/2018/jun/08/argentina-loan-imf-protests-peso.

11. Dom Phillips, "Accused of Corruption, Popularity near Zero—Why Is Temer Still Brazil's President?," *Guardian*, October 17, 2017, http://www.theguardian.com/world/2017/oct/17/accused-of-graft-popularity-near-zero-so-why-is-brazils-president-still-in-office.

12. Joe Parkin Daniels, "Iván Duque Wins Election to Become Colombia's President," *Guardian*, June 18, 2018, http://www.theguardian.com/world/2018/jun/18/ivan-duque-wins-election-to-become-colombias-president.

COVID-19 POSTSCRIPT

1. Michael Stott and Andres Schipani, "Poverty and Populism Put Latin America at the Centre of Pandemic," *Financial Times*, June 14, 2020.

2. Pan-American Health Organization, "COVID-19 Americas' Region Dashboard, Geographic Distribution," updated August 3, 2020, https://www.arcgis.com/apps/dashboards/efb745c3d88647779beccb91c0e715f9.

3. Antoly Kurmanaev et al., "Latin America's Outbreaks Now Rival Europe's: But Its Options Are Worse," *New York Times*, May 12, 2020.

4. Julie Turkewitz and Manuela Andreoni, "The Amazon, Giver of Life, Unleashes the Pandemic," *New York Times*, July 25, 2020.

5. Pan-American Health Organization, "COVID-19 Americas' Region Dashboard."

6. FT Visual and Data Journalism Team, "Coronavirus Tracked," *Financial Times*, updated August 3, 2020, https://www.ft.com/content/a2901ce8-5eb7-4633-b89c-cbdf5b386938.

7. "Mortality Analyses, Deaths per 100,000 Population," Coronavirus Resource Center, Johns Hopkins University and Medicine, updated August 8, 2020, https://coronavirus.jhu.edu/data/mortality.

8. ECLAC, *Preliminary Overview of the Economies of Latin America and the Caribbean 2019* (Santiago: Economic Commission for Latin America and the Caribbean, 2019), 110.

9. ECLAC, *Preliminary Overview*, 59.

10. ECLAC, *Social Panorama of Latin America 2019* (Santiago: Economic Commission for Latin America and the Caribbean, 2019), 16.

11. ECLAC, *Social Panorama of Latin America*, 16.

12. ECLAC, *Social Panorama of Latin America*, 17.

13. ECLAC, *Social Panorama of Latin America*, 18.

14. ECLAC-PAHO, *Health and the Economy: A Convergence Needed to Address COVID-19 and Retake the Path of Sustainable Development in Latin America and the Caribbean* (Santiago: Economic Commission for Latin America and the Caribbean; Washington, DC: Pan-American Health Organization, July 30, 2020), 7–8.

15. ECLAC-PAHO, *Health and the Economy*, 9–11.

16. ECLAC-PAHO, *Health and the Economy*, 10–11.

17. ECLAC-PAHO, *Health and the Economy*, 14.

18. ECLAC-PAHO, *Health and the Economy*, 12.

19. ECLAC-PAHO, *Health and the Economy*, 12.

20. Róbert Nárai, "Choosing between Life and Capital in Latin America: Interview with Jeffery R. Webber," *Marxist Left Review* 20 (Winter 2020): 165–189.

21. Tom Phillips, "Brazilian President Jair Bolsonaro Tests Positive for Coronavirus," *Guardian*, July 7, 2020.

22. Forrest Hylton, "Brazil's Gravedigger-in-Chief," *London Review of Books* (blog), April 27, 2020, https://www.lrb.co.uk/blog/2020/april/brazil-s-gravedigger-in-chief; Forrest Hylton, "A Hemisphere in Freefall," *London Review of Books* (blog), July 24, 2020, https://www.lrb.co.uk/blog/2020/june/a-hemisphere-in-freefall.

23. Pablo Stefanoni, "Brasil: Pandemia, guerra cultural y precariedad: Entrevista a Lena Lavinas," *Nueva Sociedad* 297 (May–June 2020): 53.

24. Stefanoni, "Brasil," 54–57.

25. Claudio Katz, "Confluencia de virus en América Latina (I)," Comité para la abolición de las deudas ilegítimas, May 19, 2020, https://www.cadtm.org/Confluencia-de-virus-en-America-Latina-I; Diego Cazar Baquero, "La salud ecuatoriano, el botín político que cuesta vidas," Fundación Rosa Luxemburg Oficina Región Andina, June 2020, https://www.rosalux.org.ec/la-salud-ecuatoriana-el-botin-politico/.

26. Katz, "Confluencia de virus en América Latina (I)."

27. Kim Moody, "How 'Just-in-Time' Capitalism Spread COVID-19," *Spectre*, https://spectrejournal.com/how-just-in-time-capitalism-spread-covid-19/; Juan Grigera, "Sal en la herida: La crisis del COVID-19," *Revista Intersecciones*, April 13, 2020, https://www.intersecciones.com.ar/2020/04/13/sal-en-la-herida-la-crisis-del-covid-19/.

28. Gideon Long, "Bolivia Delays Presidential Election Again over Pandemic," *Financial Times*, July 23, 2020.

29. Rossana Castiglioni, "La política chilena en tiempos de pandemia: Entre la (des)movilización social y la crisis sanitaria," *Nueva Sociedad* 207 (May–June 2020): 69.

30. Karina Nohales, "Nos organizamos para ir hacia la vida," *Contrahegemoniaweb*, May 5, 2020, https://contrahegemoniaweb.com.ar/2020/05/05/nos-organizamos-para-ir-hacia-la-vida/.

31. Benedict Mander, "Chile Poised to Let Pensioners Withdraw Savings Early," *Financial Times*, July 24, 2020.

32. Claudio Katz, "La economia de la pos-pandemia en disputa," *La Haine*, April 7, 2020, https://www.lahaine.org/mundo.php/la-economia-de-la-pos.

33. Michael Stott, "A Plague on All Your Houses? Pandemic Politics in Latin America," *Financial Times*, July 27, 2020.

34. Humberto Beck, Carlos Bravo Regidor, and Patrick Iber, "El primer año del México de AMLO," *Nueva Sociedad* 207 (May–June 2020): 92.

35. Jude Webber, "Mexico's Economy Records Fifth Straight Quarterly Contraction," *Financial Times*, July 30, 2020.

36. Nárai, "Choosing between Life and Capital," 171.

37. Marc Frank, Michael Stott, and Andres Schipani, "Pandemic Deepens Divide over Cuba's International Medical Squads," *Financial Times*, July 24, 2020.

38. "World Economic Outlook Update, June 2020: A Crisis Like No Other, an Uncertain Recovery," International Monetary Fund, June 2020, https://www.imf.org/en/Publications/WEO/Issues/2020/06/24/WEOUpdateJune2020.

39. World Bank, *Global Economic Prospects* (Washington, DC: World Bank, June 2020), 10–11, https://www.worldbank.org/en/publication/global-economic-prospects.

40. "Global Trade Continues Nosedive, UNCTAD Forecasts 20% Drop in 2020," United Nations Conference on Trade and Development, June 11, 2020, https://unctad.org/en/pages/newsdetails.aspx?OriginalVersionID=2392.

41. Adam Hanieh, "This Is a Global Pandemic—Let's Treat It as Such," *Verso Blog*, March 27, 2020, https://www.versobooks.com/blogs/4623-this-is-a-global-pandemic-let-s-treat-it-as-such.

42. Hanieh, "This Is a Global Pandemic."

43. James Kynge and Sun Yu, "China Faces Wave of Calls for Debt Relief on 'Belt and Road' Projects," *Financial Times*, April 30, 2020.

44. Rob Wallace et al., "COVID-19 and Circuits of Capital," *Monthly Review*, May 1, 2020, https://monthlyreview.org/2020/05/01/covid-19-and-circuits-of-capital/.

45. Tithi Bhattacharya, ed., *Social Reproduction Theory: Remapping Class, Recentering Oppression* (London: Pluto, 2017).

INDEX

abortion rights, 23, 57
accumulation: capital, 8, 9, 15, 17, 42, 131, 140; Correa's model of, 122; extractive model of, 81, 84, 116; global, 145, 164; Latin American patterns of, 77, 87; of political force, 141, 142
Acosta, Alberto, 68, 124
agrarian reform, 16, 21, 27, 30, 41–42, 56; counterreform, 82
agro-industry, 7, 85, 124, 146, 165; extractive capitalism and, 77, 79–81, 107; GM crops, 41, 42; small producers, 82–83
ALBA. *See* Bolivarian Alliance for the Peoples of Our America (ALBA)
Alencar, José, 31
Alianza País. *See* PAIS Alliance (Proud and Sovereign Alliance)
Allende, Salvador, 11, 42, 58
alter-globalization movement, 15, 22
Álvarez, Víctor, 122
Áñez, Jeanine, 4, 14, 54, 59, 66, 141, 158
anti-capitalism, 9, 31, 70, 73, 76, 121, 143; anti-neoliberalism and, 4, 111; Bolivarian economic policy and, 62; democracy and, 122; left critics of, 148
anti-imperialism, 3, 6, 32, 75, 109, 114, 148; Brazilian, 105; progressivism and, 25, 115; unity, 104; Venezuelan, 27, 102, 117, 123. *See also* counter-regionalism
anti-neoliberalism, 1, 2, 4, 28, 104, 121, 133; birth of, 110; in Chile, 58; consensus around, 7, 109, 111; governments, 113, 117, 134; movements or resistance, 114, 139, 142, 148; in South America, 32

antipoverty programs, 7, 153, 157
anti-terrorism legislation, 48, 67
Arce, Luis, 158
Argentina, 1, 14, 38, 75, 117, 123, 164; center-left governments, 5, 6, 76, 145, 150; COVID-19 and healthcare, 155, 160–61; economic crisis, 18, 28, 77, 150, 160; feminist movement, 69, 166; GDP, 83, 153; industry, 83; Left and Workers' Front (FIT), 70–71, 141; minimum wage increase, 39; *piquetero* movement, 20, 28–29, 46; return of the right, 4, 66, 104, 138, 139–40, 150; trade unionism, 24, 29, 47, 70. *See also* Fernández de Kirchner, Cristina; Peronism
Argentinian Workers' Central (CTA), 24, 47
Arkonada, Katu, 170n13, 188n15, 189n19, 190n31
Arze Vargas, Carlos, 122
authoritarianism, 33, 54, 74, 121, 148; Brazilian government, 67; Correa's, 64; right-wing, 150, 156; state, 11, 65, 73, 132, 145; Venezuelan government, 62, 63
autonomy, 43, 46, 47, 94, 141; critiques of progressive governments, 125–26, 191n61; demands for, 21–22, 25; economic, 192n66; hegemony and, 7, 9, 128, 149; institutionalization and, 136; relative, 99, 104, 105, 108, 131, 147; subalternity and, 133, 137

Bachelet, Michelle, 32, 33, 36, 42, 50; anti-terrorist legislation, 48, 67; New Majority, 56, 187n1

banks, 100–101, 146–47, 163; Bank of the South, 102, 105, 108, 147; BNDES, 105–6. *See also* Inter-American Development Bank; World Bank
Betto, Frei, 33
Bianchi, Álvaro, 127
Bolívar, Simón, 33, 102
Bolivarian Alliance for the Peoples of Our America (ALBA), 36, 94, 102, 104–7, 108, 147
Bolivarian Armed Forces, 35, 38
Bolivarian Revolution, 27, 35, 37, 44, 113, 117, 141; authoritarian drift and, 15, 51–52; *misiones* (missions), 40
Bolivarian Socialist Central of Urban, Farming and Fishing Workers (CBST-CCP), 47
Bolivia, 1, 13, 65, 118–19, 158; agribusiness, 41–42; anti-imperialism, 117; critiques of progressive governments, 122, 124–26; eradication of illiteracy, 38–39; indigenous people, 45, 46, 67–68; popular movements, 11, 14, 25–26, 29–31; poverty rate and GDP, 37; shift to the right, 4, 141; socialism, 34, 116, 117, 189n19; US relations, 35–36; violence, 66. *See also* Morales, Evo; Movement toward Socialism (MAS)
Bolivian Workers' Central (COB), 11, 45, 68
Bolsonaro, Jair, 4, 14, 160; ascent to power, 60–61, 144, 150; COVID-19 pandemic response, 151, 152, 156–58; government, 66, 67, 72
Borón, Atilio, 61, 111, 114, 115, 188nn14–15, 189n19; on US military activities, 95–96
bourgeoisie, 6, 34, 50, 126, 131, 188n15; bolibourgeoisie (Bolivarian), 51, 53; Bolivian, 35, 53, 141; hegemony of, 12–13; Uruguayan, 56
Braga, Ruy, 127
Brazil, 1, 4, 39, 72, 82, 130, 140; agrarian policy, 41; center-left governments, 6, 14, 31–32, 56, 76; Chinese investments and loans, 100–101; collectives, 14; COVID-19 and healthcare, 151–53, 156–57; critiques of progressive governments, 123, 126–27; democracy, 60; economic crisis, 18, 77–78, 157; Family Allowance program, 38; *favelas*, 67; GDP, 31, 153; household debt, 87; industry, 83; political posts, 176n98; presidential elections, 31–32, 60–61, 71, 104, 150; social movements, 21, 22, 26, 69–70; sub-imperial role, 105–6; trade unionism, 23–24, 47, 54–55. *See also* Bolsonaro, Jair; Workers' Party (PT)
Brazilian Democratic Movement Party (PMDB), 56
Brazilian Social Democratic Party (PSDB), 31, 61
Bucaram, Abdalá, 27
buen vivir (living well), 20, 34, 43, 74, 122, 124

Caesarism, 40, 129, 133, 137, 139, 149
Canada, 91–92, 103
capital, 55, 81, 89, 139, 149, 166; accumulation, 8, 9, 15, 17, 42, 87, 131, 140; big, 50; flight, 52, 163; foreign, 13, 32, 43; imperialism and, 87–88, 101; transnational, 19, 80
capitalism, 12, 19, 62, 73, 124; extractive, 7, 48, 77, 79–80, 107, 165; global crisis of, 9, 49, 60, 74, 84–86, 105, 107–8, 163; green, 68; Kirchner's, 116; neoliberal, 88–89; state, 3, 5–6, 8, 13, 49, 53, 189n19; trade union, 55
Caribbean, 79–80, 87; Chinese investments and loans, 99–101; economy, 84–86; GDP, 153; healthcare, 155, 165; US military operations, 95–96
castes, 8, 53, 55, 57
Castro, Fidel, 16
caudillo figure, 72, 133, 148
CELAC. *See* Community of Latin American and Caribbean States (CELAC)
center-left governments, 120, 123–24, 139, 148, 160; in Brazil, 14, 31–32, 56, 76; in Chile, 49, 150; electoral trends, 4–5, 6, 32–33; in Mexico, 66, 104, 149, 161; overview of, 143, 145; political-economics and, 77, 79; popular movements and, 25–26
Central America, 12, 16, 79, 85–86; US military presence, 95, 96; War on Gangs, 97
Central Intelligence Agency (CIA), 35, 61, 92, 96
Chávez, Hugo, 12, 25, 40, 51, 76, 144; coup attempt, 35; creation of communal councils, 44, 188n9; criticism of, 122; death, 49; elections, 8, 27, 32, 33, 44; founding of Network of Intellectuals and Artists in

Defense of Humanity, 113; mining projects, 52; petrol dealings, 42–43; socialism, 117
chavismo, 35, 40, 44, 46, 113, 117, 136; critics of, 71, 122; electoral base, 36, 59
Chile, 11, 17, 36, 42, 93, 98; anti-terrorist legislation, 48, 67; Concertación governments, 25, 33, 187n1; COVID-19 pandemic, 151, 152, 159; feminist movement, 58, 69, 159–60, 166; fiscal reform, 56–57; GDP and household debt, 57, 153; public transportation, 58; right resurgence, 4, 144, 150; street politics, 159. *See also* Bachelet, Michelle
China, 7, 85, 107–8, 147, 163–64; demand for commodities, 79–80, 84, 146; FDI, 91; imperial strategy, 9, 77, 98–102, 108, 146; mergers and acquisitions, 91–92, 99; world power, 90–91
churches, 14, 65
CLACSO (Latin American Council of Social Sciences), 111, 114, 187n8
class structures, 6, 8, 75, 81, 82, 146
class struggles, 53, 72, 126; from below, 8, 15, 88, 123–24; main branches of, 16; popular movements and, 12, 13, 15, 24, 143
clientelism, 33, 40, 121, 132, 136, 142, 148
CLOC (Coordination of Latin American Peasants' Organizations), 171n29
cocaleros (coca growers), 29, 45
collective actions, 13–15, 28, 35, 119, 170n7; subaltern bloc for, 30, 173n46
Colombia, 152, 155, 161; right-wing government, 36, 66, 75, 150, 162; US military activities in, 95–96
commodities boom, 6, 9, 76–77, 152, 153; exports, 82; extractive capitalism and, 7, 79–80, 146; prices, 84–85, 86, 107–8, 116, 163; resource rents from, 81, 107
commons, the, 74, 124–25, 191n61
communal councils (Communes), 44, 125, 136, 188n9
community land, 41–42
Community of Latin American and Caribbean States (CELAC), 36, 95, 102, 103–4, 108, 147
compensatory states, 81–82, 107–8
Confederation of Indigenous Nationalities in Ecuador (CONAIE), 20, 27, 48, 64, 65, 68, 142

conservativism, 130–32, 139, 149
constitutions, 43, 48, 56, 75, 124, 136, 144; Venezuela (1999), 63–64
construction contracts, 101
Continental Social Alliance (ASC), 22
Coordinadora de Defensa del Agua y de la Vida, 30
corporativism, 118–19, 142
Correa, Rafael, 36, 39, 47, 59, 142, 173n53; "change of epoch" usage, 33, 187n3; Christian socialism, 117; comments on environmentalism, 48, 119; criticism of, 122–23; Moreno and, 64; presidential elections, 28, 32, 71; Yasuni ITT project, 68
corruption, 46, 51–52, 74, 125, 144, 190n31; anti-corruption mobilizations, 14; of governments and elections, 54, 60, 62, 64, 136; Workers' Party (PT), 54–55, 140
counter-regionalism, 99, 102, 104–7, 108, 147
coups d'état, 16, 59, 145, 170n15, 187n1; attempts, 27, 35, 61, 97; of Morales, 1, 14, 53, 65, 158; of Rousseff, 53, 60, 106; of Zelaya, 60, 94
Coutinho, Carlos Nelson, 127, 193n80
COVID-19 pandemic, 7, 9, 151–66
critical thought, 109, 110
Cuba, 33, 40, 115, 151, 155; healthcare system, 155, 161–62
Cuban Revolution, 11, 16, 73, 115, 188n14
cultivable land, 41–42
CUT. *See* Unified Workers' Central (CUT)

debt, 18, 32, 88, 126, 160; crisis (1980s), 77–78; Ecuador's, 36, 158; foreign, 17, 52, 58, 171n16; Global South, 164; household, 57, 87; Latin American and Caribbean, 87, 99; Venezuela's, 97
D'Elía, Luís, 46
democracy, 17, 110, 111, 122–23; Brazilian, 60; Chilean, 57; governability, 18; participatory, 21, 43, 120, 134, 135–36, 169n1; protagonist, 44; self-managed, 20; social, 50, 187n7; state and, 8, 112, 135, 148; US promotion of, 92; Venezuelan, 44, 136
Democratic Unity Roundtable (MUD), 52, 59
de Oliveira, Francisco, 127, 140
dispossession, 45, 81, 82

division of labor. *See* international division of labor
Drug Enforcement Agency (DEA), 35, 96–97
Duque, Iván, 66, 104, 150, 161
Duterme, Bernard, 19

ecological crisis, 80–81, 162, 165
Economic Commission for Latin America and the Caribbean (ECLAC), 48, 91, 116, 153–54
economic crises, 138, 139; in Argentina, 18, 28, 150, 160; in Brazil, 157; COVID-19 pandemic, 163–64; in Ecuador, 27; global (2008), 76, 77, 84–86, 96, 107–8, 146, 163; in Mexico, 161; neoliberalism and, 77–79; in Nicaragua, 149; in Venezuela, 97, 117, 141. *See also* recessions
economic growth, 7, 79, 81, 87; global, 163; rates, 78, 84–86, 153–54
Ecuador, 49, 59, 149; anti-terrorist legislation, 67; Citizens' Revolution, 34, 36, 38, 68; COVID-19 pandemic, 152, 158; critiques of progressive governments, 124–25, 127; debt, 36, 158, 164; economy, 64–65; GDP, 50; indigenous mobilizations, 20, 26, 27–28, 65; left criticism, 120, 122–23; oil, 68, 101; poverty rate, 37; presidential elections, 1, 64, 140; socialism, 117, 189n19; trade unionism, 47. *See also* Correa, Rafael
education, 40, 56, 76, 165
El Alto (Bolivia), 30
electoral systems, 17, 26, 32, 70–71, 79, 149–50; abstention, 57; fraud and, 54
elites, 16, 40, 55, 73, 149; economic, 17, 39, 57, 64; neoliberal, 4; new, 53, 126, 133, 144
environmentalists, 48, 67, 121, 126, 148. *See also* socioenvironmental movements
"epoch of change" concept, 2, 33, 138, 187n3
European Union (EU), 91–92, 93, 99
exports, 6, 8, 65, 76, 83; agricultural, 41, 42; Brazil's, 106; commodity, 79–80, 125, 146; global economic crisis and, 85, 86; prices, 82, 163; raw-material, 122, 124, 130; taxes, 14, 39; to/from China, 98–99, 100
extractivism, 13, 68, 73, 116, 165; commodities boom and, 79–81, 146; dependency and, 7, 112, 115, 124, 148; movements and resistance, 48, 67, 121, 125, 148, 162; progressive governments and, 77, 107, 123

Falconi, Fander, 169n1
feminist movements, 22–23, 58, 69, 159–60, 162, 166
Fernandes Dias, Edmundo, 128
Fernández, Alberto, 5, 59, 104, 140, 145, 150, 160
Fernández de Kirchner, Cristina, 32, 46, 47, 70, 76; agrarian producers' unions and, 14, 39; vice-presidency, 5, 140
foreign direct investment (FDI), 78; American and Chinese, 98, 99–102, 146; Brazilian, 106; trends in Latin America, 77, 91–92, 108
foreign exchange, 83, 90, 97, 162
foreign policy, 106
Franco, Marielle, 66
Free Trade Area of the Americas (FTAA), 22, 93, 102

García Linera, Álvaro, 45, 114, 118–19, 173n46, 188n15, 189n26, 193n83; capitalism of, 49; defense of statism, 115, 116; progressivism of, 189n22
gas wars, 30
General Confederation of Labor (CGT), 24, 47, 175n81
general strikes, 28, 72, 160
geopolitics, 76, 104, 148; American and Chinese, 9, 92–94, 146; Brazilian, 60, 106, 156
Glas, Jorge, 140
global trade, 90, 163; US dollar and, 89
global value chains, 88, 163, 165
Goldberg, Paul, 35
Gómez, Gonzalo, 51
Gómez, Javier, 122
Gramsci, Antonio, 2, 26, 114, 119, 128, 139, 189n26; passive revolution concept, 8, 109–10, 129–31, 135, 149
gross domestic product (GDP), 18, 31, 155, 164; Argentina's, 83; Bolivia's, 37; Chile's, 57; Ecuador's, 50; PT governments and, 38; totals for Latin America, 80, 83, 86, 153, 154; Venezuela's, 98
Guaidó, Juan, 53, 61, 97
Gudynas, Eduardo, 124
Guevara, "Che," 170n15
Guillier, Alejandro, 150
Gutiérrez, Lucio, 28

200 · *Index*

Haddad, Fernando, 60–61
healthcare systems: Argentina's, 160–61; Bolivia's, 158; Brazil's, 38, 156–57; Chile's, 57, 159; Cuba's, 161–62; lack of access, 154; Latin America and Caribbean, 155–56; Venezuela's, 40, 62; women and, 165
hegemony, 1, 15, 127, 133, 134, 193n83; autonomy and, 7, 9, 128, 148; Bolivian, 35; bourgeoisie and, 12–13; loss of, 138, 139, 141; neoliberal, 5, 8, 13, 25, 32, 142, 143; new right, 149, 162; progressive, 4, 5, 6, 7, 10, 59, 143, 146; trans-class, 131; US, 89, 94, 103, 107, 108, 147
Herrera, Ernesto, 56
Homeless Workers' Movement (MTST), 69, 71
Honduras, 94, 146; Zelaya coup, 53, 60, 187n1
Houtart, François, 13
human rights, 94, 95; movement, 46–47, 49
hydrocarbons, 42, 46, 51, 59, 81, 101

Illanes, Rodolfo, 53
imperialism, 11, 16, 73, 77, 148, 164; aggression, 63, 123; Bolivarian Revolution and, 35, 61, 113; Brazil's sub-role, 105–6; capitalist, 87–88; Chinese, 9, 98–102, 108, 146; green, 49, 119; in Latin America, 74, 90, 91; unity against, 120; US, 9, 77, 89, 92–98, 108, 114, 146. *See also* anti-imperialism
income inequality, 7, 76, 84, 152, 153–54, 157
indigenous movements, 14, 22, 29, 124, 171n29; in Bolivia, 45, 67–68; in Ecuador, 20, 26, 27–28, 65; extractive megaprojects and, 48, 81; Mapuche struggles, 48–49, 66, 67; recognition of rights, 43, 52; violence and, 66
industrialization, 6, 23, 106, 123, 163; decline, 80, 83, 90, 103, 181n28; job precarity, 20, 84; raw-material exports and, 122, 124. *See also* agro-industry
informal employment, 39, 84, 154, 159, 160; growth of, 17–18, 23
infrastructure projects, 38, 101–2, 106, 125
Initiative for the Integration of the Regional Infrastructure of South America (IIRSA), 105–6
institutionalization, 13, 25, 99, 118, 137, 141; popular movements and, 6, 15, 22–23, 45–46, 136

Inter-American Development Bank, 64, 101, 146, 164
international division of labor, 88, 91, 108; of Brazilian society, 105, 157; Latin America's subordinate position within, 6, 75, 82, 145, 163
internationalism, new, 22, 171n29
International Monetary Fund (IMF), 31, 89, 150, 158, 161, 164; protests against, 18–19, 64–65; structural adjustment policies, 17, 92

Katz, Claudio, 17–18, 26, 61, 75, 90, 103; on China, 98; on debt repayment, 160; on imperialism and capitalism, 87–89; on neo-developmentalism, 123, 188n17; on Nicaragua, 158
Kirchner, Nestor, 29, 46, 47, 49, 76, 116
Kirchnerismo, 117, 126–27, 140
Klachko, Paula, 170n13, 188n15, 189n19, 190n31

Lacalle Pou, Luis, 4, 56, 141
Laclau, Ernesto, 72, 114, 188n10
Lander, Edgardo, 40, 63, 122
Landless Rural Workers' Movement (MST), 21, 22, 41
latifundio, 16, 41, 42
left intellectuals, 147–48, 187n7; anti-neoliberal debate, 110–11, 187n2; critiques of progressive governments, 121–28; debate on progressivism, 113–20, 129, 187n7. *See also* Gramsci, Antonio; Marxist tradition
"left turn," 13, 18, 25, 36, 77, 82, 98; renewal, 150. *See also* "pink tide"
left-wing governments, 6, 59, 66, 67, 93, 107; hegemony, 149, 162; independent candidates, 70–72, 179n135; presidential elections, 32–33; retreat or absence of, 141–42, 149–50, 162; trade unionism and, 39; two kinds of, 36–37. *See also* center-left governments
Lenin, Vladimir, 115, 188n15, 189n26
libertarian-autonomists, 115, 121, 147, 148
loans, 64, 146; Chinese, 98, 100–102, 164
Lobo, Porfirio, 94

López Obrador, Andrés Manuel ("AMLO"), 4–5, 66, 104, 145, 149, 161
López Segrera, Francisco, 118, 119
Löwy, Michael, 60
Lugo, Fernando, 32, 53, 60, 94, 187n1
Lula da Silva, Luiz Inácio ("Lula"), 41, 60–61, 70, 105–6, 140, 149; election victory (2002), 31–32; trade unions and, 55
Luslismo/Lulification, 113, 127–28

Machado, Decío, 125–26, 192n66
Macri, Mauricio, 4, 59, 72, 104, 150, 160
Maduro, Nicolás, 45, 46, 51, 63, 71, 97, 144; coup attempt, 61; creation of SEZS, 52; reelection, 149
Mahuad, Jamil, 27
Mandetta, Enrique, 157
Mapuche people, 18, 48–49, 66, 67
Marxist tradition, 15, 30, 111, 113, 115, 128; Chavismo and, 117; feminist analyses, 165
MAS. *See* Movement toward Socialism (MAS)
Menem, Carlos, 17, 24, 25
Mercádo Común del Sur. *See* Southern Common Market (MERCOSUR)
mergers and acquisitions, 91–92, 99
Mesa, Carlos, 30, 53–54
Mexican Revolution (1910), 11
Mexico, 6, 22, 36, 79, 166; Chinese investments, 100; COVID-19 pandemic, 151, 152, 161; economy, 18, 77–78, 85–86, 161, 163; GDP, 153; presidential elections, 66, 104, 149; trade agreements, 93; War on Drugs, 96
Michels, Robert, 50
Middle East, 90, 92, 106
migrant labor, 85, 163, 165
military, 2, 35, 36; dictatorship, 60; US, 61, 89–90, 92, 95–97
mining, 42, 53, 80–81, 92, 100; Orinoco Mining Arc (Venezuela), 52
Moncayo, Paco, 71
Mooers, Colin, 88
Morales, Evo, 29, 32, 50, 173n53, 187n7; coup, 1, 14, 53, 65, 158; elections and referendums, 1, 35, 53–54, 141; gas wars, 30; government, 41, 45, 68, 122
Moreno, Lenín, 1, 64–65, 140, 142, 149, 158
Moro, Sérgio, 60–61

mortality rates, 151–52, 158
Mothers of the Plaza de Mayo, 46–47
Movement toward Socialism (MAS), 26, 31, 42, 45, 53, 126, 158; union organizations and, 29
Movimiento Sin Miedo, 141
Moyano, Hugo, 47
Mujica, José "Pepe," 49, 56, 118, 140
multiclass alliances, 9, 32, 147, 148, 149
multinational corporations (MNCS), 20, 30, 35, 39, 88, 107; agro-industrial, 82; FDI and, 91; mining, 53; *multilatinas* (regional scale), 55, 83–84; natural gas and oil, 42–43
Muñoz Jaramillo, Francisco, 127

narcotics, 96–97
National Constituent Assembly (Venezuela), 63, 72
National Council for Change (CONALCAM), 45
National Council of Ayllus and Markas of Qullasuyu (CONAMAQ), 45
National Electoral Commission (CNE), 68, 179n135
nationalism, 6, 34, 51, 64
nationalizations, 37–38, 42, 120
national-popular, 18, 19, 35, 37, 138, 144, 147; left intellectuals and, 114–15; progressive governments, 8, 37, 117, 121, 145
National Workers' Union of Venezuela (UNT), 47
natural gas: extraction, 7, 76, 77, 79–81, 107, 146, 165; job opportunities and, 84; Morales and, 30; prices, 85
natural resources, 19, 29, 37, 52, 80–82, 85; Chinese investment, 99–100. *See also* raw materials
neo-developmentalism, 3, 6, 34, 38, 110, 144, 187n5; extractivism and, 124; Lula's, 55; profit from, 50; of progressive governments, 116, 123, 132, 188n17; revolutions and, 130–31; socioenvironmental movements and, 48–49
neoliberalism, 1, 2, 16, 123, 130–31, 133, 191n61; Chilean, 57–58; "combat," 66; counterreform and, 127, 193n80; crisis of, 9; critical conception of, 110; end of, 13;

202 · Index

healthcare and, 160; orthodox, 6–7, 77, 81, 82, 149, 150; "perfect," 55; political-economics of, 76, 77–79, 82, 148; popular movements and, 15, 18–20, 22, 110, 193n82; trade unionism and, 24; transition to, 80, 163; US, 92, 102, 104; "war," 33. *See also* anti-neoliberalism; post-neoliberalism
Netherlands, 91
new right, 6, 59, 118, 150, 162; rise of, 109, 143, 144, 190n31. *See also* right-wing governments
Nicaragua, 1, 11, 33, 54, 149, 158; trade union movement, 47–48. *See also* Sandinistas
Nohales, Karina, 159
Norfield, Tony, 90–91
North American Free Trade Agreement (NAFTA), 22, 93

Obama, Barack, 92–95
oil: Chinese loans for, 101; Ecuador's, 68; Petrobras scandal, 55; prices, 85, 105; progressive governments and, 76, 77; rents, 7, 35, 51, 62, 146; underwater reserves, 80; Venezuela's, 35, 42–43, 62, 67, 97–98, 105
oligarchy, 4, 34, 45, 50, 51, 82, 139; mestizo, 35; neocolonial, 30; state property and, 59
Organization for Economic Cooperation and Development (OECD), 155
Organization of American States (OAS), 55, 95, 103–4
Ortega, Daniel, 1, 32, 33, 47, 54, 149, 158
Ospina, Pablo, 122–23

Pacific Alliance, 93, 94, 102
PAIS Alliance (Proud and Sovereign Alliance), 1, 26, 28, 64, 140
Pan-American Health Organization (PAHO), 151, 152, 154
Paraguay, 96, 151; Lugo presidency/coup, 32, 53, 60, 94, 187n1
passive revolutions, 109–10, 138, 139, 142, 193n80; demobilization and subalternization and, 133–35, 141, 149; epoch of, 2; as neo-developmentalism and statism, 130–32, 187n5; progressive governments and, 8, 126–29, 137
peasant movements, 11, 27, 121, 148; in Bolivia, 29, 41

pension funds, 23, 38, 72, 149, 160; PT's management of, 55, 127, 140
Pérez, Carlos Andrés, 19, 62
Pérez Jiménez, Marcos, 27
Peronism, 5, 25, 29, 59, 117, 140
Peru, 75, 93, 96, 98, 100, 187n1; COVID-19 pandemic, 151, 152, 159
Petras, James, 123
Piñera, Sebastián, 4, 57–58, 144, 150, 159–60
"pink tide," 8, 13, 75, 163, 164
piquetero movement, 20, 28–29, 46
plebeian upsurge, 5, 24, 69. *See also* popular movements
plurinationalism, 34, 43, 121, 148
political economy, 9, 75–77, 79, 107, 148, 149; compensatory states and, 82
popular movements, 2, 5–6, 8, 43, 141–42; demands for autonomy, 21–22; of the early 2000s, 26–31; economic reforms and, 64–65, 142, 149; institutionalization of, 45–46, 118; of the 1990s, 16–19, 110; overview of Latin American, 11–15, 72; progressive governments and, 25–26, 45, 134, 144; renewal of, 145, 162; territorial and traditional aspects, 19–21; trade unionism and, 23–24, 69; urban youth, 69–70; violence and, 66–67. *See also* feminist movements; social movements
popular power, 12, 30, 44, 120, 137
populism, 25, 64, 127, 135, 187n5; left and left criticism, 4, 59, 70–72, 114–15; "radical," 93, 94; Svampa's critique of, 173n53
postcolonialism, 9, 121, 147–48
post-neoliberalism, 2, 3, 48, 58, 111, 147, 191n61; cycle, 37, 50; discourse, 113, 114; governments, 118, 120, 123, 148; passage to postcapitalism, 13, 119; passive revolution and, 130, 187n5; projects, 116
poverty: cash transfer programs, 81, 84; housing vulnerabilities, 155, 157; rates, 7, 37, 62, 76, 78, 122, 152–54
power index, 90–91
Prado, Ángel, 179n135
private property, 33, 43, 46, 59
privatization, 17, 20, 23, 52, 76; credit and, 87; labor market and, 84; PEMEX, 100; water, 30

progressive governments, 54, 74, 80, 81, 117, 146; authoritarian drift and, 51–53; failures of, 6–7, 75–76; leftist critiques, 120–28, 147–48; neo-developmentalism of, 116, 123, 188n17; overview of Latin American, 1–4, 8–9, 109, 187n1; popular movements and, 5–6, 15, 24, 26, 45, 48, 134–35, 144; regressive turn, 138–42; revolutions of, 130–31; social policies, 37–41, 50, 56, 76, 116; the state and, 66, 132; support for, 113–14, 118, 187nn7–8

progressivism, 13, 36, 41, 57, 69, 93, 126; coups and, 59–60, 145; debate on the meaning, 111–12; end of cycle, 1, 6, 64, 70–71, 73, 138–42, 144; high period or golden age of, 6–7, 8, 47, 59, 143–44; historicity of, 2; intellectual context, 113–20, 129; notion of, 3–5; passive revolutions and, 8, 110; political economy of, 76, 77; self-determination and, 136; two levels of, 189n19

proletariat, 16, 24

property relations. *See* social-property relations

PSUV (United Socialist Party of Venezuela), 51, 72, 136, 179n135

PT. *See* Workers' Party (PT)

public policy, 36, 37–40, 46, 116, 132; communal councils and, 44; passive revolution and, 127, 137; popular movements and, 133, 134; privatization and, 17; regressive turn of, 139, 140. *See also* social policies

public transportation, 58, 70

radicalism, 15, 23, 108, 113, 121; anti-systemic, 9, 147; Bolsonaro's, 157; democracy and, 44, 51; populist, 93, 94

raw materials, 39, 42, 49, 73; exports, 122, 124, 130. *See also* extractivism

recessions, 19, 57, 77–79, 89, 108, 157; COVID-19 pandemic and, 154, 161, 163

referendums, 43–44, 54, 65

reformism, 117, 130–32

religious movements, 66

remittances, 83, 85, 86, 162, 163

rentierism, 51, 107, 122, 124, 146

repression, 16, 19, 46, 126, 134, 149; of revolts and movements, 24, 27, 28, 30, 54, 66–68, 72; of trade union leaders, 40

right-wing governments, 4, 36, 75–76, 79; hegemony and, 149, 162; response to COVID-19, 156–61, 161; resurgence, 10, 59–61, 66, 138–42, 144, 150; US and, 94. *See also* Bolsonaro, Jair

Rousseff, Dilma, 14, 32, 41, 67, 70, 140; coup, 53, 59, 60, 65, 106

ruling classes, 11, 16–17, 32, 39, 144; Chilean, 57; fractions within, 51; power of, 50, 73; trade union structure, 55. *See also* bourgeoisie

Sachs, Jeffrey, 25

Sader, Emir, 111, 114, 115, 119

Sánchez de Lozada, Gonzalo, 29, 53

sanctions: on Cuba, 162; on Venezuela, 53, 97–98

Sandinistas, 11, 33, 47, 54, 149, 173n50

Sandino, Augusto César, 11

São Paulo Forum (1991), 33, 173n50

Scioli, Daniel, 140, 150

self-criticism, 119, 120, 190n31

self-determination, 21, 43, 104, 136, 137

self-organization, 12, 15, 20, 25, 44, 72

Singer, André, 55

socialism, 11–12, 75, 111, 113; in Bolivia, 34, 116; in Brazil, 31, 71; eco, 68; in Venezuela (Bolivarian), 34, 39, 44, 62, 116–17, 188n17, 189n19

Socialism and Liberty Party (PSOL), 71

social justice, 20, 114, 115, 118, 126, 138, 148

social-liberalism, 33, 36–37, 56, 64, 144; in Brazil, 31, 127

social movements, 5, 9, 12, 21–22, 75; Argentine, 160; concept and overview of, 13–14; demobilization and passivization of, 127, 134, 137; neoliberalism and, 19, 78–79; "new," 170n7; over public transit, 58, 70; progressive governments and, 26, 45–46, 109; renewal in Chile, 159–60, 162; repression and violence of, 66–67. *See also* popular movements

social policies, 37–41, 43, 56–57, 76, 116, 125; redistributive impact of, 15, 118, 122, 126; spending, 81–82, 107

social-property relations, 8, 81–82, 107, 122, 146

social reproductive labor, 154, 165

socioenvironmental movements, 20, 48, 124
Somoza, Anastasio, 12, 54
South America, 79, 80, 107; GDP, 31; global economic crisis and, 85–86, 108; income growth rate, 76; US influence, 94–95
Southern Common Market (MERCOSUR), 94, 103, 108, 147
sovereignty, 62, 75, 114, 118, 138, 148; Bolivarian notion of, 33, 103, 104; food, 22, 41, 42
Special Economic Zones, 52
state power, 3, 5, 25, 29, 114, 120, 143
statism, 114–15, 128, 132, 137, 148, 191n61
Stefanoni, Pablo, 187n7
structural adjustment policies, 17, 78, 92, 164
Suárez Salazar, Luis, 94
subaltern classes, 8, 11, 16, 118–19, 131, 141–42; collective action, 30, 173n46; demobilization and passivization of, 126, 127–28, 133–37, 149
Sucre currency, 102, 105, 108, 147
Summit of the Americas: Mar del Plata (2005), 22, 93, 102; Puerto España (2009), 94
Svampa, Maristella, 80, 106, 141, 181n28, 187n3, 187n5, 190n36; characterization of Kirchnerismo, 126–27; critique of extractivism, 48, 125; on populism, 139, 173n53

taxes, 39, 43, 46, 107, 138
Teich, Nelson, 157
Temer, Michel, 14, 60, 66, 72, 106, 150
Thatcher, Margaret, 34
TIPNIS (Bolivia), 67–68
tourism, 83, 162, 163
trade agreements, 22, 103, 104; bilateral, 93, 99, 102
trade union movement, 46, 66; in Argentina, 28–29; in Bolivia, 29, 45; capitalist corporations and, 54–55; in Chile, 69; in Nicaragua, 47–48; overview of 1990s, 16, 23–24; in Venezuela, 24, 40, 47, 67; workers' rights, 39–40
Transatlantic Trade and Investment Partnership (TTIP), 93
transformism/transformations, 8, 127, 129, 133, 148, 149; progressive governments and, 130–32, 137; social, 28, 56, 64, 74
Trans-Pacific Partnership (TPP), 93
Trump, Donald, 53, 61, 97, 104, 151, 156

unemployment, 20, 28, 83, 165; insurance, 155, 157; poverty and, 78, 122, 153; rates, 17, 154
Unified Workers' Central (CUT), 24, 31, 47, 54–55, 72
Union of South American Nations (UNASUR), 36, 95, 103–4, 108, 147
United Kingdom, 90–91, 156
United Nations, 72, 163; Economic Commission for Latin America and the Caribbean (ECLAC), 48, 91, 116, 153–54
United States, 6, 7, 91, 102, 163–64, 173n55; Brazil relations, 106; currency, 89; economy, 79, 85; hegemony, 89, 94, 103, 107, 108, 147; imperial strategy, 9, 77, 92–98, 104, 108, 146; influence in Latin America, 34–36, 147; military and police, 89–90, 92, 95–97, 106; Nicaragua relations, 54; sanctions, 53, 97, 162
Uruguay, 1, 4, 6, 49, 144, 151, 155; Broad Front, 32, 36, 56, 57, 118, 140, 173n50; minimum wage, 39; water reform, 38

Valéri, Arcary, 14
Vargas, Getulio, 56
Vázquez, Tabaré, 32, 140
Veltmeyer, Henry, 123
Venezuela, 7, 14, 71–72, 82, 130; Barrio Adentro program, 40; Caracas, 35, 59, 67, 71; Caracazo revolt, 18–19, 27; Chinese loans, 101; crisis, 1, 63, 107, 117, 190n35; debt, 52, 97, 164; democracy, 44, 136; GDP, 98, 153; imports, 62; labor law, 39–40; left criticism, 122–24; mining operations, 52; oil, 35, 42–43, 62, 67, 97–98, 105; political polarization, 61–63, 141; poverty rate, 37; socialism, 34, 39, 44, 62, 116–17, 188n17, 189n19; support for progressive governments, 113, 187n7; trade unionism, 24, 40, 47, 67; US relations, 35, 61, 62, 96, 97–98. *See also* Bolivarian Revolution; Chávez, Hugo
Vía Campesina, 22
violence, 63, 71–72, 73, 84; militarization and, 67; political, 17, 53–54, 61; social movements and, 58, 65–66; against women, 69, 154, 165

Index · 205

Wallerstein, Immanuel, 34
War on Drugs, 66, 92, 95, 96
Washington, DC, 6, 18, 34, 36, 53; consensus of neoliberalism, 8, 80, 143; Latin American allies, 104; Pentagon, 95
water wars, 30
wealth, redistribution of, 3, 4, 114, 116, 118, 122
Weisbrot, Mark, 97
women's movements, 22–23, 159–60, 166
Workers' Party (PT), 14, 26, 33, 50, 144; cadres and, 54–55; corruption scandals, 46, 55, 140; defeat to Bolsonaro, 60–61; Lula of, 31, 105, 117; mass movement against, 69–70; as a passive revolution, 127, 128; social programs, 38, 157; trade unions and, 24, 47
workers' rights, 39–40, 47–48, 55
Workers' Unitary Front (FUT), 47
World Bank, 36, 64, 98, 146, 163
World Social Forum in Porto Alegre (Brazil), 22

Yasuni ITT project (Ecuador), 68
youth movements, 69–70

Zapatista Army of National Liberation (EZLN), 21–22, 25, 110
Zelaya, Manuel, 53, 60, 94, 187n1
Zibechi, Raúl, 125–26, 192n66

www.ingramcontent.com/pod-product-compliance
Lightning Source LLC
Chambersburg PA
CBHW051124160426
43195CB00014B/2338